THE WOO WOO

D0052896

PRESS

2019 SELECTION

CANADA
READS

CBC BOOKS

cbc.ca/canadareads

WRITERS' TRUST OF CANADA

WT

HILARY WESTON WRITERS' TRUST PRIZE FOR NONFICTION · FINALIST

LINDSAY WONG

HOW I SURVIVED ICE HOCKEY, DRUG RAIDS, DEMONS, AND MY CRAZY CHINESE FAMILY

MORE PRAISE FOR

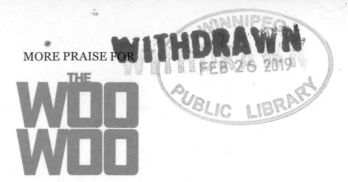

"That Lindsay Wong is even alive to write this book is amazing. Her black humour combines with compassion: she represents the realities of mental illness in her family while still telling us the story from their perspective: that of people haunted by the woo-woo. After you read this book, you may be, too—in the best way."
—Sarah Perry, author of *After the Eclipse:*
A Mother's Murder, a Daughter's Search

"You'll find yourself wincing and snickering and possibly weeping long after reading the last eloquent sentence. *The Woo-Woo* is both heart-wrenching and batshit insane, and is also beautifully rendered and fearless in its whip-smart humour."
—Sean Madigan Hoen, author of *Songs Only You Know: A Memoir*

"Equal parts appalling and riveting, *The Woo-Woo* proves that a sense of humour can get you through the most dire circumstances. A riveting, unbelievable family epic told in exquisite, visceral prose—you won't believe it's not fiction."
—Elizabeth Greenwood, author of
Playing Dead: A Journey through the World of Death Fraud

"No definition of 'dysfunctional' in any language on earth can hope to adequately describe the bizarre, darkly hilarious antics of Lindsay Wong's extended immigrant family. Every page of this no-holds-barred memoir will leave you astonished and incredulous."
—Andreas Schroeder, author of *Renovating Heaven*

LINDSAY WONG

THE WOO WOO

HOW I SURVIVED ICE HOCKEY, DRUG RAIDS, DEMONS, AND MY CRAZY CHINESE FAMILY

ARSENAL PULP PRESS
VANCOUVER

THE WOO-WOO
Copyright © 2018 by Lindsay Wong

THIRD PRINTING: 2019

ARSENAL PULP PRESS
Suite 202 – 211 East Georgia St.
Vancouver, BC V6A 1Z6
Canada
arsenalpulp.com

The publisher gratefully acknowledges the support of the Canada Council for the Arts and the British Columbia Arts Council for its publishing program, and the Government of Canada, and the Government of British Columbia (through the Book Publishing Tax Credit Program), for its publishing activities.

Arsenal Pulp Press acknowledges the xʷməθkʷəy̓əm (Musqueam), Sḵwx̱wú7mesh (Squamish), and səlilwəta?ł (Tsleil-Waututh) Nations, speakers of Hul'q'umi'num'/Halq'eméylem/hən̓q̓əmin̓əm̓ and custodians of the traditional, ancestral, and unceded territories where our office is located. We pay respect to their histories, traditions, and continuous living cultures and commit to accountability, respectful relations, and friendship.

Cover and text design by Oliver McPartlin
Edited by Shirarose Wilensky
Copy edited by Doretta Lau

Printed and bound in Canada

Library and Archives Canada Cataloguing in Publication:
Wong, Lindsay, 1987-, author
    The woo-woo : how I survived ice hockey, drug raids, demons, and my crazy Chinese family / Lindsay Wong.

Issued in print and electronic formats.
ISBN 978-1-55152-736-9 (softcover).--ISBN 978-1-55152-737-6 (HTML)

    1. Wong, Lindsay, 1987-. 2. Wong, Lindsay, 1987- —Childhood and youth.
3. Wong, Lindsay, 1987- —Family. 4. Wong, Lindsay, 1987- —Mental health.
5. Chinese Canadians—British Columbia—Vancouver—Biography. 6. Psychoses—Patients—British Columbia—Vancouver—Biography. 7. Psychoses—Patients—Family relationships—British Columbia—Vancouver. I. Title.

RC512.W65 2018   616.890092   C2018-901954-9

                                                                  C2018-901955-7

I dedicate this book to my past, present, and future selves, in all variations and parallel dimensions. For why else would anyone write a memoir?

Joking aside, this book is for anyone who has ever felt like an extraterrestrial bystander on Earth.

CONTENTS

AUTHOR'S NOTE

Everything in this book is true to my memory of the weirdo happenings of my life. Several character names and identifying characteristics have been changed. In some cases, details and timing have been compressed, expanded, or rearranged to facilitate a coherent account. I have done my best to portray these events accurately, despite the fallible nature of memory.

WONG FAMILY TREE

The Family in Hongcouver (the Chan Clan)

Cloudy Heroine (great-grandmother, mother of Poh-Poh)

Poh-Poh (maternal grandmother, a.k.a the Grand Dame of Woo-Woo)

Gung-Gung (maternal grandfather)

Beautiful One (youngest of the Woo-Woo, a.k.a the Bridge Jumper of Hongcouver)

Uncle E.T. (husband of Beautiful One, L.'s uncle)

Flowery Face (younger daughter of Beautiful One, L.'s cousin)

The Residents of Pot Mountain

Confucius Gentleman (father of L., husband of Quiet Snow)

Quiet Snow (mother of L., wife of Confucius Gentleman)

Lindsay, a.k.a Retarded One (eldest daughter and narrator)

Deep Thinker (younger sister of Lindsay)

Make Lots of Money (brother of Lindsay, the youngest of the family)

BRAIN CHILD

"**M**iss Wong, you are seriously ill," the neurologist in a midtown office said, preparing to offer me a sympathy tissue. But I was dry-eyed and benignly frosty, my way of responding to shitty news. It wasn't like me to fake a ladylike smile, or even to cry.

"The visual disturbances aren't going away," he continued, as if he were delivering a lecture in one of my writing workshops at Columbia University. "Migraine-related vestibulopathy isn't like having a cold. Objects and people are going to float around you. You're going to see bright auras. You're going to feel like you're moving when no one else is. This means that you could have vertigo for the rest of your life. You might have to spend many more months in bed. I don't even know if you'll get your ability to read back. You might not be able to finish school. What this means is that you have to start thinking about your future."

There was a dramatic, intentional pause—the kind that customer service representatives and people speaking at funerals like to use.

"Have you thought about who will look after you? Do you have any family that you can go to?"

I was twenty-two years old and had been on my own in New York City for four months, a good 2,000 miles away from my crazy Chinese family, who were still exorcising fake demons—the Woo-Woo—they called them, from anyone whose opinion they flagrantly disliked. That had included me, and it looked like the Woo-Woo had caught me anyway.

This was normal in our family, who believed that mental illness, or any psychological disturbance, was caused by demonic possession. The Woo-Woo ghosts were sometimes responsible for cancers, unexplainable viruses, and various skin afflictions like mild psoriasis.

Growing up, my superstitious mother always believed that going to the bathroom alone could lead to possession, whereas my father said any emotional weakness would bring on symptoms not unlike those dramatically thwarted in *The Exorcist*. "Lindsay, you cry and your eyeball will fall off," he would explain seriously, while clutching his head like he was having a moderate seizure. "Ghosts use any opportunity to possess you, okay? Don't be weak, or it's game over for you."

According to the neurologist, I had an extraordinary disease with no cure and a mysterious source. My brain was one hell of a light-headed mess. Electrical nerves had somehow gotten tangled and unplugged from their loose sockets. The feral wiring had somehow gotten wet and the damage had zapped the pupils and left me scrambling to understand why everyone and everything was jumping and leaping in polar directions; why the sky sometimes swapped with the versatile ground; why I had fallen face down in his office when he asked me to walk in a straight line.

My vestibular case (migraine-associated vertigo, or MAV) was particularly rare (unlike anything the doctor had ever treated), and he seemed impressed by how severe my symptoms were and very excited to investigate my monstrous head. In Canada, I had not been able to get off the waiting list to see a decent neurologist, but in New York City, you could book one on a Sunday afternoon in less than forty-eight hours—a mind-shocking luxury of American health care, which I was happy to have access to as a student.

The neurologist thought I'd be particularly thrilled to know that a famous pop star, Janet Jackson, shared this exclusive brain disorder with me. How nice to know that I was officially un-Woo, I thought, though he was diagnosing me with a lifelong disorder which left me confined to bed and frequently unable to read or write. I had a disease that gave me strange visual hallucinations like my severely schizophrenic grandmother on my mother's side whom we called Poh-Poh. I had a brain affliction, which made me feel like I was falling with a broken parachute and coated my vision with a dirty angelic glow. For several months now, for twenty-four hours a day, the intensity of these visions and nausea had worsened. I could not sleep. I could not eat. I frequently shat myself when I could not make it to the bathroom on time.

"Well," I said, "you never want to have anything in common with the Jacksons."

And that was all I said to him in our three-hour examination that wasn't related to my bizarre symptoms.

I must have taken my diagnosis remarkably well, because the doctor looked a bit startled by my comment, and I had waved away every tissue. The truth was: I was in shock. I had been trained not to cry in front of strangers; I was trained not to "boo-hoo"—as my father called it—at all. "Crying will turn you into a zombie like Mommy," he would often announce, making the cuckoo sign around his earlobe whenever he referenced the wild breakdowns on my mother's side. In our family, crying was considered contagious; it made you extremely vulnerable to the Woo-Woo ghosts, which was why, as an older teenager and then an adult, I became too scared to cry, convincing myself that I did not suffer from any extraordinary affliction of sadness.

There was no cure for my disease, the neurologist said, but we might be able to control it by experimenting with a concoction of epilepsy drugs and beta blockers and anti-anxiety medication; eventually, we'd concoct a potent mixture that "might make things better." There would be blood and stool tests every month, and the side effects would include balding, epic constipation, weight gain, liver destruction, hearing deficiencies, kidney failure, migraines, etc.

Of course, he had no idea that the childhood I had survived in my neighbourhood of meth labs and pot grow-ops, and—the most dangerous of all—my crazy parents, made this look like a cakewalk.

I had stopped listening to the neurologist, and I saw myself being chemically dissolved, every part of my body disfigured, just so they could stabilize my brain, whose instability—my father had already explained when I was sent to special ed in elementary school for not speaking English—was caused by my low IQ. Born from the extreme darkness of the Chinese loony bin by way of Vancouver, I had been already diagnosed by my parents as "crazy." To freeze the vertigo, the neurologist had to Botox the rambunctious nerves in my head, which had previously defined me as "slow" and "dumb-thinking."

I had never acknowledged that there were other genetic diseases, besides mental illness, that affected the structure and neurons of the brain.

After all, how could I? My mother said that if I left home, an angry ghost would murder me. My father said that if I demonstrated stupidity or vulnerability in my graduate studies at Columbia University, New York City would make my brain implode violently. Of course, what made it dark and frightening and semi-prophetic was here, coming true in a doctor's office.

I hadn't begun a separate, Woo-Woo–less life yet. I had no close personal connections or relationships or whatever normal people in their early twenties were supposed to cultivate, at least no one who would look after me, and I was being sent back to my childhood home. New York had been disorienting—Americans, especially ones my age, were obsessed with discussing their feelings and always wanted to know how you felt, enthusiastically greeting you at least a dozen times a day. My Columbia classmates, roommates, and professors had seemed to me obscenely Santa Claus–like, unreasonably cheerful, and I didn't know where one crazy ended and the other began.

Not to mention, I had no money. And I worried that my untrustworthy brain—defined by my father as the Woo-Woo—meant that I was not employable. At the risk of sounding nauseatingly self-pitying or self-important and even a little tragic, just after leaving the doctor's office, the news that I had a rare form of migraine vestibulopathy snapped me. At first disbelieving and disoriented, I finally let myself break into insect-sized pieces of sludgy sadness and disgusted, paroxysmal rage. I became a nasty vortex as I stalked around the midtown shops, as the vertigo, sensing my dark mood, began to swirl faster and transformed me into a gloomy human cyclone. Miserable, I elbowed a woman in front of me for walking too slow, but this didn't make me feel much better.

At the subway station at Columbus Circle, I surprised myself by suddenly having a first-rate cry. I didn't know what the hell was wrong with me. I hunched on the people-swarmed stairway and wailed so much I thought my eyes must have been bleeding. So I cleared out my clogged eyeballs. The water had probably been sloshing around for decades and frying my disgruntled nerves in their sockets. Yes, that was it. I needed to cry to clean out my dirty, robotic system.

Even though I had done my best to reinvent myself, I still felt that I was some *thing* with the emotional capabilities of a second-hand appliance. Here I was, trying my best not to excavate my tumultuous childhood, but it had soccer-kicked me in the ass.

17

I couldn't remember the last time I had cried, but the best thing about crying in New York was that I could sprawl on a chaotic staircase and Whole Foods fabric grocery bags and designer purses might thump me on the forehead, but no actual person would really notice. I could be as noisy and sloppy as I wanted, howling all day as the trains zoomed by.

Eventually, I became hungry from my wailing. But I learned a valuable lesson I never got growing up: it was very relaxing to cry, and I could see why people did it so often.

Then I started laughing. I couldn't stop giggling because I wasn't what my family had termed Woo-Woo: I was only medically damaged—the spirits that have plagued my Chinese family for years be damned. Thank God. I was a freak with terrible, mutinous genes, but at least I was not turning into my permanently sad mother, my suicidal auntie Beautiful One, or my maternal grandmother, Poh-Poh.

There might have been a horrible tsunami of hatchet-thumping pain walloping inside my scalp, sadistic firecrackers blowing up in my frontal lobes, but at least I wasn't Woo-Woo (for now). A certified neurologist had declared me sane, so I wasn't like my family, and even if I couldn't walk straight or saw everything through a hellish hallucinatory vision, I wasn't nutso. Who cared if I couldn't read or finish graduate school? I wasn't Woo-Woo. It was fitting that my brain was malfunctioning, but at least I had my own type of illness that was different from my family's.

I laughed so hard from pent-up relief that I vomited on the stairs from the nausea of swaying back and forth and got beige-coloured puke on my shorts. As far as I was concerned, laughing was the same as crying, and the only similarity between real people and those of us who originated from the Woo-Woo was that laughing was much easier on the eyes. I must have looked so incredibly monstrous because someone stopped on the staircase and handed me a dollar. This did not make me feel better, but I got on the 1 train and spent it on a chunky chocolate chip cookie at Nussbaum & Wu at West 112th Street.

I knew that I could not reinvent myself anymore. The Ivy League graduate student in New York City who had escaped her crazy Chinese family: it was such a trope, a perfect reality show. That summer, I also had a prestigious publishing internship, where I was supposed to compete with other millennials, jostling with them like affectionate piranhas on the subway, in our glass midtown office, in fancy fish-tank bars. And I had been so desperate to outrun the wreckage of my ghost-fettered past. I had tried to leave my family's mental illness behind, to abandon the Woo-Woo in Canada, as if it could stay there, rain-drenched and forgotten.

But that summer, balancing had become impossible and I could not toddle in a near-perfect straight line, like I had suddenly become rubbery and inflatable. I could not make soup on the stove without my brain making me think that I was falling inside the pot and being dissolved. So I had no choice but to go back to Vancouver, or Hongcouver, as we not so affectionately referred to it.

This was how it ended, how running away worked: a tremulous, circular route through the tricky universe that brought you back to the arthritic Pacific Northwest of your crazy family's cul-de-sac, where the world thought you belonged.

Laughing hysterically, because I was both sad and relieved, I continued my walk to my apartment on West 114th Street and passed out on the floor before I could get to bed, right before the ceiling dropped on me and the walls turned into squirming black holes.

CHAPTER 1
FROM DUMPSTER

We were supposed to be nice people, at least by our choice of Chinese immigrant decor: yellow-white wallpaper and kitschy knick-knacks of prancing bovines clutching signs that said, "Udder Chaos Lives Here." My mother, who was known as Quiet Snow in Cantonese, even had a miniature teaspoon collection of twenty or twenty-one exotic American states that she asked people to pick up on their travels.

I think there's this stereotypical belief that Chinese people are docile, or at least muted and agreeable most of the time. After all, you typically don't see ballistic freak-outs of my people on the news. But like any other people of colour, the news and the truth were separate.

"Oh, fuck you!" my mother screamed, and hurled her dinner at my father. At six, I was terrified, squatting under the table as I watched her spongy chicken thigh tumble to the floor. My mother's plate had become a flying mallet, cracking a cupboard door off its hinges.

My father, rolling his eyes and imitating her jerky facial spasms, mimicked my mother's high-pitched hysteria. "Why you trying to renovate the house, huh? Nothing wrong with kitchen. But everything wrong with your head!"

This was normal in our family, downplayed as the Woo-Woo's fault. The ghosts had possessed my mother again. Yet it was always frightening to be in the midst of such a supernatural siege, to pray that I was invisible under our plastic IKEA table.

Even as a child, I could see that our household's World War III was going to be won with wooden chopsticks and cheap dishes. The kitchen hadn't been cleaned in a week: newspapers strewn in precarious towers, mouldy teacups and chicken carcasses mountained on the counter. Definitely not the houses on the Chinese soaps my mother watched or the homes of playmates whose counters were sparkling and commercial clean. One of my mother's tantrums had sprinkled clumps of maggoty-looking rice and fermented fish on the linoleum like confetti. There was even some mice poop, which I had hungrily mistaken earlier for chocolate chips.

Until I left home at twenty-one, I never knew when the domestic wars would break out. But my mother knew where all the kitchen utensils were, which meant that my father, whose name meant Confucius Gentleman, was at a distinct disadvantage.

"We're moving to the mall, you retarded piece of shit!" my bony, bird-like mother, all five feet and ninety pounds of her, yelled at my father as he fled to the bathroom, where he would hide for hours.

"Good idea!" my father would holler through the locked door. "I get whole house to myself. Save money on electricity and heat!"

And I would usually remain huddled beneath the table, a small kid trying to find the humour to cope with what terrified me: a bizarre volatile world steered by my mother's fierce and unpredictable mind.

M y world became a strange and terrifying place when our family first became sad, unearthly versions of ourselves.

The Woo-Woo ghosts first came to visit when I was six, in 1992, when my baby brother was born. A month later, at two or three a.m., "the aliens" supposedly had an interplanetary stopover in our kitchen. My mother knew that she had acquired powerful psychic abilities, "like Superman," she said excitedly, and because she had a fourth-grader's English vocabulary and loved swear words, she often described her ability to see what was coming as "Batman's spidey sense or some shit." Yet she'd never cuss in Chinese, arguing that it was repulsive. Later, I'd recognize that her fireball language was unlike most mothers. After all, what mom wakes up her daughter in the middle of the night by long-jumping on her bed and yelling that she was "very afraid, help!" Most nights, she'd sleep opposite me on my kid-sized mattress, her bunioned feet resting on my head.

Most mothers do not need to be comforted by their six-year-old daughters, but as a child I found her physical presence to be both comforting and terrifying; her feet, funny-shaped, Spam-smelling, and certainly irritating, were a means to receive her attention. I see myself as that chubby little girl, moon-faced and urgently afraid of the dark, needing my mother to be more typical and less fickle—to generously soothe my whirlwind nightmares when we dozed together, yet she was always gone when I needed her most.

My mother's delusions started early one morning; it all began as she had fumbled for baby formula in the pantry at my brother's feeding time. She later told me the next morning that there had been a hot, staticky voice in her head that seemed to possess her. *Look over here*, the voice had demanded, and my mother's eyeballs and neck robotically swivelled to the doorway as if by pure synaptic sorcery. *You're okay*, the voice reassured her. *You're going to be absolutely A-okay*.

"Lindsay, it was an alien or a ghost!" she wailed, grabbing my shoulders. "It took possession of my brain and body!"

Too young to understand, I shrugged her off and walked away. But I wanted to know why we weren't happy or even nice to one another, like *The Flintstones* or *The Jetsons* on Saturday morning television.

This was the first hallucinatory "vision" that made her insist she had played host to the Woo-Woo. "They came here, right into the kitchen and hugged me!" she continued, clutching her belly, following me to the kitchen, where I was searching for leftover Halloween candy for breakfast. "Oh my God! Then the ghosts or aliens put fire in my body and gave me magical powers! So everyone in our family has to listen to me from now on!"

"Okay," I said, wanting to show her that I heard her, "but does that mean I can have more chocolate?"

Unfortunately, in our large Chinese family, mental health was not a strong suit. I had a grandmother who had been diagnosed with serious paranoid schizophrenia, who everyone said was mentally weak (or suffered from embarrassing extrasensory perception, a.k.a. "fucked-up ESP"). Too many of us were inclined to nervous breakdowns, mainly in exciting, psychotic instalments. And many years later, when I was twenty years old, on Canada Day 2008, my Auntie Beautiful One, the youngest of my mom's five sisters, would take the city of Vancouver hostage, trapping more than 200,000 people as she threatened to leap off the Ironworkers Memorial Bridge.

According to what I would now describe as seventeenth-century Chinese psychobabble, it was thought that we were somehow more prone than other people to "demonic possession." This wisdom, said to be common knowledge, was superstitious folklore that my family wholly believed in. It was a standard practice, like brushing your teeth, which had been handed down by my ancestors and perpetuated among our clan. My family was so mistrustful of all breeds of outsiders and North American newspapers, choosing to champion instead rambling phone gossip and ancient bullshit tradition: "Aiya! If you have the shit gas, go outside and hit yourself fifty times in the ass with a bamboo stick and it will go away! Fever? No problem. Run around in the snow. Naked."

Later, when I was in high school and briefly took psychology as an elective, I saw my mother's picture next to the definition of psychotic delusions, but of course there was no mention of the Woo-Woo, whose foul moods ruled our household. Our family insisted that supernatural outcasts chartered our bodies because we were born with watery minds and squishy hearts, which meant that anything dead could rent us for free. Randomly leaping inside us, these ghostly villains rotated among their hosts at least once a week. It's in the DNA and cultural beliefs of almost every village Chinese family to think ghosts, *gwei*, are haunting them every so often, especially if a new baby is born exceptionally ugly or someone gets a shocking grade on the SAT. But our family's Woo-Woo was the most horror worthy and innovative.

As a kid, unlike my mother, aunties, and grandmother, I did not have this peculiar superpower, and upon finding out that my mother was in terrible trouble, and not entirely understanding the consequences, I desperately wanted to belong. No matter how hard I tried, or how much I peeked inside cupboards and closets, I could not see a single ghost.

As a small child, not having the Woo-Woo power was like not being invited to a birthday party whose host you detested, yet *everyone* you knew had been invited and came back raving about the laser tag and the seven-layer ice cream cake. Even though my parents' fights scared me as a child, I also found their brand of crazy fascinating, like a car wreck. I couldn't look away.

To solve her supernatural problem at home, which in the real world of our kitchen was a case of severe depression and anxiety, my mother took my two siblings and me to our suburban shopping centre after school. At the beginning, the mall, with its colourful stores and cheap deep-fried smells, was thrilling—a novelty fairground that was a parallel reality to school and home. It was where you could chug down unlimited Pepsi, choose sugary candy bars from magical vending machines, and ride a purple choo-choo train for seventy-five cents—a burgeoning wonderland scene where my mother wanted to exclusively spend time with me, a mini holiday.

"You can have whatever you fucking want," she would say, handing me her purse like she was the patroness of both Lunar New Year and Halloween.

But by the third day, I was so tired of the unrelenting chaos and crowds I just wanted to stay at school, hurling sand in the playground and enthusiastically challenging other kids to ant-eating contests and kicking them if I didn't win.

But Monday through Friday we stayed in the food court from opening to closing time, only leaving to attend school. Eventually, I became sulky and punched the back of her seat whenever she drove—I did not want to stay in the food court, but at three p.m., she robotically scooped up my sister and me and we sat there until nine or ten p.m. Anxious and infuriated after the first week, I was forbidden to return home if my father wasn't there, because she said we were all in terrible end-of-the-world jeopardy.

"Sears is not as safe as Hudson's Bay because it's not as bright," she would exclaim. "Look for lots of lights and sunshine!"

She thought that if we hid out in retail paradise, then the elevator music, the hot dazzling display lights, and the blasts of delicious fatty-food smells would comfort and sustain us. There was less chance of getting killed if we were always surrounded by an anonymous daytime horde of housewives with strollers, all unaware of the vicious Chinese Woo-Woo who was afraid of crowded places, according to our mother. Our situation was not unique, as my extended family would often hang out at shopping centres after funerals or crises to cleanse us from bad luck. In our family, we were simply saving ourselves.

To keep us busy and to find answers to her scary "vision," my mother usually made all of us loop around the mall thirty times, my sister and me barely keeping up with the stroller while she forged ahead. Since I complained that I did not like to run around the mall non-stop, she promised me a bucket of cheese fries and maybe two hot fudge sundaes if I did.

"What do you do if an alien or Woo-Woo attacks you?" my mother asked us, insisting that running would help us if the evil ghost somehow found our mall outside Vancouver. This was the only way that she knew how to care for us.

"Go to the Bay!" I screamed in a convulsing sugar-high monotone, while my sister nodded. This seemed to satisfy my mother, but then she'd ask us again, needing our unwavering childish reassurance, a million times.

We wore mismatched, unwashed sweatshirts and leggings with weird kaleidoscopic patterns because our mother didn't pay much attention to our clothes. The Wongs, she said, were not a vain people, unless there were family connections to impress. She dressed herself randomly and handed us whatever—I wore fluorescent-green overalls and boys' orange T-shirts, all from my older cousins who had outgrown their wasted, shitty, are-you-sure-they're-not-from-the-sixties clothes, most likely passed on from other people in Hong Kong. The hand-me-downs were sequined leftovers with funny, misspelled messages, which I didn't notice until I learned how to read. My overalls had glittery *Rain in Spring run Mainly in Plaine* on the sides and my beachy orange T-shirt said, *Luff Thee Mother.* We were thriving suburban bums, self-made Hongcouver hippies, living in our self-imposed exile. It bothered me on some instinctive level that my clothes looked like figure skating costumes, but it did not become so apparent until kids in the older grades started to mock my outfits, which meant that I had to chuck rocks at their brains during recess.

We showered twice a month to save money, and a kindergarten teacher at the new Montessori school called my mother in one day to convey the stinky verdict.

"Does Lindsay shower?" the woman asked, a naive new teacher straight from college, having absolutely no clue that she was confronting an ogress. "We've had countless complaints."

"Do you think my kid smells like shit?" My mother became enraged. I stared at my desk, which I was defacing, intently, with a felt-tip marker. "Tell me, out of all the teachers in this school, how come we got stuck with a bitch?"

She suddenly turned to me. "Come on, Lindsay, let's quit this school!" she snapped. "You won't learn anything from a crazy woman who thinks you smell like poo. She's picking on us because we're Chinese."

But the next week, as was customary, she forgot about the argument and sent me back, because we had tried almost every elementary school in the district, and I was already very resistant to any education that did not have an immediate cash reward. Although I was six, I could not read or write, and I wasn't even sure if my parents knew the English alphabet—no one had bothered teaching me letters or numbers. But to instil in me a burgeoning work ethic, my parents paid me to go to school: twenty-five cents per day. My Chinese parents understood the value of monetary pride, but my teachers complained about my compost stench and were too stingy to part with a nickel or a dime, which annoyed me, like a nagging stomach ache. I tried not to show it, but it worried me that I was the sad, radioactive source of such freakish ping-pong screaming between my mother and teachers.

I did not know this at the time, but my mother liked to lose herself at the mall, a kind of fragile ghost woman—enormous caterpillar-brown eyes and fried hair from the eighties that made her look permanently electrocuted—who was teetering into a protracted nervous breakdown with three little kids in tow. She must have wanted to be a proper suburban housewife. Even though it was 1993, three kids meant that you had achieved a certain financial status. She could not stop having children until she had produced a boy because she would not be blessed according to our Chinese superstitions. And after all, a son made you the envy of everyone in the Chinese community, no matter where you were in the world. It was like suddenly becoming the owner of a fancy new Porsche, whereas being the mother of a girl was like leasing a Toyota.

This was what, I would come to believe, also led to her breakdown—she had been waiting and waiting for the birth of my baby brother and when it arrived, there was no starry-eyed revelation where the skies ruptured and the universe thanked her by raining pellets of gold.

Instead, my mother got depressed—in retrospect, I see it might have been postpartum depression and treatable. But instead, she used the mall, where she was hoping to be saved, muttering apprehensively to herself about divine intervention. But what I also didn't see then was that this nervous breakdown was supposed to be fun: she enjoyed the frenzied bustle in her own emotionally stunted way—freedom from our asylum-coloured house.

"Pizza? Hot dog? French fries?" she would yell enthusiastically when she picked me up from school. "At the mall, you can eat whatever you want! We'll be safe and I don't have to ever fucking cook!"

"Whatever," I said, ignoring her heady excitement and secretly wondering when we could permanently move back home. To emphasize my monstrous displeasure, I kicked the back of the driver's seat over and over, but she didn't seem to notice or care.

Maybe my mother also saw our relocation as an active unwifely rebellion against my father, who was afraid and unsupportive of her reaction to her ghosts, so he would be responsible for making his own wonton noodle lunches and ironing his own collared shirts.

Looking back, we were superstitious, paranoid Chinese suburbanites who were trying our best to fit in. The Woo-Woo ghosts haunted us to the point where if someone fell down or cut their finger, it was blamed on a nasty spirit—"Aiya! Get the Polysporin! But make sure there are no ghosts in the fucking medicine cabinet!"

After a week of whirling around the mall, all I wanted was a mother and father who inspected what I wore to school, made me lumpy purple jelly sandwiches for lunch, and read to me at night. As fascinated as I was by my volcanic parents, I thought maybe I had been born into the wrong family. That loud-mouthed aliens with poor hygiene and cantankerous manners had kidnapped me. It was devastating, no, a pure tragedy, in my probing kid-mind that we weren't similar to any cartoon family on TV.

As the eldest child, I did not appreciate my brother and sister, certainly had no attachment to these screaming things, and assumed these noisy creatures had been shipped overnight in the mail.

Although I wished my sister and brother no harm, if it came down to them or a treat, I'd trade both siblings, even if it were only for a bag of gummy bears or powdery sour keys that stuck in the uneven gaps of my teeth. If a stranger waltzed up to me in the food court and asked to see my assembly of toys (yes, my sister and brother were life-sized dolls that belonged to me), out of perverse familial loyalty, I told myself that I would only sell them for a decent sum. *My sister is worth at least $2.50!* I would argue heatedly.

Like many first-born kids, I now know that I wanted the world to be exclusively mine. Until I was about thirteen, I refused to imagine that other children besides me could exist in our family. Each mother, especially mine, who had such limitations to begin with, should only be assigned one child in case they do not have enough affection. Mine didn't, as she tossed us spare change from her purse in lieu of physical warmth, as if feeding bread to ravenous geese. "Just buy candy from the machine, okay?" she said, half crying and shaking violently. "And don't talk to me until you've eaten at least twenty gummies each. I have a fucking headache, okay?"

Moaning like an undead cartoon monster, my mother fed us candy for breakfast, lunch, snack, and dinner but would forget to brush our hair and did not scold us for not cleaning our yellow-splattered teeth. In our family, a mother was someone who made sure her children were never hungry, and she tried as much as she mentally could. But at that point, fed up with our life in the court, I saw that my mother had been born with a heart the size of one of my doll's shoes and would have benefited from some family downsizing—like maybe if it were only me.

Besides, even though I was only six going on seven, I didn't think I had ever been a baby or a toddler because of the famous Wong family procreation myth, delivered with the also famous Wong half-funny-half-cruel-all-too-confusing-to-untangle wit, which explained that my parents had fished me out of a downtown Dumpster.

"That's why you're garbage," my father would explain, boasting that my origin story was extraordinarily funny. "All garbage have low IQ. Not like Daddy at all. I'm very, very smart because I'm from library."

"Then why you get me from Dumpster?" I had asked once after starting elementary school, speaking in a churlish, babyish Chinglish. Being sensitive yet spacey, I took his every word at hurtful, no-bullshit face value.

"It's free," my father declared, sounding sombre. "You think we want to pay money for you? Mommy and I know how to save money on unimportant things."

"Why I not important?" I said, sad and a bit resentful.

"Because you are from garbage."

This was my father's typical response, a robotic, jokey, unhelpful statement that drove my mother absolutely batshit; it was characteristic of him to carelessly wave a hemorrhaging red cape at a rabid bull, for my mother did not understand humour or indirectness. How they met and married is still a complete mystery to me. It was never once spoken about in our family and deemed irrelevant and irritating as small talk.

"I found your mommy in garbage can," my father joked when I asked.

"What she doing there?" I said.

"Just like you, no one want her. Like Mommy, like daughter."

They did not have any wedding photos, and I imagine that my parents' courtship was non-existent, their wedding a dour but efficient signing of papers. To this day, I have never seen my parents touch one another, as my father kept my mother and everyone at an emotional and physical distance of exactly two feet.

Now it seems exceptionally cruel to mock a small child while taunting a panicky wife, but all this happened before cable television became mainstream affordable, and there were no strong male role models, like Dr Phil, to provide complementary domestic counsel.

"It's like talking to the fucking answering machine!" my mother often complained about my father when he joked about our Dumpster origins or made fun of her thinning hair. "What the fuck are you supposed to say? Talk to you later? Have a nice fucking day?"

My parents possessed no shared interests and didn't seem to communicate in the same language.

And even though I find my father's jokes funny now, his black humour wounded me as a child. Believing that I was from an indiscriminate downtown Dumpster, instead of a clean office wastebasket like my engineering father's, was like a dull axe through the skull. As adults, my father and I speak an analogous dialogue to each other now: one that is equally foul-mouthed, sarcastic, blunt, and dark. We can laugh sadistically at ourselves, but back then his jokes could break my papery sense of self.

I was so desperate to be noticed that I would do nearly anything for attention. After all, my parents were too busy battling the Woo-Woo between themselves. In those food-court days, just a sprinkling of my mother's strange affection, even a mild scream-ing, some trademark volleying of swearing, would make me feel appreciated—anything to make me as important as her ghosts, whom she spoke to at length, saying, "Hello, good morning, good afternoon, leave me the fuck alone, goddammit!" And if I couldn't get it from my mother, I'd get it from the teachers at the Montessori, earning me a reputation as an above-average bully who used her superpowers to irk the headmistress and special needs teachers who believed that I had ADD and autism. I screamed and howled like a wounded rhinoceros for their attention—mimicking my parents because I thought this was acceptable social behaviour.

"Lindsay, why did you take off your clothes and throw them in the garbage can?" the headmistress asked me in her office, her face haggard with worry.

"I don't like clothes," I announced, jumping on her desk and beating my chest. "I'm from garbage!"

"Put your clothes back on or I'm calling your mother!" she yelled. And my mother would arrive two hours late, shrugging and unapologetic, with two McDonald's cheeseburgers and a carton of fries. It seemed that she existed just to feed me.

And her arrival with tasty McDonald's only encouraged me: I punched a little girl with Down syndrome, snipped another girl's braid off, and then happily smashed a little boy in the back of the head with my favourite Dr. Seuss book (*Green Eggs and Ham*), which got me sent to time out in the cloakroom.

At first, I was terrified to be left alone in the dark, my nose pressed against the cold tiled wall, among the mildewed jackets and the sweetly sour smells of half-eaten sandwiches and fruit. After all, the untrustworthy gloom was where ghosts took your unsuspecting body hostage, which I imagined, based on my parents' constant neuroses about corporeal possession, was supposed to be as unsettling and scary as visiting the doctor for my biweekly suppository. Prone to bouts of heart-heavy insomnia and eye-twitching paranoia from kindergarten to the twelfth grade, I was always cranky and constipated it seemed. Yet after my second or third transgression at school, I felt hope and optimism. Alone, I could imagine that I was my mother, surrounded by shadowy shapes, and that shoes and backpacks and gym strips were whispering ghosts too.

In the cloakroom, a nasty desperation was brewing inside me, something so frantic and similar to my raging mother's. It was like a poltergeist was trapped inside my ribcage, banging against my small and insignificant heart. It was like a cyclone of rank supernatural premonition.

It was like waiting for someone in my family to get possessed.

Essentially, there was too much sadness boiling inside us, which was why, I like to explain, we blew up.

CHAPTER 2
POT MOUNTAIN

I f you do not make friend at school," my father said, "you will turn out Woo-Woo like your mommy." Attempting to be funny, he made a cuckoo sign around his earlobe and a face that was supposed to be a drooling, pop-eyed zombie—he liked to imitate his wife to relieve the tension in our household. "Do you want to wake up and look scary?"

"But you don't have friend," I said after the teacher called my parents to tell them that I had difficulty adjusting to middle school.

I had gnashed my half-formed molars, frustrated. For how could I adapt? The formative years of elementary school had been squandered in the food court until my father, fed up, hired a woman from Hong Kong to raise us until my mother's phobias subsided. It was she who equipped my mother with an arsenal of recipes for Chinese cuisine and taught her how to properly clean.

Middle school was a thrilling possibility for the Wongs to start over, perhaps even a real chance for ostensible middle-class respectability.

"Daddy doesn't need friend because he is not retarded," my father continued his humour that edged on spitefulness. He liked to quip that I was mentally disabled since my school had me tested (results: TBD) for everything from Asperger's to hearing impairment. He went on cheerfully, "Retarded people need friend to help them."

"How much will you pay me if I make friend?" I asked.

"Five dollar?" my father said.

"Ten dollars," I said, "and ninety-nine cents."

Unlike my mother, my father would leave the house for work and somehow, two-faced, was able to form business alliances to function in the professional world in a way I was learning to function in school. In his own sad, peculiar way, I think he worried about his children's mental and physical well-being, even if he could be like a standoffish circus clown: preaching advice through hurtful humour and shrill, exaggerated pantomime.

My upbringing made me feel alone. I was a bully without realizing that I was a pretty decent one who casually told teachers to "Fuck off!" when I did not want to participate in class, which was often. After all, this was what my parents would do. But I was certainly not charismatic enough to build up a loyal mean-girl following. My sister and brother were cute, popular children, who seemed easy with others on the playground, but as the eldest, my parents' sour-faced guinea pig in childrearing, I was afflicted with my mother's neurosis and father's zealous anti-social tendencies.

Our Chinese names were supposed to be personal blessings, our parents' magical gifts for showy, boastful success. My sister's name was Deep Thinker, but rather than becoming an intellectual, she sometimes seemed to me to be cursed to agonize her thoughts aloud with worrying frequency. CBC Radio 1, an auntie once called her. My brother, Make Lots of Money, was supposed to be blessed to attract abundant wealth, yet he has struggled with unemployment. And I had been named Talented One at birth but because of my hissing lisp and other wild behavioural issues was mostly called by my English name—it didn't seem as if I had been born with that much talent (I had the gross misfortune not to live up to my name during childhood). It made me sad that I was considered less than my siblings, so I was determined to prove that I was better than them in every way, which would cause a deep and despicable rift between us, a gully of vicious contention.

Still, my father insisted that I should have at least two friends, so I could alternate between them, "like shoe," he said, even though he had no friends himself.

At that time, I thought that this double standard was supremely unfair. "I had whole entire village of friends in Hong Kong when I was your age," he bragged when I protested. "I'm so nice that when someone nice to me, I'm ten times nicer. But when someone is mean to me, Daddy is ten times meaner."

"Why?" I said, confused. "I can play by myself."

"You are too retarded to not have friend," he said, frustrated, and then went back to his AutoCAD blueprints. They were usually spread on the dining room table when he decided to work from home to keep watch over my mother, who was still scared of the Woo-Woo ghosts and couldn't be alone. At least she stopped taking us to the mall's food court after school when we got older, and her moods seemed to slowly improve. She spent her days and nights in the kitchen, compulsively practicing what our former caretaker had taught her: sometimes origami-wrapping more than a thousand cardboard-coloured wontons and filling two giant freezers.

As an adult, I can see the likelihood that my father did not know enough English to explain the subject of friendship properly, and he was genuinely worried about my happiness, which was already spotted and sour, like my gym strip that hadn't been washed in more than a year. Having friends was something I couldn't understand. Although my father had professional acquaintances, and my mother had five close sisters and two brothers, neither of my parents had any friends—my father, I later realized, did not want me to become like my mother.

Our house had been christened the Belcarra by its builder in an effort to make everyone forget it was a boxy McMansion. The name was supposed to give us an element of inflated class and imply an aristocratic lineage that would never exist on a mountain two hours from the city of Hongcouver, a place known for its gigantic Chinese population.

By looking at us, people with no obvious interest in personal hygiene—my mother, siblings, and I had greasy rag-like hair plus *eau d'ogre* breath—you wouldn't expect us to be comfortable suburbanites. I was not (still not) allowed to know our finances. But even though I thought we were very poor, we must have been at least comfortably middle class, but not small-time millionaires like some of my aunties and uncles, though Westwood Plateau was an affluent neighbourhood with a few well-known NHL players. My father had purchased the house because it was the cheapest one on the market in the area. The kitchen, dining room, and living room were on the very top floor, which had turned away every potential buyer except him, as our family did not invite people over.

To any sane person, the house's interior probably resembled a type of rat-like, labyrinthine madness, a privatized mental institution of tiny, almost claustrophobic rooms. This was where our Woo-Woo dwelled, it seemed, inside the Woo: a netherworld aquatic tank swarming with foggy, morose ghosts.

Our isolated mountain had recently been renovated into Stepford suburbia: real Canadian waterfalls competed with obnoxious fountains, green grass carpets, and dour-faced garden gnomes. You wouldn't know it now, but only twenty years from when I was growing up, the mountain was known as the boondocks where the pizza guy absolutely did not deliver.

For millionaire migrants of Asia, this was must-have property and everyone snatched up these luxury boxes like accessories. The Chinese loved the mountain so much because the upward slope meant that the money would supposedly stay in our pockets. Many of the white families moaned about the "Asian tsunami" that had flooded their community and lamented the neighbourhood's terrific ethnic decline into "Chinky Chinatown."

But the isolation of the Plateau, shrouded by a canopy of black evergreens, was ideal for illegally growing and harvesting pot. The Poteau, as it was mocked in the newspapers, had been declared "a narco-terrorism zone" because of many moneymaking Asians who acquired luxury real estate for grow-ops and meth labs. This was the hottest Gold Mountain in history. The Poteau had become a neighbourhood of Chinese drug millionaires, and it seemed that everyone's hardworking Chinese parents (three out of seven houses on our cul-de-sac) were cultivating BC bud for $250 an ounce, helping to generate a $6 billion industry for the province. No one ever suspected a hastily constructed show-off McMansion was manufacturing drugs.

When the story of the many marijuana plantations finally broke in 2004, the local newspapers exaggerated the Poteau's crime rate, making it seem like everyone was always waking up to find a dead body on their flawless turf or a bullet hole in their front door. There was an exciting world that seemed more appealing than scary, from my child perspective. No matter how hard I prayed, I could never come across a corpse sprawled grotesquely on the Belcarra's ample driveway.

Only once, in 2008, when I was twenty years old, did a meth lab a few streets down go boom, the palatial roof blasting high into the gloomy mountain sky, the glass shards from the foyer's skylight lashing into the lush fronds of banana trees and splashing into the concave fountain like coins. For weeks, the newspapers raved and gushed and gossiped: "Posh Westwood Plateau House Explodes!"

As kids we heard our parents joke that if you purchased a multi-million-dollar toy castle with a multi-million-dollar view, the sellers threw in the Westwood Poteau Asian Barbie, toting her very own hot-pink meth lab starter kit.

Before the scandal in the news, my family, like everyone else on the block, was on the payroll for our silence. Every week, our neighbours brought over tinny buckets of clacking crustaceans, fine wines, chocolates, and a maybe a small cash gift of fifty dollars or more. There were usually two or three grow-ops on our small cul-de-sac at any given time, which would be immediately replaced after a police raid. At five p.m. at the end of the week, my mother, even when she was unwell, would wait with her carpenter's hammer, ready to bash our live lobsters before boiling them for dinner. She would gouge out the crustacean's beady, panicked eyes, and for another week, we would ignore the marijuana plantations reeking next door, and the methamphetamine fortresses down the street that oozed fresh cat piss and dizzying ammonia fumes.

It was only fair that we were paid to tolerate their moist toxic smells.

I grew up to love and expect my bounty of free chocolate—every week was trick or treat, except my neighbours came to me.

Just a year after we bought the Belcarra, the pinkest Barbie house in the middle of the cul-de-sac, mutual acquaintances whispered that the builder could not pay his debts, so his head was blown off at the Poteau country club, i.e., by Chinese gangsters. His death was hush-hush and did not make the news. I wondered if one of our criminal neighbours had discovered a creative way of killing him.

"What do you mean his head blew up?" I had asked when I was eleven years old, not so secretly thrilled with the wildness of his death. "Was it, like, a bomb? Did his head explode? Did his brains go everywhere? Was it hard to clean up?"

But all the grown-ups in the room told me to shut the fuck up.

"His brain go kaboom because he have low IQ," my father said, turning this rumour into a lesson about school. He sounded tired and superior, which made me believe him.

There was nothing to see or do on the Poteau, except when our neighbour down the street got her brains eaten by a rebellious teenage black bear (the animal, not the woman, made the news). Everyone who witnessed the attack said the bear had somersaulted through her basement window and eagerly eaten half her head before the police arrived.

I had missed the incident, and then I was at school when another neighbour got his thigh chomped by a coyote when he was out gardening—the coyote only digested a little before deciding he didn't like the chewy texture of old man. People seemed to forget this was a mountain in rural Canada masquerading as suburbia. You were more likely to be mauled by a gang of homeless bears while unloading groceries than to be bludgeoned to death with a trowel by the Chinese pot gardener.

My fascination with other people's tragedies made me feel better about my own. I was convinced that nothing would happen while I waited for neighbourly maimings, so I was reduced to spending my summer hiding behind our scraggly bamboo bushes, my double assault Super Soaker sniper rifle pumped full of water and ready to spray at any neighbours I didn't like. Rowdy and unafraid, I was a yodelling sixth-grade warrior, an assassin orangutan who'd leap out of the shrubbery and soak my screaming victims.

Eventually, on my block watch, a black BMW came to survey the neighbourhood and a smartly dressed Chinese couple and their daughter got out. They stopped in front of the beige McMansion across from the Belcarra, the one with medieval turrets and bulky buttresses that made it look like an obscene Disneyland theme park castle. There was no moving van and minimal luggage (a carry-on per person), which meant they had to be in the "gardening business."

The man was young and ordinary and looked like some kind of professional, but the woman, an aging beauty queen, was wearing expensive clothes and five-inch stiletto heels that made her legs look like they belonged to a spidery silicone flamingo. She looked like a once-glamorous Hong Kong movie star with her crimson lipstick, except her teeth were blackish yellow and fanged. The skin on her face had been badly bleached (there were still slug-coloured spots that someone had missed), and this was why people on our block would call her Lesser Michael Jackson. She beckoned me over, but I was unsure if I should talk to her. Looking at her wobbling heels, I decided that I could definitely outrun her if she gave me any trouble.

The woman grinned, flashing her terrible fangs, and asked me which house I belonged to. I pointed at our pink Barbie house, and she nodded. "Tell your parents we'd like to meet them. Are you Hong Kong Chinese? Taiwanese Chinese? Singapore Chinese?"

"Hong Kong," I said, and she looked incredibly relieved. She must have believed that her kind of Chinese was the best. "Us too. We'll come by later with your presents."

"Presents" confirmed that our new neighbours were savvy and practised pot growers, who would do their best to guarantee our silence with gifts.

"You may come play with my daughter," the woman said, trying to make her voice sound less authoritative and more gracious. She pointed at the miserable-looking girl behind her.

The woman then pulled out a red envelope from her purse and stuck it in my sticky palm. "Here's a small forty-dollar present for you, little sister. Please remember to tell your parents we'll come by soon."

Their daughter, also dressed in beautiful clothes, a pink silk tunic with a collar of boisterous red animal fur, looked seriously unhappy at our introduction, and I decided that she might be acceptable company. She was squat, with a brown dumpling-shaped face and some kind of raccoon snout for a nose. I sensed kindred deformity and shoulder-cringing anguish in her, like head lice that are helplessly drawn to clean hair. Her name was Terrifical Blossom, but everyone, including her own parents called her Pizza Head, on account of her blotchy scalp. She was noticeably bald, her head scabby and red.

She kept clawing at her scalp, and when she thought no one was looking, she stuck her hand inside her pants and scratched. I didn't know what was wrong with her; it appeared to be some kind of psoriasis, which made patches of her skin look like ancient cottage cheese, but she seemed like she was my age, and I could show my father that I had quickly made a friend. It wasn't as if we had to even like each other. She was brand new to the neighbourhood and would earn me an easy $10.99.

Unsure of what to say, I blurted hurriedly, "Do you want to be my friend? If you don't, it's okay. I don't want to waste any time, so you should tell me right away."

Pizza Head blinked and took a few seconds before she said, "Can I think about it?"

It seemed fair; after all, she needed time to decide if I would be a good friend. She didn't know me. Her English was more stilted and awkward and confusing than mine, except I lisped and she didn't. In those days, I had trouble with everyday talking noises. My tongue and lips and distended dinosaur teeth (stegosaurus underbite) didn't like each other, and were at a constant three-way war. My father said that I looked and talked like "the Frankenstein," which didn't bother me until I learned what it meant when I was forced to read Mary Shelley in tenth grade.

"Fine," I agreed, and quickly turned around and marched back to my house, thinking that I had a fifty-fifty chance.

The next day, Pizza Head told me that we could be friends on a trial basis, just in case she found other kids on the block that she liked better. Having no clue that this was a bad idea, I agreed. Pizza Head wasn't sure if we would get along, and she really wanted to know why I dressed so funny.

"What you talking about? I said, confused. "I'm wearing shirt, you're wearing shirt. I'm wearing pants, you're wearing pants."

"Yes," she said, wrinkling her compact little nose so that it disappeared inside her face, "but why you wearing boy clothes? And why your sneaker too big?"

"What you talking about?" I said, not realizing she was embarrassed that I was dressed like a cellphone advertisement. I rotated between baggy men's Motorola and LG logo T-shirts sent over by a rich uncle who owned a cellphone chain store in Australia. I had noticed a distinct difference between our clothes, but I assumed it was because my family was extremely poor (we lived off hand-me-downs) and she was in the "gardening" business, which meant that her parents had to spend a lot of money on finessing their upper-class appearance. It was like comparing someone who owned all the Manchu Wok fast food franchises in the province to someone who owned just one lowly Chinese restaurant in a rundown strip mall. Besides, she was the typical overseas Hong Kong princess who demanded everything that was girly, pink, and designer, and I was the rough tomboy CBC (Chinese-Born Canadian), which meant that I only liked food and all forms of hockey.

"But your house look way bigger than my house, so why you dress like that?" Pizza Head persisted.

I shrugged, and then her mother came out to give us glutinous red bean candies and a dish of deep-fried hot dogs drowning in black garlic bean curd, so I forgot what we were talking about.

You knew someone had a successful drug business when they wouldn't tell you their real name, or their parents claimed they were successful travel agents but didn't know the name of the company they worked for. Those in the standard marijuana occupation or the riskier meth business did not allow visitors inside. If their children invited you to play, you were confined to the front steps or the rusty backyard swings, where dishes of semi-frozen hot dogs and gluey sweets were served, their bowing parents apologizing about the sad, skunky smell.

This was our immigrant interpretation of suburbia: Chinese parents trying to be accommodating and white and country-club attending as much as possible. Pot was something assimilated people mass produced and distributed in British Columbia; it was a marker of success, like sending your children to Ivy League schools.

In fact, Lesser Michael Jackson proved to be a fabulous Poteau hostess, always smiling and bowing; she rotated between serving us the usual fried rice and undercooked spaghetti glued together by mustard, relish, and coagulated ketchup. Having been raised on fast food from the mall and easy Chinese food (fried rice, lo mein, chop suey), I could eat anything and didn't yet know the difference between margarine and mayonnaise. My taste buds for Western cuisine were seriously undeveloped, and if someone handed me a sandwich full of gummy bears and potato chips, I would gladly eat it with a handful of sugar.

When Lesser Michael Jackson, who also didn't quite understand Western cooking, brought out jumbo marshmallows smeared with mayonnaise and strawberry jam, I thought I had found my fairy godmother. Did this woman also exist just to feed me? She was the only Chinese lady I knew who cooked North American food, which made her a celebrity chef in a way. No grown-up I knew could read the English directions on packaged food, but Lesser Michael Jackson claimed she could, which is why she had mastered chicken nugget rice, spaghetti with ketchup like "the Italian," and mayonnaise marshmallow casserole. She invented Western dishes like she made up stories about her life as a travel agent.

In contrast, at our house we ate a simple buffet of steamed fish, chicken, or pork on dry, gravelly rice if my mother was in a cooking mood; if she wasn't, we devoured turd-shaped beef jerky from the box and slurped peppery instant noodles. Although she was a drug lady, Lesser Michael Jackson constantly fed Pizza Head home cooking and decorated her front steps with cheerful paper plants from Costco. My mother couldn't be bothered to cook or clean the house when she was afraid and depressed, so I preferred Lesser Michael Jackson's ersatz gourmet version of motherhood.

Because of their daughter's memorable nickname, our newest pot-growing neighbours became known as the generous Pizza Family: friendly Mrs and Mr Pizza (Lesser Michael Jackson and Three Decade Younger Husband behind their backs), who had produced such a yeasty Pizza Head. It was rumoured that Pizza Head wasn't really their daughter, just some sad, unfortunate girl who had been assigned to the sensational drug couple. The adults in our neighbourhood did not seem particularly concerned about Pizza Head, but there was an unspoken policy on the Poteau to never get involved if you didn't want "your head blown up."

Truthfully, she did not look like either of her enigmatic parents, and she bitterly referred to her mother as "That Woman" and her father as "Him." I could certainly relate and began addressing both my parents as "You," which they did not like.

Whether this was unsophisticated adolescent rebellion, or she had truly been sold/kidnapped/hostaged, poor Pizza Head despised both her parents and did not consider That Woman and Him to be her family. There might have been some unhappy truth to her story because the Poteau was known for stranger things, but I had been raised not to interfere or ask questions, especially when I had two or three delicious meals on their front porch a day. Like me, Pizza Head had an overbearing, dramatic mother and an emotionally distant, unavailable father, and I thought I knew why she loathed me so much—because That Woman and Him insisted that we be "the best friend OR ELSE."

The "OR ELSE" in an immigrant Chinese family could mean many different things, and if your parents were old-fashioned like mine, you might have to sleep outside for talking back and relinquish half your Lunar New Year money. My parents believed that punishment was supposed to be practical and intensive, none of that go-to-your-room-and-meekly-apologize Western bullshit. Punishment had to hurt a little bit. In Pizza Head's case, she had to sleep on an air mattress in the garage and hand over her platinum credit cards, which was just considered *average* according to my lofty Chinese Old Testament standards.

You really had to feel sorry for that Pizza Head. First, her head was always snowing like textured confetti, and second, she had no choice but to be my friend. Even I did not want to be friends with myself. In retrospect, I felt alien and apart from my surroundings, believing myself to be disgusting, inferior, and brain-damaged—a carbon copy of my parents' projected phobias and insults. Because I struggled socially, I felt as if I had crash-landed from Pluto and could not fathom how to interact with the human species. With no idea how to be kind or generous or even mildly entertaining, I admit that I was lousy company. If I did not make friends with Pizza Head, I would not have $10.99, and I would incur the wrath of my father, who did not like losers and wimps.

"This is the only reason why I'm talking to you, you know," Pizza Head explained to me. She had the refreshing honesty of someone who had to lie about everything else. "Otherwise, we wouldn't be the best friend at all."

Because childhood misery tends to cut off oxygen to the brain, it makes the sufferer not only irrational but also irritable—it puts everything in a wholly negative and nightmarish light. My gloominess was like being a portly hamster forced to run on a never-stopping wheel, whereas Pizza Head was like a timid ladybug that had been inelegantly stuffed into a jar, taken from a lush botanical garden, and forced to live among a few scraggly maple leaves. We should have been miserable together, forced into unsavoury surroundings and situations by unstable adults who were too busy looking after themselves.

Unfortunately, even such a low-bar friendship wasn't going to work—my father had elbowed me towards sociability, but he didn't seem to think Pizza Head was good enough, even for me.

"Out of all the kid on the block, you choose *that leper* to be your friend?" he had asked me, shocked, when the smiley Pizza family first came by to pay their bribes, giving us three dozen fresh lobsters and two bottles of good merlot. "She looks like a fucking potato! There are fleas eating her head!"

I didn't look much better, my father finally conceded, but thank Buddha I didn't have a pepperoni pizza for a head.

Accustomed to his outrageous remarks, I could only pretend that I hadn't heard, secretly rolling my eyes. It was an early defence mechanism that I was slowly developing, not engaging fully with either of my parents; that is, if I didn't want to hear any stomach-churning screaming that could shatter my precarious, indistinct sense of self. The answer seemed so simple: if you didn't react, you didn't receive a fat stake in the chest. Yet it would take me many years before I could fully disengage. I was learning self-preservation, in the same way it was better not to walk outside during a lightning storm or to be caught outside when the black bears and coyotes were out. Unfortunately, it wasn't enough, and through adolescence to adulthood, I had to adapt: retreating so wholly into myself that I was afraid to convey any pulp-like vulnerability.

In short, there were times when I became too much like my father—assholian and unliked.

I figured that as long as my father paid me for acquiring my new friend, which he eventually did, I would not tell him that it all seemed like a very poor investment. Besides, I was the first-born and the first generation of Chinese immigrants, and I knew that if I did not succeed, there would be punishment. For instance, once my father forced my mother to buy me a box of cookies from the grocery store and ordered me to hand them out to some random kids playing roller hockey on the street. But they didn't like me and said I looked and talked funny. So I took back all my cookies, including the half-eaten ones (they were worth $2.99 each), and everyone got incredibly upset, and I couldn't see what the big deal was. I could not bear to go back on the street and hand out cookies like flyers to kids who had previously rejected me.

During the first two weeks of our friendship, Pizza Head and I sat companionably on her front steps, devouring whatever food Lesser Michael Jackson brought out. Our eating continued uneventfully until one day we had made our way through two plates of That Woman's chewy specialty spaghetti and, for dessert, twenty plain soft taco shells (she had mistaken tortillas for puff pastry) when Pizza Head told me that she could not be my friend anymore. Without an ounce of false remorse, Pizza Head explained that there was a potential opening for her in someone else's friend group and they had invited her to play tennis. This was a private invite-only audition, and I was not welcome, on account of my smell and terrible clothing choices, which had never even occurred to me. It wasn't just one bad choice that I had made, she said, but I was wearing too many unforgivable choices that could not be ignored.

The news was shocking—when was clothing a decision-maker in this petty game called friendship? I certainly did not smell like pee anymore and washed my hair with some regularity, so why wasn't that enough? Besides, we had spent a lot of time sitting and chewing on the porch together, even if we hadn't ever talked. After all, I might have argued, in movies and television shows, cows and other intelligent livestock that grazed together often seemed to form silent and intense bonds. I was shocked at this sudden betrayal and testy judgment, especially from someone who had such an obvious skin affliction.

"I don't smell!" I protested. "I shower every day now because the teacher said so. Before I didn't, but I do now!"

"Well, a lot of other girl say you smell funny," Pizza Head pointed out, as if this were an encyclopedic fact. "They say you go to special ed because there's something wrong with you. I guess you should probably leave soon because I don't want the other girls to see me talking to you. If they like me, they might invite me to go to mall."

"I order you to be my friend!" I shouted, furious at her for dismissing me so easily.

In her place, I would have probably done the same thing except I would have ended our friendship with a strong farewell punch. I'd have given myself a broken or bloody nose if I'd been Pizza-Head, if I were ever so lucky as to be invited anywhere. She was exactly the type of friend that I would latch onto as an older teenager and adult, someone who had access to foreign food and money, and maintained a cool deformity. At the time, though, I saw her through my father's eyes: she wasn't even a delectable frozen pizza from Safeway; she was just a spud. A cheap potato.

Even though I was not fully attached to our version of friendship, I felt that I should have gotten a little more return for the efforts I had made. It was like handing over all your Lunar New Year and Christmas money to a jerky older cousin who promised you his Pokémon trading card collection and did not follow through, but what you really should have done was deposit the eighty dollars from your aunties and uncles in a savings account until you could afford the Pokémon deluxe collector's edition.

I stomped off into the evergreens and chucked a rock at a fat singing blue jay, which missed. I felt wounded and bewildered. What just happened? My father had not explained the bratty betrayals of little-girl friendships. He made it seem like you showed up, paid a person in cookies or cash, and were thus entitled to make them do whatever you wanted.

Furious, the next time I saw Pizza Head lounging alone on her front steps, minus her new cool friends, I stuck out my tongue and gave her the finger—the only thing I knew how to do.

The very next morning, a pouting Pizza Head came by with a necklace, a lumpy translucent rock on a flimsy silver chain—a peace offering.

"That Woman says I have to be friends with you or I can't use my credit card anymore," Pizza Head announced, huffily. "That Woman says our job is to make the entire block like us, so you better take this stupid necklace. If I don't like you, then your parents won't like us."

"I don't want your necklace," I said, which was true. "Why would I want to wear necklace with an ugly rock on it?"

"What wrong with you?!" Pizza Head said, horrified. "It's Swarovski! What you want instead? Chocolate? Money?"

"Maybe," I admitted, and thought that if she had just brought over five or ten bucks, I could forgive her for dismissing me earlier. I did not know what Swarovski was and did not want a gigantic, heavy rock. How could she think that she could repair our friendship by giving me a collar for a St Bernard?

"Fine," Pizza Head snapped. "Let's go back to my place and That Woman will give you present. I'm gonna keep necklace, but don't tell That Woman."

"Whatever," I said, trying not to let her see that I cared very much.

I still felt hurt and betrayed, so I did what I thought would cause anyone else pain. I stomped at the back of Pizza Head's heels as I followed her across the cul-de-sac—the quickest thing I could think of.

"Owwwww!" Pizza Head complained, rubbing her heels so that more of her skin flaked off. "Watch where you going, idiot!"

"Don't be baby," I said, recognizing that I was being as callous as I could, and stepped on the back of her flip-flops again. Soon, this turned into a competition of cruelty: name-calling and grass-flinging. Eventually, I decided that I didn't want a friend anymore.

"Where you going?" Pizza Head asked me, a little shocked when I turned to go. "Come back right now!"

It took a long time before I could see that Pizza Head was permanently stuck with That Woman and Him, as I was stuck with my own parents, and that we were like unfortunate amphibians locked in the same pet store terrarium. She was most definitely a victim of her circumstances, as unhappy and surly as I was. Whereas her sores were bright and open, mine were dark and hidden inside, like termites or a dead body in an eccentric uncle's freezer.

Certainly, I recognized her misery on some fundamental level, as much as I accepted essential forces like hunger or schoolyard malice, yet instead of making me feel a little more sympathetic, it just made me dislike her even more. I saw my ugliness and short-tempered wretchedness mirrored in her scrunched-up skin and glassy, bewildered eyes. It was as if I was hearing my voice for the first time on a tape recording and was shocked by how strange and tinny it sounded.

Suddenly, I despised her for being so goddamn sad all the time. Of course, later I realized it was because I was seeing myself.

As a Neanderthal sixth grader, my first instinct was to scream and make the monster go away.

So in that moment I reacted instinctively and cruelly. I threw a rock at Pizza's head before stampeding away.

Maybe the openly generous Pizza Family drew unwanted attention with their exorbitant hydro bills because a month later there was a major police raid and all the neighbours were ordered indoors for the day. Three police cars and a special unit van containing a narcotics team kicked open the Pizza family's McMansion doors. One of the mahogany panels fell off, and a police officer lugged it out of the way as if he were dragging a body.

From our front window, I watched a team of eight cops smash their basement windows, the glass falling like wilful icicles, the sound deafening and frightening. One by one, officers with heavy shields and gas masks confiscated more than 500 marijuana plants in black pots. I had never actually seen a grow-op before and was so disappointed—these were just plants that anyone, rich or poor, might grow in a garden. I had envisioned marijuana to be beautifully packaged candies, delicious despite the stink. I didn't understand all the fuss over a bunch of potted plants that made our neighbourhood smell like dead skunk and old man breath.

Pizza Head and her parents were not home that day. Maybe a loyal neighbour had tipped them off. For the next six hours, I peeked through our foyer's grimy windows to see what the exciting Pizza family would do next. When the police raid was finally over, and it was dark and only the coyotes were prowling the garbage for dinner bones, I saw the Pizza's family's BMW creep into the cul-de-sac. As soon as they saw that half their front door was missing and that their first-floor windows had been boarded up with planks and industrial garbage bags, they backed up and vanished.

I wondered what was going on inside that car: were they yelling and screaming and blaming each other for something that had gone terribly wrong like a real family would, or were they unsentimental professionals, stoically accepting the setback and moving on? Had this happened in their last-cul-de-sac? Did they have multiple backup marijuana houses and fake passports and IDs? I imagined Pizza Head would be scratching her flaky pie-crust arms in agitation, and when they reached their new destination, there would be nothing left of her except a mound of dead skin, like a pile of unbleached flour collected in the backseat.

If this incident had happened in my early twenties, I'd have packed a bag, rushed over, and begged to become a member of their absurd little tribe, offering to pose as someone's big sister or bratty niece, if it meant getting my hands on some free weed. Instead, I just stared passively through the blinds. In the mountain blackness, which meant total darkness at five p.m., the house, without its door, no longer looked like a fun Disneyland palace. It was menacing and unclean. Just a broken, deserted junkyard castle.

I called Pizza Head and tried to message her online, but her cellphone and MSN account were suddenly deactivated. Eventually, I gave up and watched their house with a voyeuristic, vulture-like curiosity. That week, several police cars patrolled our cul-de-sac, but all of our neighbours insisted that they didn't speak English. They were not talking.

During my watch, I once saw a chrome-coloured Mercedes slowly drive by with a group of youngish Asian men in business suits, who must have seen the boarded-up windows, because they shouted something panicky before zooming away. The house stayed shut down for only a few weeks. Then some real estate tycoons fixed it up and two grinning, charismatic Vietnamese men named Moolah and Poodle purchased it for a bargain price of $1.9 million to manufacture more cash-crop drugs.

For a while, our cul-de-sac began to see female carriers on foot, hired catalogue models dressed like country club tennis players—at least fifteen different girls each day—in brand-new sun visors and sporty white dresses, their identical blue duffel bags most likely stuffed full of drugs. They looked too upscale and sophisticated for weed, so it must have been cocaine or ecstasy. The hired girls would jog their circulatory route back and forth from the ex–Pizza home, always looking over one shoulder, eternally smiling—a perfect J. Crew catalogue of our specialized Poteau lifestyle. They'd deliver their moneymaking goods to different houses on the mountain, never once stopping at the Poteau country club where they were supposed to be playing tennis.

When I look back at this, I think about how amazing it all was, and how you could make people do anything for free lobsters and chocolate. It wasn't as if you couldn't acquire live crustaceans or sweets from the local supermarket, but people, no matter how much money they had, enjoyed free things. It seemed that as long as you hid behind your immaculate house with its green lawn and were kind to your neighbours most of the time, you had absolutely no one to answer to, except yourself.

I too then convinced myself that I was inherently special, exempt from and above the rules, better than many people, or at least better than everyone else my age, so I continued skulking behind my grisly bamboo bush. And with grand and unmistakable glee, I resumed my illicit water-gun activities, soaking anyone dumb enough to wander into my staked-out territory.

CHAPTER 3
ON THE ICE

After a year without paranormal incident, when I was twelve years old, my mother suddenly checked out again. It was just before the semifinals of my peewee winter hockey tournament at our home rink, Planet Ice, and I still had to play.

During the year without incident our family had been surviving, at least to our very minimal standards, and one night, my mother and father had woken my siblings and me at two a.m. and ordered us into the van because they had suddenly decided to drive from Vancouver to California.

"No ghost follow Mommy to Disneyland," my father happily promised us, as he handed out Costco-sized bags of discounted Halloween candy for the trip. During those three weeks we were frighteningly spontaneous, and I think it was the only time my parents seemed like they weren't furious at each other and themselves.

And then, without consulting any of us, when I was at the start of seventh grade my father signed us all up for little league hockey, which was supposed to keep us "busy" and distract my mother from her ghosts. She had no choice but to become a hockey mom of three, a transformation that bewildered and terrified her—*What the fuck is the point of this Canada sport?!*

Our manic hockey extracurricular was also supposed to make our family assimilate faster into North American culture. As if possessing enough money to throw three kids into organized sports meant that we had achieved a recreational version of the American sitcom dream. Hockey practice was also a way to toughen us up, which I didn't realize until I was fully grown—my father wanted his children to learn discipline and heroic fearlessness by participating in a sport condoned by our country's culture. He did not want us to be terrified and seemingly "weak" like our mother.

Unfortunately, he did not consider that the hectic four a.m. practice schedules and nine p.m. away games on school nights would make my mother crankier and more volatile.

At three one morning, she finally drove off. "Sorry," she apologized to my sister, who was nine years old and an excellent worrier. "If you're hungry, Daddy only knows how to make rice, so it sucks to be you."

I said nothing, because this was her blunt way of stating a fact (Daddy *was* indeed a shitty cook). I watched her stomp away with her winter coat and car keys, disappointed. I felt like her least favourite child; she did not even acknowledge me, and I was already insecure, so this further unsettled me in a jealous, mercurial way.

"If you won all your hockey game," my father said to me before the semifinal game, "she'd have stayed. No one like to watch loser. You need to win MVP so she will like you."

He may have been attempting a joke, but at this point, I think even he knew he had failed at keeping her on track towards middling sustainable sanity. It was getting harder and harder to conceal his sadistic shame with humour—and his humour was becoming uglier and blacker.

"Okay," I said, not understanding the whole situation, but I was dumb—i.e., desperate and hurt and disturbed—enough to try to please him.

During the preceding year, when the ghosts seemed to have forgotten about my mother, I contentedly spent an hour or two at craft classes at a local arts school, where I learned how to weave Eastern patterned tapestries and operate an old-fashioned printing press. But weaving and papermaking were not as stimulating or exciting to watch as real-time hockey for my father, who felt that I had a second-rate talent for crafts, so I was paid to hit other little girls in AA hockey.

Whether my father was training a small-time thug or just another pragmatic Chinese kid who valued money, I was paid a decent goon's commission: twenty dollars per penalty, five dollars per goal, three dollars per assist. I did not particularly enjoy organized hockey, but it was a job, much like attending middle school.

In sixth grade, a dirty game of hockey could mean an easy sixty bucks. I became a little sumo wrestler, who leaped around on pointy designer blades, custom-made double E size 3 boy's skates because I had fat, archless feet that seemed to expand sideways. I just had to vary and combine the main offences: charging, body-checking, tripping. Throw in some comedic high-sticking. If I busted my stick and still played during my shift, it was an automatic penalty (I ruined a couple good sticks before each game). My father checked with the scorekeeper, tallied up the money, and coughed up the cash when we got home, because otherwise, I refused to participate. Paying someone to partake in an organized team sport was much easier than spanking them or hitting them with plastic hangers, which was something he did when money failed him.

"She pull diva again," he liked to complain to my mother when she called, always a little disappointed that I did not wholly appreciate a game that defined an entire nation. "Lindsay wouldn't put on her gear, so I had to pay her extra. She doesn't like to move, that's why she's a fat piggy. At least we know our kid will do anything for money."

Hockey was my stop-and-go routine, as if someone punched play and fast-forward repeatedly on a remote control. Bundled in modern gladiatorial gear, I disliked the grid mask of the helmet. It was like squinting through a frightening checkered prison. And I hated the hefty shoulder pads—perverse spaceship armour that bulked up our wimpy girlish shoulders to look more astronautic. The hockey pants were basically oversized girdles developed by NASA. With three private coaches specializing in applied physical theory (skate, pass, slap shot) and abundant private ice time, I made assistant captain within a year and performed until the end of tenth grade.

Hairstyling was my father's ritual before any hockey performance. It seemed to relax him and appeal to his grand and obsessive tendencies. He would compulsively fix my hair into a tight, twisty ponytail for a regular game or French-braid it beautifully for a tournament. He was responsible for hair because my mother was rough-handed and could pluck a strip raw by accident. My father's only hobby, besides his family, was gently sculpting hair into tidy creations. This was his only attempt at bonding with me pregame; he did not know how to use words in encouraging ways, so he embraced drugstore hairbands and elastics, just like a girl feebly twining friendship bracelets for her first-grade class.

"Hair okay?" he would ask. "Now go kick ass."

But if I lost, he sometimes became too involved with the game and punished me by letting me choose a plastic hanger from his closet. He would chase me around the house like a cartoon grizzly, swinging my pink or yellow hanger of choice. I would sprint to the bathroom and lock the door, wondering for how many hours or days or weeks I would have to hide.

Looking back, this is where my father snapped; all humour flooding from him, he resorted to transparent brutality—he intended to smack. He claimed it was to make me harder on the outside, "less of a loser like Mommy." Once, I stayed in the bathroom for eleven hours, hoping that he might get bored and give up. Even though I had stolen twenty dollars from his wallet, I did not think I deserved a whacking. Hockey was a terrible idea for a parent who was already so tortured. The ritualistic team practices, the demanding tournaments with the finger-biting fifty-fifty raffles, the fierce head-cracking penalties—it was too much for a man who loved to win.

To make my mother come back from her three a.m. drive, that weekend I hustled in the semifinals against the Alaskan team so I could become MVP. In our league, I was known for playing brutal defence, and bloodthirsty parents liked to watch my "mean streak," which flowed through me like an all-you-can-eat meal.

I believed that if I won a medal, there was a slim chance my parents might like me, that my mother might come back, even if the kids at school despised me, because it seemed fundamental that one of your parents should feel obligated to you via genetics or societal pressure. Wasn't the main reason you reproduced to create the same, if not a better, version of yourself? I sensed that I was an irritation—like dust lodged in the eye or a small piece of meat stuck between the teeth. And friendless, still, I was horribly lonely. However unmotherly my mother was, I needed her home.

On my shift, I charged down the ice, delicately stick-handling our prized puck, but tripped over someone's stick and somersaulted into the wooden boards like an amateur acrobat. A girl punted me with her skate. I was trapped on my back, and another four or five piled up and pummelled the shit out of one another—our fathers' live weekday entertainment. This was guerrilla hockey for girls who were practically apes, and I thought I was the baddest King Kong in the arena (a result of watching too many *Sailor Moon* cartoons). Boxy gloves were flung down. Black helmets were snapped off and tumbled onto the shimmery ice, little guillotined heads bouncing happily along.

To survive this beastly brawl, I was sly enough to shut my eyes and play dead. But a sick feeling lurched in my tummy, like I had swallowed a writhing beetle or part of my own tongue. It was a feeling that I didn't understand—absolute wrongness.

Suddenly queasy, I threw up a little in my mouth but couldn't tell if I had smacked my head too hard on the boards. I blacked out for a second, abruptly falling asleep. When I woke up, the paramedics said I had a minor concussion. But I could still perform to win back my mother, so I jumped up and insisted I play *now*. My skull thumped, helmet suddenly squeezing too tight, something perhaps not right. I felt my front teeth with my tongue, the bottoms were lightly chipped, my mouth guard stupidly left at home. No blood—not like last time I was clobbered in an offside fight. And not like when my father splintered his molar chomping into a walnut, gargling up gritty crumbs of ground-up enamel and nut.

I was going to be okay, and I was going to be victorious. I did not care if my team won, only if I won MVP overall. This was my deeply troubling mindset at the time: to appease my father and fix my mother.

A period later, I charged a girl centre ice and attacked ferociously, cracking the fleshy back of her lower leg with my stick. The shin guard obviously did not extend fully around. There was just the fuzzy, soft hockey sock to defend her spongy skin, and we both knew something had gone very wrong. She dropped. The linesman and referee allowed us to skate around for a few fast seconds. But then there was a sick little animalistic scream in the arena that got louder and louder. The girl I had whacked was flat on her back. Thrashing her arms in a useless backstroke, she looked like she was having a psychotic break, gone ridiculously mad.

This did not feel real to me at all, as I was back on the bench seeing it all through the plastic screens of the ice rink. I felt that I was watching the action like it was a video game manoeuvred by a disembodied controller.

"How come the girl cry when she get hurt?" my father later asked me in the truck when the girl had been cleared off the ice by the paramedics and the game was finally over. In my fugue-like state, I did not even remember how we had won. "You know if she retarded? Possessed?" he asked. If there were a ghost in the hockey rink, we would know that my mother had inadvertently caught it too, much like how someone could accidentally encounter a ravenous bear in our backyard—shitty luck.

"I broke her leg," I said, unsure whether I should feel guilty. His was a real question, like someone asking for the time or directions—my father didn't seem to understand what crying was for and thought that I could clarify it for him.

In the backseat, I did not feel well, and I did not feel as if I deserved my thrilling victory. The coiling BC freeway loomed like a concrete serpent, and I could feel my insides twist dangerously, as if I were becoming unravelled, while my father drove us home. The foamy blackness outside felt like it had transferred inside me, gurgling like unruly diarrhea, and I wasn't sure what was consciously right; I was afraid I didn't know the answer. While my head tingled from lack of sleep and excitement, I thought about the screaming girl; how much was her own noise, and how much was the wicked ghost inside her?

It would take a while for me to understand that this incident was just another casualty of my father's war for control, just an effortless battle outside the house that he could win: he needed to blame someone for his wife's sudden disappearance, and I was desperate and gullible. He could have blamed my sister, who would have cried for at least half an hour, but I was a better scapegoat because I would be tormented for longer. Prone to guilty sulks, like my daily nosebleeds and constipation, I would have done anything to make things better, even though I had pretended not to care that my mother hadn't said goodbye to me.

"The coach says it was just an accident," I eventually blurted, ignoring the slimy blackness in my gut, which was expanding, like a serving of cold, hard rice, which I then mistook for indigestion. "But I have to write her a nice sorry card."

"Don't bother," my father said, miffed because he hated inconvenience. "It's just a game. And postage all the way to Alaska—yikes. I'm happy we won. Are you happy? If I'm happy, you should be very, very happy. Are you loser or winner, Lindsay? No loser in this family, okay? We have to beat up loser. Now because we won MVP, Mommy will come back."

"Okay," I said, because I really believed him, or because I really wanted to. That there was magic in the bronzy medals that my father hoarded like Viking treasure. These prizes from the tournament somehow made me worthy of his parental respect. Nothing in our family came at a low cost—we paid for everything. If I took home a prize that night, there was hope that my father would not blame me for my mother's absence. I had done my delusional duty, like a good daughter, and my actions, the last ingredient in our homemade spell, would bring back my ghost-driven mother.

Nearly twelve hours later, at home, we pretended my mother didn't desert us. That she was on an extended grocery-shopping trip because of all the food she was collecting for hot pot. This was a special household feast that had everyone in the family cooking pimply cow tongue and squashy white longevity noodles that went on forever; if you choked on them, it meant you were going to die within the year. I imagined the wrinkled bundles of bok choy, the silly confetti tails of limp enoki mushrooms, all gurgling in our burner tabletop.

"Are you worried about Mom?" I asked my father, wanting to know if I should be unhappy or frantic or both or neither. I took my visual emotional cues from him, as I was twelve and a half and didn't know quite how or what to think.

"Why the hell do you want to know for?" he asked, perplexed and scandalized, as if I had asked him to expand on his bathroom habits. "Are you conducting survey on bullshit? Why do you think the answer is important? I worry you are all mentally challenged. First, Lindsay has to go to retarded class because she is dumb and can't talk properly. Then the second one is so bad we need a translator. Don't get me started on the third. You got your genes from Mommy!"

In middle school, my lisp was so bad he thought there was a Talking Demon that made me unable to sound out the letter S correctly. However, my sister was definitely worse off than me and visited the speech therapist every day, whereas I went twice a week. My sister automatically added "ded" to every past-tense verb.

"I ate-ded the sandwich you made-ded me," she once whispered at school. "It tasted-ded bad."

"Thut up," I snapped. "You thuck."

As my sister sobbed non-stop, we were supposed to mock her for crying and not hiding her weakness, for surely she was headed for a bout of demonic possession, which was like deliberately going outside in the snow without a jacket and catching pneumonia.

"Only idiots cry," my father explained to my sister, looking ashamed of her. His parents had taught him that it was ungainly and annoying to others if you blubbered. Emotional displays, like begging on the street, were a burden on everyone, not just the health care system, who had the grisly misfortune to be nearby. "I never cry," he continued, pleased. "Learn to suffer in silence. No more talking until tomorrow. Lindsay got concussion and didn't complain. People who cry become Woo-Woo."

Over the years, we only saw our crazy grandmother blubber, so we believed him. We never knew when our father was truly sad. If someone cried, he believed, you were supposed to quit the room immediately, which I now recognize as a cultural but mostly idiosyncratic belief that was specific to my father.

Growing up, even if I felt a little miserable, I blamed it all on serious dyspepsia, believing that heartburn or gas was the cause of all my unadulterated sadness. I had no useful or tangible name for the Woo-Woo sickness that afflicted us, which was as difficult and impenetrable and coded as a high-clearance intelligence secret. All I knew was that if I appeared weepy and afraid, "a ghost" would slip inside my brain.

Later, my father demanded that I give him my MVP medal, and he dumped it in his special bedroom drawer with all the other warrior possessions—cheap metal trophies that he almost loved more than the game itself. I didn't especially like to relinquish my winnings, but I subconsciously knew that he needed them more than me, like beer or black coffee. My awards built up his confidence and fatherly identity. He must have convinced himself that we were on the most righteous path: we were noiselessly suffering while winning medals, which meant that the universe would reward us and bring my mother back. I would be generous and donate my earnings to our cause.

We then took a seat in the piano room and he proudly insisted we practise for the upcoming concert, which was a year away.

For a week, maybe two, we still didn't hear from our possessed mother, so we decided not to speak about the missing time. But all the while, as he neared the edge of all he could take, unused to being a single parent of three, my father reacted by telling more of his perplexingly harsh grown-up jokes. In movies, a missing person always meant a dramatic suicide, like the bad dreams that kept my sister up all night cradling the cordless phone. But we continued with our hockey games and intensive immigrant piano practice schedules—three to four hours of Beethoven, Piano Sonata No. 1 in F minor, after a sadistic bout of hockey. You didn't need a metronome if you had my father: "One-ee-and-ah-two-ee-and-ahh-are-you-fuck-ing-deaf-why-does-it-say-canta-bile-and-then-over-there-it's-all-eegretto? Why are you so fucking retarded, you buy Beethoven written in French not English?"

He pretendezd nothing was wrong by throwing himself into my piano practice, kept stubbornly counting off beat. He refused to look for my mother or call the police. He did not trust outsider *lo-fahn* authority with such horrible family matters—if they located our mother, they might lock her up. Apparently, we just had to wait. Chomp on chocolate bars until our molars decayed. Order in cheap Chinese takeout—hard salted rice with fish bits that looked like overcooked boogers, gooey beef chow fun congealing in shiny fat.

This was the candid, respectable, saving-face Chinese way: doing absolutely nothing.

This was how the stoic Wongs fiercely handled their spazzy, unmanageable family crises.

"Go do battle," he insisted before every hockey practice, as if he could fix our problems with a simple directive. His pep talk referenced a legend from the Northern and Southern Dynasties. "Hua Mulan saved her daddy from going off to war. She disguised herself as a boy because her daddy was old. So she went off to war for him and killed lots of people and the emperor gave her tons of awards and, most importantly, money. So put on your fucking gear and do battle for me, okay? Her daddy didn't pay her, she went for free. Would you go to war to save me?"

"I really have to think about it," I said, not knowing how to lie yet (this was a trick question that I always failed), but my sister, who was a show-off and brat, always agreed.

Since hockey had always been my father's fixation, he required the little league violence to sustain him over the winter months; he risked the slippery, zigzagging roller coaster ride to the rink, swerving on black ice. At the time, it certainly seemed that he loved hockey more than himself, which was saying something, and he woke us up three hours before a seven a.m. game to make sure we would arrive on time.

On sunny, frostless days, it took a minimum of forty-five minutes to drive from the Poteau to Planet Ice. In the winter, it took hours, and he stocked the pickup truck with a sack of salt, flashlights, and gardening shovels. "Get ready to dig if we stuck!" he ordered, because he could be more obsessive than my mother, who did not want to be up so early, and she would be calling him "a fucking selfish retard" over a thermos of coffee in the passenger seat.

On one drive to a weekend game, I wondered aloud if she was parked at the mall, but my father refused to slow down to check, saying it was "too much bullshit."

I did not know this at the time, but his screwy Chinese stoicism made him so self-conscious that he could not be caught worrying.

"Kids, she's not on the news," he declared as he drove us to the rink, as my heart tumbled into my stomach, like something poisonous, cheap, and deep-fried. I didn't want to cry—just to throw up—which I took as an excellent sign that I was strong enough not to get possessed by some nasty Woo-Woo.

"Good enough!" my father continued, trying to reassure us in a much cheerier voice. "Means my wife didn't bang into a lamppost. She's such a terrible driver we'd hear it by now. It'd be a domino effect, she'd take down five cars with her and they'd all be lying in ditch."

For that week, my poor, obedient nine-year-old sister tidied up the house every day and waited anxiously for our mother. She was a good daughter: my father certainly thought so and paid her fifty dollars to do the chores. My brother slumped after her and called my sister Mommy, and I was relieved that he did not follow me. Even then, I knew I was not a role model or any kind of rousing cheerleader and would gladly relinquish the role of eldest to my sister. She was the most responsible and screamed at my father and me if we did not clean up our messes or if we abandoned her with the dirty dishes. But being the one in charge, she'd still scrub all the plates with sulky diligence. While she mopped the floors, I took advantage of her work ethic and my father's distraction and watched an R-rated horror movie, which I would not have been allowed if my mother were home. She was always scared that Jack Nicholson in *The Shining* might lunge out of the TV, smashing the screen with his axe.

Unfortunately, my sister did not know how to do laundry and my father, useless at domestic annoyances, could not teach her:

our hockey gear, three black duffels that looked like frumpy body bags, and our soiled clothes were rotting in the laundry room that we could smell all the way upstairs—our yellow skull-esque helmets and sweaty girl's jock straps smelled like fresh cat piss. He suggested that my sister and I check the internet for instructions, but our dial-up connection was too slow, and no one knew how to spell "laundry" for the search engine. My sister and I had been tested for dyslexia and the results were inconclusive.

My brilliant solution was to shut the door, and my sister spritzed it with my mother's terrible Givenchy perfume, which gave the house a tangier scent of pee and yesterday's compost. My father said he would just replace the bottle later.

I decided that my mother was making a retail tour of all the malls in suburban Hongcouver with her Woo-Woo ghost. I was confident that she was having a blast: a real vacation away from her demanding husband and offspring. And no one would hurt my sick, broken mother—she could kick terrific ass if she needed to. At times, she might seem vulnerable, but my mother had a ferocious tongue on her, and she would not hesitate to use it on any poor stranger. Looking back, the woman whose desire for kids at all is still unclear must have really hated driving us to hockey practice at four in the morning three or four times a week.

"I tried-ded to call-ded Mom," my sister whispered to me one night, as she cradled an ancient-looking stuffed animal. Our bedrooms were at opposite ends of the hallway, and she had suddenly appeared like some starving ghost-child, in an ugly undershirt with a gaping hole in the chest. "She's not picking up, Lindsay. I called-ded and called-ded. What if she dead-ed?"

"People only die in movies," I said, but she was a precocious kid and she immediately knew that I was lying.

My sister began to cry, and somehow we ended up arguing because she called me "a stupid idiot," so I got angry, leaped out of bed, and punched her in the mouth. I couldn't help it: my nerves were ablaze and it scared me that I couldn't control myself. Punching others was how I communicated my unfiltered sorrow, and it let me feel powerful and peaceful again. No pre-teen was more furious, near-sighted, and deluded than I was. I didn't regret hitting her until her front tooth got wobbly and tumbled out. I did not mean to smash out her tooth in an episode of older-sibling brutality. But my mother should have been there to pluck it from her slippery gums, as she had done with all my movable baby teeth, like she was yanking out an unremitting weed. She enjoyed pulling our teeth, like other mothers took to baking or aerobics.

"At least Dad will pay you two dollars for it," I said, trying my best to cheer her up. "He's a really cheap tooth fairy. But you'll get two dollars!"

"WAHHH," she sobbed, not at all comforted by the fact that she would earn two whole dollars. At her age, I'd have happily taken the money and bought two hefty candy bars from the vending machine. Already, my sister and I were very different people; she feared the loss of only two teeth when she still had, like, twenty extra ones with no cavities. We may have shared the same parents, but we did not understand the other—we were already evolutionary strangers, a billion genetic mutations and maybe an ice age or two apart.

Having no idea how to calm her down, I ignored her wailing and made her an offer that I thought was more than generous at the time: "Do you want me to punch out all your other baby teeth? You could make twelve whole bucks, which is a lot of money!"

She did not stop crying.

"Thut-up," I said. "Do you want Dad to hear?"

At six one morning, my mother came back. It had only been a few weeks, but to a kid it felt as if it had been a year. It seemed that my life had an open-door policy: adults magically appeared or reappeared—it was like Narnia or a two-star motel where anyone could check out whenever they pleased. During this period of my life, I was embittered, plagued with blistering spasms of anxiety, which manifested in the form of dry-eyed insomnia. I'd lie awake on my mattress for hours, heart thumping in zombie time, listing out loud the ways that my mother could die. This sounds very gruesome but was bedtime meditation for me.

And then she was suddenly back, in our kitchen, carelessly frying up green onion pancakes and pork dumplings, the plump milky fists ballooning and popping in a heated pan. She looked ghoulish, her eyes engorged, skin like our wallpaper: fluorescent yellow-green.

"Where did-ded you go?" my sister asked, starting to whimper. "Why did-ded you go?"

"What are you talking about?" my mother barked, looking stunned. She did not like crying because it attracted the ghosts, and I knew my sister would get spanked if she continued to make that awful noise.

"You went-ded away," my sister insisted, sniffing buttery snot, and I was furious that she was acting possessed like the stupid girl at the hockey rink. Didn't she know that we had to be emotionally strong if we didn't want the ghosts to take our parents away? I decided then that I was going to punch her again if she did not immediately stop. Anything to prevent the Woo-Woo from coming back. So emotionally disabled was I, like a piece of plastic, it was a miracle that I didn't just give up and agree to be a dense, psychotic thug with a hard Gobstopper heart.

"You have too much imagination," my mother said, shaking her head as if her neck were convulsing. "I haven't gone anywhere.

I cooked you guys a big dinner yesterday and the day before. The whole fucking week and the last. No? Well, that's your problem. You guys are so fucking unappreciative."

She grunted, stared at us like we were all grotesque and nutso. Maybe she thought we were playing make-believe. Eventually, we realized she really believed what she was saying or had convinced herself to believe her own tepid lies, that she had been living at home all along. My sister, who was smarter than me, knew not to push it and pretended nothing had happened. She began setting the table. We could all see that there was white Chinese pancake dough in the frying pan, the uneasy shush of splashy oil hissing at us, mocking us. We all must have known that our mother smelled terribly rancid, as she cooked up our delicious ghostly cuisine only a few feet away. But she was our mother, and it felt wrong not to appreciate, if not *like*, every aspect and spastic version of her. It was an improvement when she wasn't sad.

"I think there's something wrong with Mom?" I said, sucking sour air through my mouth. But everyone tried not to hear me. "Dad?" I said louder, hating myself for sounding so feeble and worried. "Can't you smell her?"

"Shut the fuck up," my father ordered, in one of his intensely unpleasant suck-it-up moods. I didn't know this then, but he hated pushing his luck, and he was so glad that our lives could finally go back to "normal"—hockey practice was in a few days. "If you can't talk properly, why talk at all?" he asked, turning on me. "Why the fuck you eating, huh? Fat, fat, fat."

I was afraid to show him that this exchange hurt me, so I kept my face blank and stared past him.

Later, I saw him pacing up and down the halls, while my mother impassively watched her soap operas. In the TV room, we would sit cross-legged with our mother on the floor, because we weren't allowed to share the sofa with my father, who insisted on maintaining what he called a "personal boundary" from his wife and offspring. As usual, my parents did not touch one another after my father's frantic stumbling, because of his insistence on keeping us at least two feet away, and their eyes did not seem to leave the TV screen.

Somehow, at that age, I also knew that if my father lost himself, we were all deeply and indefinitely screwed to the exponent of 10,000. He could not afford to vanish; someone needed to make money and look after us. In that moment I was very aware that my mother might not ever fully recover. And I was scared that we were all going to be spastic cosmic orphans, pathetic little planets spinning non-stop, if my father didn't pull himself together and teach us how to effectively orbit around our out-in-space mother.

But in retrospect, I see he was afraid to catch the Woo-Woo ghost from my mother and had to physically, if not emotionally, distance himself. By enrolling us in little league hockey and ordering us not to appear emotionally fragile, he was promoting our self-reliance—in case we needed to fend for ourselves. But he seemed to be struggling with his own life lesson after my mother came home.

"What should we do?" he suddenly asked me, as the TV blasted conversation. He kept his face more empty than usual during our alien exchange. "My wife ... screw up!" he practically screamed at me, heartbroken and petrified. "She go Woo-Woo, you know!"

For a vaporous moment, I was confused by his shrill, suddenly humanlike behaviour. I think that I understood that winning another hockey game had not entirely fixed our problem, and that I had broken the girl's leg for almost nothing. But I refused to admit it: *yes,* my magic trophies and sacrifices in the arena had returned my mother, but she was as maliciously cracked as that damned femur. And she needed special help—a certainty that I was only then beginning to comprehend.

My father may have talked as if he did not care when our mother was missing, but he was as lost as I was, perhaps even more so.

"Why you asking me?" I finally snapped at him, unbelieving. "I'm the dumb one, remember?"

"Yes," he agreed, and went to ask my sister for unswerving, no-bullshit answers.

CHAPTER 4
YOU CAN'T ESCAPE THE WOO-WOO

I thought Auntie Beautiful One, my mother's youngest sister, was the sanest in our extended family, as she, unlike my mother, was a thriving franchise restaurant queen of salty Vietnamese food, i.e., a very successful business owner, which seemed separate from the Woo-Woo. Although she had always been moody and vain, I did not think that she could be a lunatic because when I was an adolescent, I thought anyone who, like my father, performed tasks outside the house and was decently paid could not be insane. However, her husband, Uncle E.T., was another matter entirely. Like my mother, he stayed home, as if he had to be hidden from public judgment, so I viewed him as Woo-Woo too.

With his abnormally large head and thin, crooked tree-branch limbs, Uncle E.T. had been a victim of malicious childhood polio and was nicknamed after Spielberg's deformed alien. Rumoured to be an ex–Vietnamese gangster, my uncle was an extreme man who spoke in sickly grunts and guttural screams. We were all immensely frightened of Uncle E.T., who force-fed his three misbehaving children cheap supermarket cat food. I am not joking when I say that if you were insolent, you got a container full of crusty kibbles for a school lunch the next day. We had all witnessed Uncle E.T., who supposedly came from Asian street-gang culture, tie his children to a chair with skipping rope if they did not finish all the vegetables on their dinner plates.

Uncle E.T. was every kid's number one bogeyman parent and the reason I was afraid to be invited for sleepovers at the Beautiful One household. But what terrified me most was that Uncle E.T. kept a militant Poo Schedule tacked to the bathroom door. In the Beautiful One household, a bowel movement was an extraordinary privilege, and the Poo Schedule was meant to keep you safe from Woo-Woo ghosts, who attacked lazy children who sat too long on the toilet. It was considered unhealthy to be alone and very hazardous to your mental health, so your bowel-movement time was closely monitored and checked off by a responsible adult.

Once, when I had been invited to spend a long weekend at their home, I had been too mortified to sign up for a three-minute slot. The bathroom door was always locked, unless you could prove to Uncle E.T. (who had the key) that you had registered. For seventy-two hours, I clutched my aching abdomen and thought about digging a latrine in the backyard with my bare hands, while my cousins argued over double-booking. Finally, I became so constipated and hysterical that I was rushed to the emergency room for what everyone thought was aggressive appendicitis.

Perhaps marrying Uncle E.T. and then allowing him to run their household was a precursor to my aunt's breakdown, but at the time, it just seemed to me that she had poor judgment and a very picky husband, especially since Uncle E.T. insisted on tracking the amount of toilet paper that had been used. They were much wealthier than us, but if you dared use more than three pieces, Uncle E.T. accused you of being wasteful.

My mother liked Beautiful One the best of her seven siblings, so it meant that we often took our holidays together. My mother was the only one who wanted to go with what my father, not realizing the irony, called "that freak show family." The sisters gossiped on the phone for hours each day, and it saddened my mother that I did not get along with my sister, Deep Thinker. At this point, my sister and I were sworn enemies. I was savagely jealous that she was much smarter than me, knowing instinctively how to mimic her peers' smiley-faced social cues and receiving all As in school. Unlike my sister, I was hypersensitive despite being a bully, and I allowed my home life to interfere with my gross misperception of the exterior world. And Deep Thinker was furious because she thought that I was the favourite child—"the bestest kid," who received the most criticism from our parents, which in our Chinese family meant lavish attention. "Fuck you!" somehow meant "I care about you!" because everyone knew that there were multiple ghosts listening to us, so it was better not to show any weakness.

Most summers, we went camping with Auntie Beautiful One and her family. Our standard vacations often meant RVing, i.e., luxury camping, in Canada's only desert, in southern BC. To get to Osoyoos, a dry pouch of town in wine country in the Okanagan Valley, we drove five, six, sometimes seven hours on dipping and twisting cement, the fat home-away-from-home trailer bumbling behind our copper pickup truck. From Osoyoos, off Highway 97, you could walk to the Washington State border, bypassing mounds of urine-coloured grass before veering into orchards vending red, swollen fruit. The highway was a callous hummock folding outwards like uncertain origami—a potholed journey that was supposed to take us away from the darkness of our house. But Beautiful One's family madly pursued us, towing their large trailer—our families had identical pickup trucks, because we had gotten a cheap two-for-one bargain. We did not stop, driving like we were all being chased by some very murderous Woo-Woo, which we were, in a way. My parents suffered from a permanent refugee mindset, acting as if we could be deported or mass murdered anytime, especially when a new prime minister was elected.

This particular holiday to Osoyoos, during the summer of 2000, was also supposed to be a month-long mental escape from my maternal grandmother, Poh-Poh, who had gone off her medications and believed the refrigerator was out to assassinate her. She wanted to move in with us. This was unacceptable, and my parents commanded us to pack the RV and abandon house immediately. My grandmother was always shit news because she brought the Woo-Woo with her, and as extreme people, we believed that we could avoid all our problems by declaring ourselves "Vacation." Like declaring ourselves "Not It" in a game of constant and childish tag, "Vacation" meant that we could abandon our responsibilities and current lives for as long as possible, because it was far too hard and heartbreaking to live in the present.

At the time, I couldn't imagine the impossibility of staring your mother's vortex of insanity in the eyeballs, as though seeing your future before you, in the form of a person, crumbling—though I would soon enough. Looking back, I can see the two sisters must have been finding comfort, even a sense of normalcy, in each other.

All the way to the desert, my mother cracked sunflower seeds with her back teeth, spitting out the grainy, streaked carcasses as she screamed at my father in the harassed bluntness of her bazooka Chinese. When in "Vacation" mode, my parents' fights escalated, and we all knew my mother would lose, because she was sitting in the passenger seat in a car driven by a very bad-tempered man.

"Why are you so negative all the time, huh?" she spat, annoyed at my father for his sulking.

"I hate Beautiful One. I thought this was a family vacation, but you bring that crazy harpy along," my father complained, making it known to all of us that we should hate Beautiful One because he hated her. Since he was the boss of our family, it was assumed that we should take on his opinions and beliefs, just as we had inherited his last name.

"She's my sister, okay?" my mother eventually said, sounding defensive. "It's not like you even have a family. You don't even call them. Beautiful One isn't crazy. You're just a fucking weirdo who has no emotions and thinks everyone who cries is crazy."

"Beautiful One is a liar, a selfish bitch, a hypochondriac who thinks she's going to die every day. I buy a truck, she buys same truck and says hers is better. Then we get trailer, she has to buy a bigger, more expensive trailer. Next time don't tell them where we're going. They can house Poh-Poh, that fucking piece of shit. You and her are both crazy, always on the phone, three hours a day. All day long, bullshitting. You tell her everything, and now everyone in Vancouver knows about my hemorrhoid."

This was a typical rant from my father, and my mother started shrieking. They continued screaming at each other, and my father drove as fast as he could, and I was scared that we would lose control and flip over on the freeway; the truck and trailer would smash us all into unrecognizable charred bits. This kind of thinking, of course, was absolutely ridiculous. If my mother had been at the wheel, I'm sure we'd have immediately crashed. But thank God my father was always on autopilot and did not seem remotely affected by the fight, except that arguing made him break all the speed limits. My siblings and I, who desperately wanted to pick on each other and fight, decided it was best to be invisible and quiet until we were closer to our destination.

But even a vacation couldn't give my mother a break from herself. I didn't realize that I too had been hoping for an interruption in her black hole of madness on this shitty vacation until one morning when it became clear that the Woo-Woo had pursued us, and my mother enacted its violence more wickedly than I'd ever thought possible.

My mother flung back my pink Hello Kitty sheets, thrust a stove lighter under my foot, and set it aflame. She had been normal the night before, serving up canned spaghetti in plastic bowls and asking me if I wanted fourths and fifths, like a very different, separate person. "Eat more," she had commanded, hurriedly piling noodles on everyone's plate, seeming excited. Even my aunt seemed to feed off her energy as she quickly dished up steamed tofu, bok choy, and sliced chicken—our families always ate lunch and dinner together when camping. Before bed, my mother began to obsessively scrub the trailer, freezing our camping meals: fried rice and lo mein. She mopped the floor, dusted the cupboards, and complained that she couldn't sleep. Usually, when she was generous and hyperactive like this, she'd let me stay up all night and we'd frantically bake hundreds and hundreds of cupcakes, decorating the counters and chairs of our house until our crumbly creations went stale and inedible.

We should have recognized this normalized calm before the eruption of a full-fledged Woo-Woo hurricane. Because this morning, she had completely lost it. We were 515 kilometres from the epicentre of crazy (Poh-Poh), but we were parked perfectly in sync beside Beautiful One and her family in a dehydrated RV resort. We had matching trailers, so how could she not go Woo-Woo?

I was beginning to realize that the madness in our DNA was a life-threatening disease, transmitted like a pesky airborne infection, attacking and mutating the pink and grey confetti cells of the brain.

It was a twenty-first-century plague that seemed to affect only the women in our family, and there was no standard vaccination. The day my mother burned me, I saw clearly: if you caught the Woo-Woo, you had to let it run its course and hope that you survived with unnoticeable scars.

Maybe she'd had just enough of fighting with my father or she was just truly insane, but I was tired and slept in past ten a.m., so she ignited my foot as if it were a backyard barbecue pit. A utilitarian gas stove. With her multi-purpose utility lighter, with its stainless-steel tip and extendable flame for those hard-to-reach places.

Clickety click-click. The flame suddenly poked the bottom of my left foot. Like something soft but raw and painful. I screamed, the shock radiating into my toes. I would never have expected it from my mother. My father, maybe—he crossed over the blackish border of cruelty so easily. But never from my mother, who was someone who disappeared whenever she couldn't take it anymore.

"Hey, fatty," she suddenly said, and climbed up to the top bunk of the RV and aimed again for my favourite cotton sheets, not caring that she could light the entire bed ablaze. But she got the piggy toes of the same foot instead and I shrieked.

That summer, my stomach had begun to protrude with adolescent misery, and my face and breasts had seemed to bloat like oversized helium balloons. Puberty had transformed me into a four-foot-eight, 140-pound goblin, more grungy and cave dwelling than the smiling, bejewelled child's Treasure Trolls that seemed to horrify everyone, my mother included.

I was used to unnecessary wake-up calls from my emotional insomniac mother, but never like this. She had always been paranoid about Woo-Woo scourging, and I believe that summer she thought a demon had squirmed inside my fragile head when she wasn't looking.

The poor woman blamed herself for not being a vigilant ghost-hunting mommy. I was fat and lazy and stupid, which obviously meant that I was possessed. My mother believed that her sole life purpose was to exorcise any family member's ailing cranium and banish the evil Woo-Woo. She believed that she had been Chosen and was taking her duty seriously.

As a child, I did not know burning someone was wrong, that violence was evil and even illegal in many countries in the world. Certainly, I felt queasy, baffled, and betrayed, but I did not understand the horrendous soul-shattering implications. How do you begin to recover from a nuclear stabbing to the heart and brain? How do you begin to understand that what was done to you is hateful and intolerable? As an adult, it is both saddening and infuriating that my mother did not seem to understand her actions or remember her potent mania. I wanted to hate her, but I couldn't. She was my mother, but I despised what she did to me when I was an impressionable young teen.

Those in our Chinese community, Little Hongcouverites who knew my mother, said she looked like the Hong Kong actress Faye Wong, sleepy eyes with a coarse, bitchy temper. Not that I could see the resemblance, but I agreed about my mother's weird, shitty moods. Her black hair was always in linty pink and yellow curlers; she weighed only ninety pounds, agile enough to swing into the top bunk of our RV to exorcise me. Uncle E.T. had forbidden Beautiful One to have frizzy hair like my mother, because he thought all the toxins and chemicals might leak into his wife's brain and make her go insane, and who knew what she could one day do?

"Curly hair means brain problem," Uncle E.T. once told me at a dinner party. "That's why I think your mommy crazy. If she straighten her hair, she won't be. Tell her that for me." Eight years later, when Auntie Beautiful One would try to jump off a bridge, he would blame her new haircut; it would be the hairdresser's fault for making his wife Woo-Woo—choppy, blunt ends meant that bits of her brain had gone missing, left on the salon's floor. We were far too literal in our family, and so quick to blame.

Apparently, I thought, my father and my sister and brother don't even understand what the world "Help!" means. English was our second language. My father could not have been more useless.

At the time, I didn't understand why my mother didn't burn the shit out of my nitwit siblings too. But the truth was, I was a convenient target for her intense frustrations. How could she scream at my two siblings when they were up and already following her orders? I was sleeping and perhaps peaceful, which may have irked her on some cruel, fundamental level; my ability to sleep soundly as a teen may have been annoying to my mother, who was lucky to have three hours of sleep per week. Until now, I had been pretty loyal to her—not exactly perfect but good enough to earn maybe fifteen or twenty bucks in my job as eldest daughter. This was the first time she had actually hurt me.

Before Osoyoos, I had trusted my mother implicitly, believing that she was going to save us from the Woo-Woo and keep me relatively safe. But loss of familial trust is like a screwdriver in the eye or a sledgehammer in the forehead—it's more the shock that causes the internal damage, and you don't even think about the pain or the bleeding or the spreading infection of hate until later. My mother had never been violent towards me—she had screamed, yelled, and carelessly threatened, but she had never caused me any real physical harm, and I think that it was this hard disbelief that kept me relatively high-functioning and level-headed in the trailer.

Although I did question whether this was my mother or an actual ghost.

To drown out my freak-show screeching, my ghoulish NOOOOOs, my father quickly turned on the radio to the staticky cackle of the CBC, his soundtrack as he skimmed the newspaper. He was often cowardly, and now I think he was afraid that my mother would set him on fire if he dared interfere, or even worse, force him to survive on nothing but burnt toast for the week. He claimed that he dreaded all "white people food" more than he disliked camping with Auntie Beautiful One. My younger siblings had avoided her anger, picked up their books, and plugged in their music players, pretending to be busy—this is what we usually did if there was trouble near us. Someone could be twitching on the floor, obviously and deliriously Woo-Woo, and we would still be leisurely slurping our breakfast of watery congee and dehydrated egg—as long as it didn't affect us.

The Wongs: Chinese stoicism gone wrong, too terrified or pragmatic to squeal for help, so we attempted to ignore the Woo-Woo.

And in that moment I felt strangely separated from my body. It was not me on the bunk bed, curled up in a ball, screaming and sobbing. I was somewhere else, watching the entire scene from a panicked fly's point of view. But that miserable moment was an indication of a loss of my dependence and ferocious loyalty, when my mother became grotesque and cartoonish, when I lost my friend (my only friend) and somewhat untrustworthy household ally. This exciting, paroxysmal woman was *not allowed* to be a monster, especially since I had always been more than a little sympathetic to her and almost always took her side when she was arguing with my father. But the truth was, like my father, she was both a hero and a villain, someone I could and could not depend on. This knowledge that she was both a kindly Dr Jekyll and an errant Mr Hyde made me fearful and mistrustful of her, and growing up, I continued to wonder (still do) who my mother was. Would she be the concerned woman who phoned me in New York at five a.m. to make sure I ate breakfast, or would she be the deranged harpy who called my midtown internship at noon to scream about ghosts?

I tried to move, but pain neurons suddenly went blitzkrieg all over my ankle. Quickly, I soccer-kicked my mother in the shoulder with the other foot—a reflex. I thrashed against the tangle of blankets and crashed out of the top bunk as she tumbled backwards to get out of my way. I lurched over the linoleum, locked myself in the bathroom, and like an evergreen, fell clumsily into the miniature trailer tub, trying not to *panicpanicpanic*. The room was getting smaller, but it could have been my woozy, flickering vision, which was blurring with little black spots, like ants crawling over a white television screen.

"It's not like you need both feet, because you don't move anyway," my mother called out, in an almost motherly, reassuring way. She was waiting for me outside because she was concerned about the ghosts getting me rather than worrying about my minor injury. Huddled in the bathtub, the white shower curtain whipping around me like a teasing spirit, I sprayed cold water on my foot, which felt like I had a horrific sunburn. I was trembling so hard I thought my heart would implode. My arms were stiff and awkward, and I had trouble aiming the shower head. It was like I wasn't in control of my body anymore, fuelled only by unadulterated survival instinct. Like a chicken that keeps going until it notices that its head has gone permanently missing. My instinct was to quickly put the fire out, and then to not think about what had happened if I wanted to get through the day.

It was what I would learn to always do: distance myself from my existing reality, shrinking inside myself, like crumpled aluminum foil, so that I wasn't a real living person anymore. An eggshell of something cruel and numb and atrocious. Like one of those permanently smiling animal heads displayed in a hunter's living room, immobilized by the time and trauma of its death. It was here that I became more monster than girl.

"Hey, you have to wake up when I fucking tell you to, okay?" my mother yelled, checking the bathroom to see if I was still alive and unpossessed.

My mother had survived Third-World poverty in what had once been the rural outskirts of Hong Kong. Her grandfather's prosperous merchant family had sold their schizophrenic daughter (my grandmother) to a poor man for just 100 bucks before jumping ship to Hongcouver. Not only had my grandmother been cut off from the family fortune, but she had basically been abandoned in a backwater village to run around barefoot and be infamously crazy. So my mother and her siblings had grown up with nothing to eat but all the cigarettes they cared to smoke. Gung-Gung, my grandfather, doled out economy packs like candy because he got them for free with his gambling, win or lose. I imagined my mother and my aunties and uncles as toddlers: squatting in ankle-deep mud, chubby black flies chewing the thick grease off their scalps, smoking cigarettes, having a blast. Because as soon as you turned two years old, Gung-Gung proudly handed you your very own pack to help with the hunger. When they were lucky enough to buy a whole chicken, only the boys could partake in the skimpy meal, and I imagined my mother as a kid, sulkily huffing and puffing on her cigarettes all day long as she watched her brothers gorge on fresh meat.

Each of the eight kids had a favourite sibling or someone they felt a little sorry for. My mother looked out for my aunt, who was six years younger. She was responsible for plucking lice out of Beautiful One's thick, horsey hair, and when Beautiful One was too vain to want an ugly boy's haircut, my mother would slap her into agreement. A sympathetic auntie once told me: "Lucky you! You got the meanest person in the family for your mommy!" which was true, because my mother was certainly the most demanding sister. In times of famine and hardship, having my mother around meant that you had a better chance of survival.

At mealtimes, the quickest or the biggest kid got the most rice through speed or physical intimidation. In those simple village days, dinners were violent world wars, so alliances and strategies had to be forged and schemed. If you were not a blessed boy, the chicken thighs were definitely out of the question, but as a little girl, you could always brawl over a measly gizzard or a bleeding poultry heart. My mother shared her dinner organs with my aunt, and sometimes she did not eat.

This was the compassionate side of my mother that I had never seen, and it seemed that it had slowly leaked out, like battery acid, during her marriage to my father, who had a selfishly polarizing effect on her. It was almost as if she had to hide any slivers of kind-heartedness from my father, to avoid being discovered for what she really was, or what she could be. Show a little self-sacrificing compassion and my father might mock you. Then a nasty ghost would take possession of you.

At dinner parties, when the aunties and uncles talked about the old days, they loved to compare the exact size and length of their parasites. Supposedly, these were dangling snakes that they had to pluck out from their assholes, and my mother always bragged about her squiggling cobra being four feet long, whereas Beautiful One said hers was a beast at six feet. They could spend hours arguing over whose monster worm was scarier, which one was hairier, whose had a googly eye. And I assumed that because they had nothing to focus on back then except their miserable poverty, this was what they discussed to pass the hours as they happily puffed a pack a day. When the dimensions and forms of these mythological serpents had been discussed to death, the siblings all complained about their terrible childhood hunger. To reassure themselves that a food shortage did not exist anymore, they ordered in dozens of cardboard pizzas, soggy boxes of saturated fried chicken, and entire menus from the greasy spoons for Lunar New Year. The sweet and sour pork bleeding a vicious celebratory red, the black fermented fish heads tossed in maggoty fried rice, everything and anything ordered to make up for not eating when they were children. Of course, all the cousins had lost our appetites by now, and we stared at the foot-long slimy rice noodles, the caterpillar-like vermicelli coagulating in sludgy sauce with queasy, unspeakable horror.

To this day, my mother will defend Beautiful One from anything, and their bond is so savage and sisterly that no one else can compete. Everyone and everything came second to their darkly indestructible friendship. The old days were full of bitter survival stories and used as modern-day scare tactics, carefully employed to guilt and manipulate my cousins and me into behaving. None of us wanted to wake up with worms wriggling out of our butts like hard leftover spaghetti. It was my mother's heart-thrashing stories about mystical parasites and violent famines that made her and my aunt seem like tough-luck people who could be capable of extraordinary sacrifice or kindness.

Numbly, I nursed my lightly barbecued foot in the bathtub. The cold water felt refreshing and extraordinary, and seemed to lessen the pain. When it puffed up pink and tingly, I decided it was no longer part of my body. It was not my foot, it did not belong to me, and I would be absolutely fine; such an offensive appendage might eventually fall off. I could have stayed in the bathroom for the entire morning or a month or a year, but it felt like only five minutes.

When I peeled back the sliding bathroom door, my mother impatiently threw the first aid kit at me, which smacked my shoulders like a volleyball. She was being what she thought was motherly and sympathetic and helpful. But at thirteen, I did not know that this whole incident and her reaction weren't remotely normal. I did not know that it wasn't socially unacceptable to go around burning people to wake them up—I thought that what she had done was brutal and uncompromising but certainly effective. Was it necessary? No. Painful? Yes. But was there a quicker way to get me out of bed? Probably not. I was beginning to come to terms with what she'd done—in the Wong way, at least. In our family, people did idiotic and medium-evil things to one another because they were possessed and not in control, so it was best not to think too much about the horrors of whatever had been said and done because there was often no answer. We excused our behaviour by blaming the ghosts.

"Finally awake?" she eventually asked me, like she was casually inquiring if I wanted eggs or oatmeal for breakfast. She was acting like it had never happened, and it irked me that the incident was not even a little momentous, like not recognizing a double-digit birthday or graduation from a prestigious college. "Did you fall asleep on the toilet? You're too young to have hemorrhoids like Daddy.

"You are going running with Uncle E.T.," she said.

In retrospect, I see she really thought that she was helping me, especially by enlisting my extreme uncle in our family weight-loss project. She looked at me as if I had somehow disappointed her, as if I did not want to get better and fight off whatever demon (i.e., puberty) was making me uncomfortably pudgy. Our family was compulsively preoccupied with an unattainable thinness, so an average-sized North American was thought to require a gastric bypass.

My mother said: "We're all trying to help you, but you'll never go anywhere in life because you spend too much time sleeping. It's twelve! It's the only way, okay?"

I was not permitted to eat breakfast, so I had to limp hungrily after scary Uncle E.T., who charged enthusiastically across the desert. I was not thrilled to be in his company. Another interesting fact about him: he had been a proud guest of multiple concentration camps and top-security prisons back in his native Vietnam. These were just basic biographical particulars that he casually told people, like you might tell someone where you had grown up or gone to school. He was a tyrant about toilet paper *and* a convicted criminal.

Uncle E.T. shouted at me to hurry up, because we were going to do what he was forbidden to do in jail: cross-country sprinting. Auntie Beautiful One marrying some moneyed gangster was not shocking to the family, but what was horrifying was that he was Vietnamese instead of Chinese, which disturbed all the blood purists in the family, who thereby considered him inferior. His nationality was thought to be more alarming than his profession and distorted appearance. No one in our family cared that he had gone to jail or maybe killed one or two people. This was all in the past, and what was done was done, and there was no point feeling guilt or remorse. It was a methodical and frighteningly effective means of survival, an inability to hold a pretty decent grudge, which meant that we had much shorter and simpler memories than pet goldfish.

"FAT, FAT, FAT!" Uncle E.T. announced helpfully, as if shouting to warn me about an unforeseen danger, and I worried that I had to go running alone with a highly probable killer; for surely, my uncle hadn't killed anyone since immigrating to Canada, so what if he were presented with this wonderful opportunity? There were so many places in a vast desert to hide my body, and how would I even outrun him with an injured foot? I was an easy victim, a quick kill. And although my parents might be sad for thirty minutes, forty-five minutes later, they would share a bottle of gin with Uncle E.T. and say it was all in the past.

I really didn't want to get murdered and then eaten by buzzards and rattlesnakes. I hadn't even figured out what I wanted to do with my life yet. Middle school graduation was in a year, and it was true that I wasn't naturally good at anything (classical piano did not count, because I had tutors who screamed at me daily, so I had no choice but to improve). Besides, I could not rely on my family to write a decent obituary for me; it'd be full of errors, and I did not think they would even spell my name correctly.

"SO YOUNG SHOULD NOT BE SO FAT," Uncle E.T. crowed, laughing, and then I was certain he was not going to kill me if he wanted to fix me. Like my mother and every adult in my life, he claimed to always have my best interests in mind. As I watched his large dented basketball head bounce up and down, he cheered: "YOU HAVE MAJOR PROBLEM, LINDSAY! I WILL REPAIR! What happen if Lindsay have to go to jail when she grow up? The fat first to get killed! Hahaha!"

The quails sang a thick and horrible song, and a few black flies buzzed near my ear, biting me and drawing blood. I could see our trailers parked beside each other and hear the eerie, wild animal noises of the desert, which seemed less frightening than our makeshift travelling asylums.

O soyoos was a popular holiday town surrounded by the scorched tangles of barbed briar bush, a fried shrubby mess. It really didn't make sense to come here unless you skinny-dipped or sailed sleepily across the country's most tepid lake. Our family preferred the vast shopping mall to desiccated nature. Mostly, my family liked how far away the town was from crazy Poh-Poh.

"It's Osoyoos, Mom," my mother had said on the phone, clearly relieved that she had an excuse not to take our grandmother on vacation with us. "If you can't pronounce it, you can't come. Boo hoo, I know it really sucks to be you."

There was nothing to do in Osoyoos for our type of suburban Chinese family, so to pass the time, we huddled miserably, suffocating in the choky desert heat, inside our claustrophobic 150-square-foot mobile cabins, skinny, rectangular travelling motels that had the frigid luxury and malfunctioning comfort of unplugged commercial freezers. This was what we thought real North Americans did: that we were fruitfully living the American dream if we owned a brand-new RV per family.

So for an entire month, to prove that we had assimilated and succeeded in the New World, we sat in our housecoats and mostly watched each other across a foldable table. The emergency travel keyboards were brought out daily for piano practice because all the cousins had a competition in a few months and we all had to learn an identical repertoire. I did not want to practise in the desert and annoyed everyone by only playing "Flight of the Bumblebee" to encourage the killer bees, which burrowed persistently through the RV's screens, to go right ahead and sting the shit out of my mother. I was still furious at her for burning me and then seeming to forget about it.

Eventually, Auntie Beautiful One complained loudly about her boredom, so one afternoon, she bought a rubber collapsible boat and told me I had to keep her company. I didn't mind; I was tired of practising the piano. Her youngest daughter, Flowery Face, wanted to come along too. But Beautiful One sent her away, because it was no secret she disliked her five-year-old daughter, blaming Kid Number 3 for her slightly saggy belly. She claimed that my cousin had stolen some of her beauty while in the womb, for which she could not be forgiven. Ours was a culture and a family of deep blame. Already I was realizing that you could easily become a leper if you were born with the wrong ears or a mole in a suspicious, unlucky place. Her other two kids were more independent and didn't seem to care what their mother was doing.

Never happy, Beautiful One had been born vain, cursed for modern-day life when my grandfather, Gung-Gung, foolishly gave her such a lofty name at birth, as he wanted her to grow up to be divinely beautiful. She did grow up to be quite beautiful, with spongy, unblemished skin and boar-like, black hair—the kind of mythological Chinese beauty that could be effortlessly auctioned. At just four years old, she had almost been sold to a man who admired her good looks, and Gung-Gung could have gotten six months' worth of food money in exchange for Beautiful One. My mother, afraid to lose her favourite sister, had begged her father not to, and promised to eat less if Beautiful One could stay. Luckily, Gung-Gung had a soft spot for my mother, whose birth been followed by two revered sons, which in Chinese culture, meant that she was Quiet Snow, bringer of boys: lucky, blessed.

"Go away! I see you way too much," Beautiful One snapped at poor Flowery Face, who cried and gave me a mean look. Auntie had never been maternal, the kind of silly, very colourful girl-woman who shocked people when she said that she had three children. "Out of sight, please! Can I just talk to my favourite niece in fucking peace?"

When I was thirteen, Auntie Beautiful One was still unfamiliar to me and therefore more exciting than my mother; she spoke to me without screaming and did not call me retard, fat, or ugly. In retrospect, I see it was because I did not live with her and only interacted with her on vacations and at family dinners that I believed, on some ideal, glamorized level, that she was sane and more human than my mother. I did not confide in her, yet she treated me like I was her only secret keeper and wholly worthy of her grown-up mysteries, which filled me with nifty, juvenile pride.

Flowery Face was the only kid who would try to talk her mother down from the bridge eight years later—everyone else refused. When I look back on this, I wonder if, when she was begging her not to jump, she remembered being shunned because her mom seemed to like me better, if she remembered the cutting warmth of the lake in summer and how alone we all felt even though we were together. Neither Flowery Face nor I received specific affection, kindness, or genuine compassion from our mothers, and I think it caused us both to feel a damp and aching sadness, a childhood arthritis in our half-grown bones.

On the bridge on Canada Day, I wonder if Flowery Face remembered how everyone always snubbed her. If she felt a little resentful or if she mostly felt it was her duty to make her mother love her back, the way I did. We were similar in that way, kids who were bruisingly sensitive and famished for what we didn't know was missing: a sense that we were valued and liked by somebody. Not just somebody, but our mothers, who were about as maternal as smiling hamsters, who are commonly known to devour their snack-sized babies at birth for fresh protein.

On the beach, Flowery Face looked like she wanted to punch me, so I made a note to buy her some candy when I had the chance. She was a skinny kid, but she was the product of Uncle E.T. and I did not want to fight her, even though there was a good chance that

I could win because I was older and sixty pounds heavier. In our floral bathing suits, competing for the attentions of Beautiful One, she suddenly whacked me in the shoulder when no one was looking and I viciously kicked her back.

"Get your own mom," she said.

"Mine's currently broken," I said, wondering if it was too late to bribe her with candy.

"Too bad," Flowery Face snapped. "You're a fat, ugly freak!"

I sighed, because I was used to fights and name-calling like this, with either my sister or my mother. Flowery Face and I would not be remotely sympathetic to one another until we got older, and back then, I viewed her as an extension of my sister—someone much younger than me, an inconvenience, someone who needed her face and eyes and gums rubbed in hot sand.

But clenching my teeth, I resisted the urge to knock her down. Because Flowery Face was just another *someone* I had to beat and be better at in every way, it was not worth my effort, as I had already won my aunt's attention. We had been raised to believe that the competition that existed in each small family unit extended to everyone; we performed the exact same repertoire at piano concerts to compare who could play a Rachmaninoff piece better, or who wore what dress better, like screaming pop princesses. At thirteen, I was competing with myself, my siblings, my cousins, my parents, my uncles, my aunties, and all the other Chinese people in the world. Another family characteristic that would make Beautiful One want to jump off a bridge, as I think she felt that she could never measure up as an immigrant, wife, mother, and woman. She strived to be the best, and I believe she felt that she had to overcome her tremendous poverty and unfortunate origin story, a cosmic obsession that would lead to her psychotic break.

"Wear a life jacket," my mother called to my aunt, genuinely worried. She was scared a ghost would pull her under and never went in water higher than her knees. "You're with fatty and the boat might sink. Lindsay doesn't need a vest because obese people float. If your life jacket doesn't work, just climb on top of her and float back to shore. We should just rent her out to people who want boats and make money."

I was glad to be with someone who liked me, even when, hypocritically, I knew Beautiful One treated her child like my mother treated me. In our family, Mother was just a name. A clumsy two-syllable English word like "river" or "building." A mother was just someone, I thought, perhaps even a ghost, who cried a lot and fought off the supernatural but fed you constantly. Both Auntie Beautiful One and my mother were decent providers of sustenance, but Beautiful One was better in my adolescent mind because she owned several restaurants.

So ignoring my own monster mother, even though I wanted to belt out a horror-movie scream, I followed my aunt to the edge of the lake, shoved our boat to knee-deep water, and hopped in.

We drifted towards the middle of the greenish lake without the rubber boat collapsing under our mutual mass (we were so lucky!), and Beautiful One, who always looked lonely and heartbroken, suddenly said, "You know Uncle E.T. had a bad life, right? He came in a fishing boat with other refugees and they drank their own urine to survive. His boat was attacked by pirates and he jumped in the water and swam to Hong Kong. That's why he's so angry all the time. That's why he's making you run. I really hate him."

"How come you married him?" I asked, hoping that she might offer me some money if I listened to her.

"Well, he came to the house with a gun and took Poh-Poh

hostage until Gung-Gung gave his blessing. You know how they hate non-Chinese. And I was pregnant."

"Oh," I said, not quite sure how to respond, because her story, which was very likely to be true, didn't seem that interesting or remarkable to me, mostly because I was thinking of all the things I could buy if I had money. Also, I was thirteen. Hers was a typical anecdote, not hyperbolic or unique to Beautiful One; if no one had died or tried to kill someone or themselves, no one in the family would think the story was worth remembering. Maybe Uncle E.T. had a pocketknife instead of gun, but anyway, he seemed like the kind of man who would cheerfully threaten a future mother-in-law. Everyone knew why Beautiful One had married him: he was so crooked and frightening that he would make Beautiful One look magnificent even as she aged. Besides, I had heard this story about a billion times, even from my mother, who had said that Uncle E.T. was carrying a bomb to blow up Poh-Poh, which she said would have done everyone a huge favour and made E.T. the best brother-in-law in the world.

As the boat floated in the middle of the lake, I tried to concentrate hard on what Beautiful One was saying. That might mean more of a payoff. If she was going to talk for more than an hour, then I could forget waiting for the money and change the subject, since I only wanted easy-earned cash for fake listening. After all, my aunt, my mother, and my father were all lonely, desperate people (which I did not realize then); otherwise, it wouldn't have been so easy to earn the contents of their wallets.

"You know they're all fucking nuts," Beautiful One said sadly, and we looked at all the lazy families sprawled on the rocky beach. Like they were some impressionistic painting or a performance piece in a modern museum: people who looked idyllic but upon closer inspection were secretly hellish and tormented. "E.T. wants to take all you kids paragliding and your mom is just like Poh-Poh, nervous about everything. She likes to invent fucked-up things to be scared of. Me and you are the only sane people in this family. We have to stick together, okay? Do you like me better than your mother?"

"Duuuuuh," I said, and she gave me twenty bucks, which I saved because I felt it was a magnificent sum, and I had found myself a new idol and ally by agreeing with her. In that moment we were partners, allies who totally understood each other, who could see whatever the others couldn't comprehend or acknowledge. Me and Beautiful One, both of us absurd and selfish and missing half ourselves, wanted to be exempt from the hot, troubling chaos of having a Woo-Woo inside our brains.

CHAPTER 5
WOO-WOO LOGIC

The refrigerator is attacking me!" Poh-Poh wailed at my mother and me.

Only a month after our lake trip, we brought her gluey radish cakes and doughy white pork buns because she said she couldn't open the refrigerator. That was where the Woo-Woo lived.

Like my mother and Auntie Beautiful One, my maternal grandmother had a way of charging her Woo-Woo directly at her female descendants. But perhaps forecasting my mother's mania, I thought, and—I feared—my own impending insanity, Poh-Poh's Woo-Woo was relentless. Her form of madness was untethered; it was chaotic and loud, like an amateur marching band. Was this who I'd eventually become, the embodiment of sickly terror, darkly hilarious only to those who didn't have any idea how else to love me? An old joke?

"Blue lightning is zapping me!" Poh-Poh yelled, her hair greasy and dishevelled. She was not wearing pants. "It doesn't want me to get my groceries! How the fuck will I eat?"

She threw herself at the old Maytag refrigerator, as if to push the ghosts out of it. Exhausted, she jumped backwards and suddenly slumped to the floor, unconscious. I stared at her on the linoleum in fascination and horror. I was tempted to poke her to see if she was pretending or if she had died, but I was afraid she'd jump up and scream at me.

This was just a typical visit to my grandmother's house.

"The fridge electrocuted me!" Poh-Poh exclaimed after she woke up. Then, shoving her hands into oven mitts, she quickly grabbed the door handle. "Eeeeee. Ahhhh," she shrieked, as she attacked the nasty aluminum beast—whack, whack, whack, poor battered refrigerator.

She was having a psychotic break, believing that all inanimate objects were threatening to assassinate her. My mother—no stranger to mental illness herself, of course—only gawked, then sighed. And even I, who was thirteen and not immune, rolled my eyes.

It didn't matter how hard you fought or what closet or refrigerator you tried to battle. The Woo-Woo ghosts were never far behind—our Chinese family still believed that these supernatural ghosts were responsible for irrational behaviour. We still didn't believe in Western medication or psychiatrists, which meant that we prolonged our suffering.

During my visits to my grandmother's house as a child and teenager, I would point to the blender, then the microwave, and finally the oven, asking: "Poh-Poh, does this have a ghost inside it?" but she refused to acknowledge my nosiness.

"Who the fuck are you?" she snapped in her usual foul-mouthed Chinese. "Never seen you before," she continued. "Must be ghost!"

"Boo!" I said, affirming her distrust.

I was frightened of her, but I had to find ways to make our visits as entertaining as possible. Otherwise, I would never have been able to tolerate her constant screaming and sobbing. But my grandmother did not feel the same way, and my jokey response made her so upset that she had to lie down. *How does someone go crazy?* I wondered. Like a rabid werewolf or a zombie, did she wake up and suddenly find herself septic? Or was her madness, slow and irrevocable, something that you just inherited, like high cholesterol and sociopathy?

And if that was the case, was that what had happened to my mother?

Especially in our trailer in Osoyoos? And if so, when would the genetic mutation awaken within me? I shuddered—real fear was beginning to override the harsh humour I'd sometimes find in my grandmother's very authentic mania.

Even though everyone in our family claimed not to believe in Western medicine, a sneaky auntie, worried about my grandmother, had taken her to a distant cousin who was a psychiatrist.

After the visit, where I now know she was prescribed the common antipsychotics lithium and clozapine, she was so doped up that she couldn't speak. It was decided that because my mother did not work outside the home, she would be responsible for looking after our grandmother as she fought off what everyone called her "demonic possession." It didn't help that my mother was fighting her own sinkhole of depressive battles, which would be worsened with my grandmother in our house.

When my father, who had somehow escaped the Woo-Woo but was nonetheless a believer, heard that we would have a new guest, *his mother-in-law*, he shuddered and announced that he would be "so very busy" at his engineering firm. It was shocking that my father agreed to house my grandmother, but he was becoming more afraid of my mother. If he insisted my grandmother not be allowed in the house, my mother would destroy cupboards and hurl dishes.

Shortly thereafter, an auntie drove up to our cul-de-sac and my grandmother appeared in the driveway, carrying a black garbage bag full of her clothes.

"Be aware," my aunt said, as she escorted my grandmother to our front door. "I try to fix Poh-Poh, but there are still many ghost. She just throw herself down the stair because she think her head is not attached to her body."

"How many ghost inside her?" my mother asked, looking concerned.

"Probably a dozen," my aunt replied, sighing. "Might take a year to get better."

Having her own mother in the house seemed to bring back my mother's childhood rage. Because when she had come down with a fever in their village in Hong Kong's countryside, my grandmother sent her outside to die without a blanket. But my mother, always disobedient, even as a little girl, spent a week shivering and hallucinating in the hellish heat and came back alive. I thought that my mother had acquired some sort of post-traumatic stress disorder from it because she always said, "I was going to kill your Poh-Poh when I recovered because I fucking hated her," and "Who sends you out to die without a fucking blanket? No common sense! Screwed in the fucking head!"

At our first dinner together, my grandmother squealed and shoved her fingers in the overcooked lasagna on the kitchen table, so no one wanted to eat anymore. My sister and brother wisely fled to their bedrooms, but perhaps because of the camping trip, I still wanted my mother's approval, so I stayed behind and grudgingly gulped down three enormous helpings of burnt noodles.

How was this crazy woman with ringlets really my grandma, someone who, according to Hong Kong soap operas, was supposed to bake almond cookies and dish out cash to grandchildren at birthdays and Lunar New Year, especially when she yanked off the lids of the salt and pepper shakers and began flinging fistfuls of seasoning all over the carpet?

"EEEEEE!" she shrieked, so I, not being one to miss out on fun, instantly picked up a handful to join her. "EEEEEEEEEEEEEEEE! AHHHH! OOOOOO!" she yelled, and I screamed too.

"I didn't sign up for this!" my mother yelled. She looked like she wanted to cry. "There is a place in hell for crazy, trouble-making people like you! Lindsay, if you don't behave, you will have to spend all eternity with Poh-Poh."

When my mother really could not cope with my grandmother's erratic and bizarre behaviour anymore, she stormed out of the kitchen, shaking.

Soon after, she enlisted me on a mission: we were going to rummage through Poh-Poh's garbage bag to search for her medication and put a stop to all this bullshit. We were going to cure Poh-Poh ourselves, she said.

"I'm helping your very lazy grandmother," my mother said, and then wondered aloud if she should bury the orange pill bottles in her own underwear drawer. Like most of our family, she believed that pills were evil and unnecessary and expensive, as people in medieval times did not need them and our brains in modernity were certainly more evolved.

Anxiously, I stood watch at the door, in case my grandmother caught us stealing her drugs—not that she would notice anyway. But because I was the eldest, I was expected to be supremely loyal to my mother. After our camping trip, I was still afraid of her spasming percussion of rage, but I was immensely curious about fate versus genetics.

I was also dubious: if a psychiatrist, someone with an advanced medical degree, had given my grandmother medication, why were we undoing the treatment? Didn't we want my grandmother to get better so we could send her home as soon as possible? Moreover, the idea that my grandmother's insanity was caused by a medical condition that could be eased simply with pills reduced my fears about my own life—pills could solve my future problems if they could solve Poh-Poh's present ones, and I was ready to find out what would happen if she popped one.

It was this new kind of thinking that had been bothering me lately—emerging like a red, bulbous zit inside my teenage nose. Daytime television had taught me that people's brains could make them do wacko things. There seemed to be a terrible disconnect from whatever I was learning on TV and at home. On the *Jerry Springer Show* and *Judge Judy,* experts were to be revered and obeyed. But in my parents' house, knowledge was feared and loudly dismissed. The more rational the information, the more they protested.

If my brother or sister and I were to succumb to a sudden fever, we were ordered to strip naked and were rubbed with foul-smelling Chinese herbs. Tylenol was the devil. If we had the common flu, we were just lazy. Viruses were caused by ghosts and exorcised by running laps around our suburban neighbourhood.

Besides, the public school curriculum in British Columbia did not include ghosts that possessed people like germs. I was finally at an age where I was beginning to question and worry that I was missing something obvious.

"Didn't the doctor say the medication was good for her?" I asked my mother, as I nervously peered down the hallway to see if anyone was coming.

"You know that doctors don't know what they're talking about, right?" she answered, as she sorted through my grandmother's unwashed clothes to find the stash of antidepressants and anti-anxiety medication that she was supposed to take, along with her mood stabilizers, sleeping pills, and tranquilizers.

"Ummm ... did you go to medical school?" I asked, a little sarcastically. After Osoyoos, I knew not to piss my mother off by being openly confrontational. But I was preteen enough to try a soft, non-neutral tone.

"I know it all!" my mother said. "These kinds of doctors don't believe in ghosts," she declared. "They can't see them. They think Poh-Poh is fucking crazy, but they can't see that she's possessed! The medication hides the demons, you see."

Later, once we got my grandmother into bed, my mother assumed her new role as Woo-Woo doctor. "This is better for you," she explained to Poh-Poh after we had hid her medication in my mother's night table and given my grandmother a generous supply of minty Tic Tacs.

"This is yummier," my mother said, using a false, cheery voice that I did not know she could mimic. "Open wide!"

Of course, Poh-Poh did not seem to notice that anything was off. Whenever she opened her mouth, my mother popped in a white Tic Tac that Poh-Poh swallowed without chewing.

A few days later, my grandmother took a turn for the worse. "Lindsay, there are Japanese soldiers here, so I can't take a bath!" she screamed, charging out of the bathroom. She was naked, flailing her starfish arms.

"There's no one there, Poh-Poh," I said, trying to sound reasonable.

"Also, my arms and legs are falling off!" she protested, ignoring me. "I can't wipe my ass! Help! Help!"

Terrified, I watched as my grandmother spun in a circle, her eyes bright and twitching.

I stood outside the bathroom door and hollered for my mother, who handed me a brand-new pair of dishwashing gloves and a spray bottle.

"Are you kidding me?" I said. "No way!"

Meanwhile, we could hear my grandmother prancing down the hall, howling, "The Japanese soldiers are here! We have to hide! Run awaaaaaaay!"

Because she did not want to shower, Poh-Poh began to smell rancid. Her hair became shiny and stiff, and her bathrobe became ratty and stained because she refused to let us wash it.

"Lindsay, my poop will save you from the ghosts," she sang whenever she saw me, and I quickly turned away, more fearful than disgusted. Would this be me by the end of the week? In fiftysomething years? I still didn't know if pills could save her. She was still taking the Tic Tacs.

As Poh-Poh detoxed from the meds, she scurried up and down the hall all night, broadcasting orchestral farts. One night, she woke me up by tugging on my ankle and insisted that I had to practise my Chinese numbers. She announced that my Chinese was cringingly shitty, and no granddaughter of hers would only know how to count to ten. This caused an internal combustion in me, triggered by severe grouchiness at the mention of mathematics.

"No way in hell!" I bellowed.

"Fuck you," she said. "You are a very bad girl ghost."

"Fuck you, no take backs," I said to my grandma, who countered by howling—she thought that this late-night exchange was hilarious.

Like everyone else in the family, back then I viewed my grandmother as something foreign and embarrassing. When she was manic, she was like a recently awakened mummy from King Tut's tomb, amazed to find itself in the twentieth century. At thirteen, my perception of my suffering grandmother was filtered through my mother's combative contempt: Poh-Poh was not someone to be pitied or babied but a wild woman to be contained.

But there was an upside: with Poh-Poh prowling our house at all hours, my mother could pick on someone instead of me. I became a semi-invisible ghost, no longer a life-sized target who disliked but desperately wanted to be accepted by my own mother. She had already given up on the notion that Poh-Poh would ever truly like her, believing that she would never be as good as a son. But I still held out hope for *my* mother, despite our daily wars. On her decent days, she was good-looking and funny; when she felt like it, she could make me laugh like no one else. I would have done anything for a smidgen of her praise. "You only suck a bit, fatty," would have been maternal and enough. I was desperate and hopeful that one day she might change, a complete 360.

The police had warned us not to stroll alone on our gloomy Canadian mountain in the summer, because wild animals often attacked the feeble or young. There were reports of coyotes that sometimes chomped on old people, but they were not usually as bold as the bears that sometimes deposited masses of shit on our doormats, muffin-shaped turds that we had to shovel before the neighbourhood dogs huffed them up. But my mother didn't care—sending Poh-Poh to exercise her demons every day for a week. We all thought she was trying to give her mother a heart attack. And Poh-Poh, oblivious, kept shuffling around the cul-de-sac like any other Poteau granny, a hot-pink beanie slapped on her head—jog-walking faster than any other senior I knew. I believe my mother was trying to quarantine the Woo-Woo, as if Poh-Poh could somehow exorcise her malevolent ghosts by completing daily laps around the neighbourhood.

I am not kidding when I say that for amusement a freakish 250-pound bear might knock you unconscious with her massive paw in our suburb, but usually, if Mama Bear wasn't ravenous, she just lumbered away. Luckily, my grandmother spoke in aggressive grunts and could communicate with the wild animals on the Poteau, even though her own family could not understand her. I imagined that on her frustrated walks around the mountain, she was complaining about us to her loyal gang of coyotes, gossiping with one or two sympathetic deer, and maybe egging on the killer black bears to eat her grandchildren as soon as we waltzed out the front doors for summer hockey camp and piano lessons.

The wild animals knew enough to leave Poh-Poh alone, but some Jehovah's Witness missionaries stalked her to our front door, thoroughly impressed by her noisy lamenting, believing that we required "recent immigrant assistance."

"Bullshit," my mother said to the missionaries, who meekly offered her a complimentary Bible when they realized that she was not someone who could be converted. "If you want to believe the Cry Wolf, you can take her with you. Goodbye!"

In the evenings, Poh-Poh howled miserably, as if she knew that her existence depended solely on her ability to make a lot of noise, and my father said, irritated: "Send outside. The coyotes will keep her company. They practise singing together and start a rocking and rolling band."

The bonds that kept our family together were like the alliances that prison inmates had no choice to form. Talk show hosts like Oprah and Rosie O'Donnell had lied: a good family was not one that forgave, but one that could bravely endure ancient grudges. Family members were people you had the misfortune to inherit, people you didn't particularly care for but felt obligated to feed and house for nothing in return.

Toe overlapping toe, my grandmother's feet were practically deformed from physical labour and rheumatism; she could only wear special black running shoes to accommodate her blocky hammertoes. Stiffly, she stamped along in her square sneakers, lurching like a miniature Godzilla. We all knew Poh-Poh had once been athletic and tough. I imagine that she had once been nice or even pretty. After all, as a young girl, Poh-Poh had chopped firewood and planted shrivelled yams when the Japanese bombed her village. She had bound her breasts and pretended to be a boy for three years to avoid being raped.

"Did she ever see anyone get bombed and explode into pieces?" I asked my mother a few days into Poh-Poh's stay, not bothering to hide my excitement. But my mother didn't know, and Poh-Poh obviously wasn't talking sense. As a kid who cherished the macabre above all else, for a little while, I felt that Poh-Poh was as interesting as cable television. But I was severely disappointed. What good was it if you had a grey-haired person in your house and she couldn't even nod or shake her head when you wanted to know if she had ever seen someone get murdered?

"Shut the fuck up," she said, when I asked her if she had lived through the Rape of Nanking.

"Mom says Great-Great-Grandpa was blind and instantly died when the bombs fell because he had a heart attack and you guys were all having dinner. Did Great-Great-Grandpa shit his pants when he died? How long did it take for his body to smell? Were his eyes open or closed?"

There was so much of me that couldn't fathom any of this as real, and it made me unknowingly cruel. That was the luxury of my generation—born in a different time and a very dissimilar place, which was what my mother both gave to me and resented about me, that First-World safety. And ultimately, that was what made me different from my mother and my grandmother, two characters that I feared I'd become. But how could I have known that then?

"No," Poh-Poh whispered.

"No to every question?" I asked, disappointed.

"Too many ghost," she said, one eye staring at a fly on the ceiling.

In her Hong Kong village, as the only demonically possessed woman, Poh-Poh had been given every generous perk of lunacy—instant fame and a scandalous reputation. When the villagers were done planting their bok choy and killing their chickens, when they had finished their meagre suppers of rice and maybe a delicious fried rat, they must have gossiped about how much Poh-Poh had been sold for and wondered what kind of man would spend his life savings on an insane woman with a low forehead, which meant, according to our Chinese beliefs, that she had exceptionally low intelligence in addition to being unfortunate-looking.

My mother said that Poh-Poh's eyesight was so poor from severe myopia that she had panic attacks when she was sent out to chop firewood during Japan's second invasion of China. Her blindness exacerbated her ghoulish terror of being sent alone into the war-wrecked woods, and this trauma caused her to also have terrible hallucinations and convulsive, raving fits. Throughout her life, she would always have paranoia about invading soldiers, confusing her heartbreaking adolescence with her present reality. Even years later, she hid from them twice a week, as she believed that soldiers stormed through the floral wallpaper of her house to attack her if she tried to sleep.

She also claimed that her father had repeatedly raped her when she was a small child, but her mother, my great-grandmother Cloudy Heroine, the tough-talking, pragmatic matriarch of the family, did not believe her. Instead, she promptly sold her sixteen-year-old daughter to my grandfather when Poh-Poh's father in Vancouver wanted to sponsor the entire family over in 1950. At $750 per head, they could save a lot of money (they had three boys) if they left someone behind.

As a female, which already made her inferior, and not even a sane one, it was mutually agreed that Poh-Poh's head was not worth the exorbitant price. This was how practical my mother's family was—you had to be worth every single penny to call yourself a member.

My grandfather, Gung-Gung, who was the stereotypical gambling man, the frivolous village playboy, purchased Poh-Poh for her family's merchant fortune and fancy Gold Mountain connections. There was no wedding celebration, just a swift exchange of $100 (in case any party changed their mind), and Poh-Poh was delivered the very next day. It was said that my grandmother understood what was happening, though the Japanese invasion had worsened her already devastating schizophrenia.

My aunties said that being left behind in a Hong Kong slum finally broke Poh-Poh.

Gung-Gung had no clue that his new wife would be cut off from all the gold harvesting (she would not receive a single cent of the escalating family fortune in Gold Mountain), and Poh-Poh was not entitled to a single cow or chicken. Being "not that smart," as the family said, Gung-Gung had not planned for this unfortunate news, and this devastated him, causing him to gamble and drink. Meanwhile, in Vancouver, the Chan Clan had taken the opportunity to buy up grotesque amounts of farmland, trading shops, and Chinese restaurants, as well as property in the city that would be developed into gigantic strip malls. And Poh-Poh was much too insane to claim her share by then, stuck in a backwater village, not knowing if she was having sex or giving birth to eight children or what to do with those kids she called "the fucking cunts."

I now wonder if I would have quickly died from malnutrition or PTSD if I had been born in her horrendous time and place. What it might have been like to be a teenage-woman in her totalitarian circumstances, her sanity and social class brutally stripped away. A war survivor and immigrant, illiterate in not one but two languages and despised by children whom she did not recall having.

My great-grandmother, Cloudy Heroine, who had sold Poh-Poh and then felt guilty about it twenty years later, finally sponsored her daughter's family of ten over to Vancouver in 1975. Cloudy Heroine died in 1995, but it didn't matter for Poh-Poh because her mother was a recurrent hallucination, a chatty breakfast ghost visitor. A foul-mouthed bedtime caller who regaled her daughter with gossipy stories from the afterlife. Poh-Poh seriously loved her mother, even if her mother had not loved her back.

Like Poh-Poh, I really tried to love my mother, but I was never sure if she had the emotional capacity to love me back.

One morning during her second week with us, Poh-Poh's mouth became unhinged. Her jaw had seized up, and her lips popped open for more than forty-eight hours. She could not close her mouth.

"Buzz, buzz, buzz," my father said, making fun of her when he came home early one morning after being gone for twenty-four hours. "Fly get in there and die! We have new fly trap, haha!" He seemed to work longer and more absurd hours when Poh-Poh was around. If I asked him what was wrong with my grandmother, he gave me his usual answer. "You can't logic with the Woo-Woo, okay?"

I had tried typing Poh-Poh's symptoms into a search engine, but only advertisements for horror movies had come up.

The family had attempted to keep Poh-Poh out of the psych ward for almost her entire life, but they did not know that my mother had stolen her medication. It would take me a while to understand this, but Poh-Poh was going through serious drug withdrawal. Years later, I'd wonder what my grandmother might have thought: one moment, she believed that she was having a tête-à-tête with her dead mother, and the next, her lips were bulbous and paralyzed. She must have been thoroughly petrified, and not being able to express it, or thinking you were crazy for doing so, had to make it even worse. Soon after, as if truly and deeply possessed, Poh-Poh couldn't even swallow water. Her mouth: yawning pure shock, a panicked, cartoonish maw. She still couldn't close it.

I could see that my mother was truly disturbed by this incredible turn of events and did not want to help her mother unless she had to—perhaps she was reliving her horrible childhood again and could not handle it.

"I fucking try so hard!" my mother yelled, throwing a porcelain bowl across the kitchen, which shattered on our linoleum floor. She refused to clean it up until my father came home.

She seemed especially fragile and furious whenever Poh-Poh was around. So when Poh-Poh's moaning became too loud, my mother quietly slipped me twenty bucks, supplied me with another pair of rubber dishwashing gloves (so I would not catch the demon), and said it was my duty to water "the monster" because she was exhausted, sad, and going to lie down.

"Bad ghost," Poh-Poh moaned, confused and frightened even after I had hastily put a glass of water to her lips. "Baaaaaaaaaad!!!!"

But her tongue wasn't working and she could not swallow. That sip of water, mixed with saliva, dribbled back out.

I backed away, afraid she was dying. It hadn't even been a full two weeks and already my Poh-Poh was falling apart. Poh-Poh's mouth had taken on the comical look of a shocked tropical fish. Her eyes bulged, her tongue did not fit into her mouth, and she looked as if we had scooped her out of a Chinatown fish tank—unable to breathe outside water.

"Do you want to suck on an ice cube?" I asked her, hoping that I might distract her from dying.

"Baaaaaad," Poh-Poh moaned in a throaty gurgle. And then my grandmother suddenly keeled over.

I needed Poh-Poh to live until someone else came into the room, like one of my younger siblings, who could share this trauma with me. Unfortunately, we weren't on speaking terms, as I had succumbed to slobbering, cross-eyed fury the previous evening and hauled both brother and sister down the hallway by their hair for no rational reason. I had always thought that I wanted to see someone explode or get eaten by a black bear, but not if it was a close family member. To a kid who had grown up with suicide threats as daily conversation, death seemed unavoidable, like a badly infected ingrown nail or a recurring eyelid boil.

But as much as my grandmother seemed like an inconvenience, she was like looking into a time-travelling mirror, where I was both appalled and fascinated to see my mother and grandmother's faces gawking back at me. It was as if my future selves had paid me an overly long and obnoxious visit.

Our peculiar family love had transformed Poh-Poh into a wild animal incapable of speech and rational thought. And lack of motherly kindness had turned her into a monster. I was thirteen, so I did the only reasonable thing: I fled the room.

Although our family could certainly be bad-tempered and difficult, we weren't indefinitely cruel, so it was decided that Poh-Poh would see an emergency room physician as soon as my mother had drowned some woolly pig hoof, a Chinese delicacy, in canola oil for our supper (Poh-Poh wouldn't be eating). My parents decided that my grandmother might be able to cure herself if given a three-to-four-hour deadline, since she, like many old people, seemed to benefit from some structure in her life.

Making me buckle Poh-Poh into the back seat when it was time to go—it was close to eleven at night—because she would not and could not touch her Woo-Woo mother, my mother declared, as if trying to convince herself: "Even though Poh-Poh was terrible to me, this is still my fucking mother, Lindsay. You know, this is my fucking mother, right? Right?"

At the hospital, when the triage nurses heard an abridged version of my grandmother's mental history, she was sent to the psych ward immediately, because the doctors believed her paralyzed jaw was part of her ongoing psychosis. I knew my mother was upset when the doctors did not diagnose Poh-Poh demonic and recommend a bath in holy water followed by an aggressive course of antibiotics to fight off the Woo-Woo.

"Those doctors," she had whispered, horrified, to me in the waiting area, "can't see ghosts, you know!"

But I wasn't sure. I thought we had done something wrong, had made Poh-Poh worse. My mother lied to the medical staff about Poh-Poh's daily medication, pretending that we had been following instructions.

My grandmother became a patient of Burnaby Hospital's psych ward for three months. This concluded Poh-Poh's psychiatric tour of suburbia, and I was admittedly relieved.

After a while, my mother, too frightened and stubborn, refused to visit the psych ward, because she did not believe Poh-Poh was trying hard enough to fight her demon. She did not like quitters or wimps, and she felt strongly that Poh-Poh was both. But it soon turned out that Poh-Poh's physical hurt was authentic; X-rays confirmed she had indeed splintered her tailbone violently crashing down a flight of stairs. For once in her life, my mother had absolutely nothing to say. Unlike her sisters, she did not feel any relief, slamming our kitchen cupboards as hard as she could when the doctors phoned with the diagnosis.

"These doctors," she finally hollered, frustrated when she had recovered from shock, "can't see ghosts! They misdiagnose your Poh-Poh all the time!"

As she stalked around our kitchen, screaming and smashing cupboards, I imagined Poh-Poh in the psych ward like a terrified phantom, trying to call "*a mo*," which means mother in Chinese. *Mother, mother, mother, are you there?* she would try to wail at no one. But my grandmother's jaw would not close no matter how hard we yelled at her to try.

CHAPTER 6

THE EMPTY

It came as no surprise to anyone that I was having a problem with a girl at school, someone in an affluent Taiwanese gang (her father was minor Taipei mafia). Having never mastered my father's orders to alternate between two friends "like shoe," I was still a loner, and those on the Poteau resented, feared, and sometimes mocked me for my meanness, fatness, and newly acquired speech impediment—an old man's stutter to join my lisp.

This unpleasant Taipei girl belonged to a gang of left-in-the-West kids, the children of overseas criminals who often bought their teenage offspring their very own Poteau McMansions and left them to fend for themselves when they returned to their home countries for business.

As a teenager, I often wondered how disrespectful you had to be, or who you must have killed, to be exiled across the eastern continent from a glittering metropolis like Hong Kong or Shanghai and dumped on such a ghastly mountain in Canada, of all places. It made me wonder if my family hadn't left the slums of Hong Kong, would I have thrived better as a street beggar than a suburban high school student.

At our high school, the Taiwanese gang was composed of the typical kind of rich kids who got BMWs and Hummers for their birthdays, but they were also the kind of Asian supremacists who would head-bash the pastiest white kids at school with baseball bats in the parking lot, making the *Tri-City News* once in a while. Anyone they thought wasn't Chinese-looking enough or was just plain funny-looking was not safe.

That year, 2002, when I was in tenth grade, classical mythology was in vogue, and all the immigrant assimilation consulting companies in Asia were recycling Greek gods to help new Westerners fit in. For a lot of money, you got a "trendy" white person's name and some lessons in North American social customs, though the companies often distributed false information. One of my distant cousins, for instance, was taught in etiquette class to say "Thank you!" instead of "Excuse me!" after burping and passing gas. His suggested English name was King Solomon until our family intervened.

This was because in Asia it was believed that Westerners couldn't pronounce Chinese names, so our high school had a lot of boys named Artemis and Herodotus, or pimply, round-faced girls called Hephaestus. One poor girl from Macau, with halting machete English, had pronounced her new name as Hepatitis in homeroom, which, unfortunately, stuck.

Somehow, people in China, Taiwan, and Hong Kong thought these names were easier to pronounce than Chow Yun-fat or Zhang Ziyi. The previous trend had been Old Testament names, which had been a lot simpler, as everyone in middle school had just been called Samson or Delilah.

Demeter, the Taiwanese girl I was having a problem with, was skinny with prickly orange hair. She didn't like that I was awkward and chunky. Where she came from, everyone was small and slim and size double zero, but my broad back and size-fourteen ass must have blocked her vision in science class because she would jab me with a ruler whenever the teacher wasn't looking. Being wide and hockey player–sized made me feel queasy and embarrassed, as if I were always wearing too many layers of ill-fitting wool clothing. In regular North America, I might have been average, but in the fussy suburbs of Hongcouver, where the standards were Hong Kong (tougher than Hollywood), where my own mother and aunties worried about their thinness, I was borderline obese.

Unfortunately, I took after the women on my mother's side of the family, who must have had some overriding troll blood in them. When they were teenagers, pus-filled boils that made acne look silly and mouldy-looking eczema like leathery lizard scales sprouted on their scalp, face, and body. Clucking at the oily scabs on my head, my mother and her sisters said, "Aiya, why so ugly-ah! You will look like a girl maybe when you turn twenty-five or forty."

My mother had been bullied for looking like a furry boy gnome in high school: in the late seventies, white kids chucked eggs at her head and told her to crawl back to the smelly hole of China. This made her angry, then sad, and then angry again, and she always said, "If some asshole wants to fight you, you don't run away, especially if they hate Chinese people. You make them cry until they are sorry." This was a life lesson that I took as seriously as I would take my post-graduate studies.

My mother never played the victim card, though she could have, so neither did I. Yet there was something complex about this decision to remain tough at all costs: I was becoming hardened emotionally to protect myself from vulnerability. Like my mother had before me, and her mother before her—you could say it was a family tradition. It would take me years to realize it didn't work. We just couldn't grapple with our feelings. We didn't have time. We just repressed them until they exploded out of us—turned us Woo-Woo. But what choice did we have?

On the Poteau, everyone said that the Taiwanese were almost as vicious as the thuggish Vietnamese, not as standoffish as the Hong Kong FOBs (i.e., fresh-off-the-boat immigrants) or as snobby as the old-money Singaporeans, but much classier than all Mainland new-money Chinese. We were all ethnically Chinese, all Asian, but we stuck to our own cliques and gangs.

Since jabbing me in the back didn't get a rise out of me, one day Demeter struck a match and decided to set my jacket sleeve on fire. My own mother and now my classmate had tried to set me alight, and it seemed to me that this was what you did to people you were not fond of. I thought that it might be my destiny to exit the world on fire and that the sadistic universe was always telling me to be near a functioning fire alarm.

Stubborn, resilient Demeter, with her Taiwanese work ethic, blew on the tiny orange spark like a giant birthday candle. I slapped the flames out, but the garment was damaged, unwearable. The fire had sizzled some of the meat on my forearm, singed the short feathery hairs. The teacher was having a coffee break in the hallway, too distracted to care.

"You'll be thorry," I lisped-stuttered at Demeter, and threw my jacket in a garbage can and skipped the rest of science class.

On the Poteau, those who knew me understood I could become a foul-mouthed, frothing bovine if provoked. I liked getting my way and would fight to the end. That afternoon, I exploded like a special-effects heavy action movie. I retaliated the best way I knew how: by bruising Demeter's kneecaps into beautiful mauve flora with a ringette stick in PE (ringette is a milder form of hockey played with a blue rubber doughnut, which was originally invented for big-boned pioneer-type Canadian females to play).

My rampage continued. Inside me was a red-eyed hockey fury,

a mechanism to cope with the blundering uncertainty of my home life, which wouldn't let me quit while I was winning. The next day, when the teachers bussed us to the Poteau country club to stand around and pretend to play golf, I struck again. Hockey had taught me to swing a golf club at someone's legs like a clumsy but powerful slap shot, and my aim was true. In those days, whenever I lashed out, I was fighting my mother, my father, and the Woo-Woo. I did not yet know that I was also fighting an aspect of myself—the part of me that always felt out of control—and losing.

"Sucks to be you," I said unhappily to Demeter, throwing the club on the grassy knoll.

I thought that the bitch really deserved raw meaty blossoms for knees, and I felt just a bit more human and three-dimensional and a little extraordinary when Demeter broke down and cried on the golf course. Like me, sociopathic toughness was in her upbringing and tempered in her DNA. But when I saw that she was truly broken inside, it did not make me feel sorry for her; it just made me feel that I was less damaged than someone else, because I had made her *cry*.

"Stop," she said, blubbering on the ground, looking afraid of me.

Crying, I cruelly thought, was for sissies and my mother's ghosts. I am ashamed to say that I thought I had won the fight because I made Demeter boo-hoo in front of a small, wonder-eyed audience, and in my aberration of black Wong logic, this meant that I was better, stronger, and tougher in every petty and sadistic way.

Unsurprisingly, the principal sent both of us home for a two-week head-clearing vacation and told us "to cool off." I was also sent to anger-management class, but my mother, who didn't believe in therapy, pulled me out after just one private session.

"Bullshit!" she had yelled in exasperation on our way home.

"White people don't understand how things are done. Don't they know that cowards don't get anywhere? I heard from Auntie Beautiful One that anger management is a cult!"

Apparently, in our sophisticated modern century, you couldn't smack people with golf clubs or ringette sticks whenever you wanted to. Life was not an epic hockey game, even though I spent four days a week at the rink and my father had paid me to hit people in the head so they might get moderate to severe concussions.

But the problem with attacking someone in a gang was that Demeter had many connections, and my parents were convinced that I would end up on the six o'clock news, my head smashed in with a custom-designed baseball bat. Their anxiety confused me (they chose odd moments to be concerned parents). But I did not want their help when I overheard my mother phoning her sisters and her brothers-in-law, casually inquiring if someone knew a dependable Chinatown gangster that we could hire for protection. It was suggested that Uncle E.T. be notified, but he was Vietnamese, and his kind of people were not to be trusted unless supervised. It wasn't an attack from that bullheaded Demeter that concerned my parents. They knew I could take care of myself. Instead, it was confronting an entire gang of angry teenagers who were too lazy to exercise their fists and preferred to use professional sports equipment to give their victims brain damage.

"They probably won't even drive you home," my mother said, a little indignant.

Was she kidding? As usual, she was worrying about the wrong thing, which irritated me like a light bulb–sized blister. I think some part of her was trying to be maternal, but she was scared and didn't know what to do, and this made her seem clueless. Like all the women in my mother's family, she seemed to repress her weaker emotions, stuffing down sadness and fear, while distorting them into other feelings.

"It's the least they can do," she continued. "We all live so close by! You know, these Taiwanese can be so rude! Not like Hong Kong or Singapore!"

"Good luck," my father said, dropping me off at school the first day I was allowed back, and he meant it. I suppose he was of the take-care-of-yourself-don't-die parenting mentality. Even though I was a disappointing extension of himself, we were still related by powerful and dangerous Wong blood, after all. I hated him for his resignation, but once again, I was facing a grave fact: how little control my parents had been given in this New World. My father didn't know what to do, either.

"Lindsay, if you get coma," he continued apprehensively, "you will be a sad potato for rest of your life and you will have no future. Remember, potatoes don't get to watch TV! So don't get fight, okay? Stay alive." As usual, he tried to lighten the mood with his signature black humour.

My guidance counsellor sounded worried. I had been sent to her office for another "casual chat" as soon as I sat down in homeroom. Our conversation mirrored the one I would have with the neurologist in midtown.

"Lindsay, your teachers say you're aggressive and display anti-social tendencies," she said. "You don't have any empathy, and the other kids have told me that they are afraid of you. Normally, I have to teach students to be less passive and more assertive. But you need to learn to control yourself, okay? I want to welcome you back to school but also to remind you to please think of others."

"Okay, I'll try not to do it anymore. No promises, though." I didn't think this was a huge deal or realize that I sounded frighteningly glib.

"You should spend the rest of the day thinking about our conversation," she said, looking unhappy. "I need you to take this seriously."

Having no idea what I was supposed to contemplate, I thought about how much I needed to work on Chopin's *Fantasie-Impromptu*, how my music tutors and judges at local competitions said I was technically good, but I had no emotions or credible feelings whatsoever; me playing Chopin, with his tricky, romanticized rubato, was a terrible, mechanical mismatch.

I had no way of understanding it then, but it was my grotesque fear of not understanding the world outside the Belcarra that paralyzed me, making me numb to everything. I decided that if the other kids did not like me, not even realizing that my behaviour was hostile, I would concentrate on hoarding piano trophies and winning glossy gold medals rather than wooing their elusive friendships. The other Chinese kids travelled in brutal teenage packs, communally smoked grade A Poteau cannabis in bathroom stalls, and attended each other's Cantonese dance parties with an eccentric, unexplainable excitement. Since I did not know how to introduce myself or integrate myself into any tribe at my high school or in my neighbourhood, I had decided to stay far away. I was envious that other kids knew how to get along, how to make friends to do things like hang out at the mall or go to the movies.

Instead, I stayed home to numbly practise the piano for eight or nine hours a day or attended private skating and puck lessons at the rink to increase my speed and improve my caveman slap shot. In my coaching sessions, we did not address wishy-washy feelings and emotions but emphasized winning and cutthroat competition. This would help me later in life: I seized obstacles like a pockmarked pit bull in a fighting ring, refusing to accept failure or long-term illness. At home, my parents did not ever ask how I was feeling; we spoke only about guaranteed results and supernatural entities. "You get gold?" my father would ask at the dinner table, whereas my mother wanted to know if I had seen a poltergeist in the living room.

"Empty?" my father asked after I grudgingly explained the events at school. "Why the counsellor think you are empty? But you show them all your big piano award and they will be impress and say you are very full. Lindsay, why they call you empty? Some new bullshit term for well rounded? You have hockey, music, and you will get all A this semester because you have tutor for everything, no excuse. Mommy and I found you the guy who write your geography textbook to tutor you because you complain you don't understand his bad writing skill and get sixty-five percent on test. No more excuse for the Empty to not understand how to read a map."

"Empathy" was not a word my family could define, so of course I was raised to be "empty." Feelings, I had been taught, were for unseemly Poh-Pohs, pathetic people prone to demonic possession. The more vulnerable emotions, such as sadness, fear, and even affection, were seen as threats. Empathy was a luxury reserved for those with enough emotional reserves to care for more than themselves, who were beyond survival mode. My family had not gone beyond survival. I frequently rotated between fear and anger, spiralling into anxiety, and then plummeting into distress, but I could not explain the godawful Woo-Woo emotions inside me.

"Hungry?" my mother or father would ask at the dinner table, which really meant, "Are you okay? Are you sad?"

I might then reply that I had gas, which meant that all was fine and all ghostly weakness would pass. Yet as a teenager, I was made from tragic turbulence, a godly 7.5 on the anger-management scale.

Really, I didn't know why the guidance counsellor was making such a terrible fuss.

There was no fixing me, but there were attempts. For example, the school guidance counsellor contrived a friend for me that I would most certainly unravel; at least, I didn't see any other way to connect with another person than through destructive means. To fix my "empty problem," the guidance counsellor assigned me a project whereby five days a week I had to push a disabled girl around in a wheelchair to learn "empty."

This Human Empathy Project truly unnerved me. How could I care for myself and someone else? I was not a natural-born nurse or kind-hearted caregiver—how would I survive? I begged the guidance counsellor to hold me back a year or give me permanent garbage duty, but she rolled her eyes and sighed.

Wheelchair "Wobin," as the other kids called my charge, was deemed by my classmates to be "strange-looking," with her hefty head and mini spider limbs. She was half Chinese, half Indigenous, which further frightened the large East Asian population at the school: "She's in a wheelchair because Chinese and Indian do not mix," the other kids gossiped, fascinated. "My parents said this is what happens if you have sex with a non-Chinese person, and that it serves her parents right."

If Wobin's boxy torso was a tree trunk, her arms were branches. And her poor fingers were practically lobster claws, clenched together in fleshy baseball mitts—she was a cruel caricature of Frosty the Snowwoman. Wheelchair Wobin had been born paralyzed from the waist down, and because fate was grossly unfair, she had a terrible speech impediment, so she could not even pronounce her own name—Robin. Kids thought this was wildly funny, even more amusing than my lisping stutter.

Wobin was also born with an electronically fried voice, so no one could understand what she was saying. My job was to tutor Wobin and wheel her to the bathroom to change her sanitary napkin and to the downstairs cafeteria whenever she had an insatiable craving for poutine. Unable to hold a fork, she'd regularly spill gravy-wet french fries and molten-looking cheese curds onto her lap. I am ashamed to say now: at first, I was afraid of Wobin, so I made excuses when she asked me to help her clean up.

Grudgingly, I accepted what I thought was my personal punishment project, one for which I wouldn't be paid or earn nearly enough high school credit. But I quickly realized that Wheelchair Wobin could help me achieve personal goals: time with Wobin included skipped classes and complimentary slurpees from the lunch ladies. I learned that Wobin loved junk food and hated classes as much as I did. And Wobin was a bright girl; she knew that people would always give her whatever she wanted because she was stuck in a wheelchair. Like me, like my mother and her family, she had learned how to survive her vulnerability—through bargaining. Immediately, I could relate.

Most teachers took one panicked look at Wobin's large head, her fluttering eyelids, and gave her preferential treatment—Wobin would put on the disabled act if she knew it'd get us both out of a math quiz, sometimes going so far as to stick out her tongue and scream obscenities as soon as we knew there would be a surprise test. "ASSHOLE!" Wobin wheeze-yelled; it didn't matter what she said—she could be reciting a scientific equation, whispering a sappy Shakespearean sonnet—it would sound excitingly obscene if you didn't have your ear close to her mouth. It was so incredibly difficult for Wobin to string together a phrase or speak in anything other than a murmur, so whenever she hollered in her garbled computer voice, the startled teachers would quickly send us outside for a walk.

In exchange for putting on her "special act" whenever I requested it, I just had to finish Wobin's homework. As her tutor, I made sure that Wobin, who read at a fifth-grade level, improved, and the teachers complimented me on my newfound teaching ability. Although I'd never admit it, Wheelchair Wobin could help me finish the school year without getting into too much trouble. We were friends, but I knew I was using her, the same way that she used me to help haul food from the cafeteria. What else, anyway, was friendship?

It turned out that I did need a friend that year. When I was in tenth grade Hongcouver's provincial government and the Ministry of Education issued an experimental psychology and personality test so we could begin to be grouped into special academic classes and prepare for our future careers. It was an intensive month-long examination of answering simple multiple-choice questions and numbering situational narratives in order of preference—1 to 4, A to D.

I thought I had no future, and I failed spectacularly.

The results of this odd psych evaluation disturbed my father, who said, "What the fuck? Tell them you have to redo it. Why you flunk this test on purpose? Is your IQ minus ten? Negative fifty?"

The computer program had somehow decided I wasn't suitable for any career, and I was surprised by the results. Not that I had been picky about vocations when I honestly answered the 300-plus questions, but not having a career path in mind had obviously been a problem for the software, which had produced strange advice:

Congratulations!
Top 3 Careers for Lindsay Wong:
1. Comedian
2. Mortician
3. Tattoo artist

If I had to choose a career from the computer-generated list, I preferred mortician. Morbidly, I thought that I could fix broken people without any long-term obligations, a new project every day of the week. Corpses had to be grateful that someone was making them perfect again, and I might do some good by helping clients who had misplaced half their faces. Besides, the school said I didn't have any empathy, which I wouldn't need if I was going to be working with people who were already deceased.

"Dead people won't care if I'm empty," I announced to my guidance counsellor, who looked at me strangely. I was good at walling off my most vulnerable emotions, but the irony here was that such a practice had caused me to feel even more vulnerable after being called out on it. I couldn't stop thinking of myself as empty, empty, empty.

Like a true teenager, I rebelled against the nutrients suggested by any adult, in this case the empathy suggested by my guidance counsellor, and embraced a humdrum future to save my pride. Mortician and tattoo artist were basically the same profession, but I thought dead people were not fussy and I would probably lose my temper with a tattoo gun.

As a tenth-grader, both eccentric lifestyle choices seemed obsessive and autonomous enough for me. But my father complained to the school, and I was permanently excused from career planning.

I could never tell my parents about my Human Empathy Project. This would have horrified them in every way. My father would have demanded that I quit the school immediately. He felt that people like Wobin should be quarantined, because low IQ and unworkable limbs were contagious. He would have worried and screamed at all my teachers for selfishly endangering the country's population.

I was scared for Wobin to ever meet him because I didn't want her to get run over by our pickup truck. She epitomized vulnerability—the very human experience my parents had crossed continents to escape and were running from now. Wobin needed me to finish her homework, and like a parasite that needs intestines and a cozy stomach lining to survive, I needed Wobin to get me out of intensive classroom learning.

As the computer results confirmed, I was much too brainless for anything professional. And Wobin said it didn't seem like she'd live very long, with her waxy skin and ninety-year-old-man slump, believing that she was already three-quarters dead at fourteen. She thought it was exciting and fortunate that we both didn't have futures. We had been given official permission by the provincial government to do whatever we wanted. At this point, I was encouraging myself to magically think that I was as emotionally disabled as Wobin was physically—I was coat-tailing her excuse to see dimly into the future, because it seemed easier than growing. And because it was a new pleasure—likening myself to someone else.

Whenever Wobin talked about dying (the only future that everyone had been preparing her for since the doctors found out that she had linguistic ability), she said that she would like to come back as a ghost to punish her parents, and she wouldn't be a boring poltergeist but a Japanese horror-movie spirit with swollen, red eyes who crawled out of televisions and household appliances. Now that was a future I found empowering.

It's not like Wobin had any reason to believe her future could be other than ephemeral when any optimistic tendencies in her present life relied wholly on her imagination. Her parents were strict but lazy: on long weekends, excluding her birthday if it fell on a holiday, they made her wear a diaper and lie in bed for hours because they were too exhausted to wheel her to the bathroom. They also let her eat whatever she wanted and drink four gallons of Coke a day, believing that she could die any day now, so there wasn't any point in trying to stay healthy.

"Last week, we had Pizza Hut every single night," she boasted, and then proceeded to recite the chain's entire menu, which she had memorized. I was jealous of her diet, but according to Wobin, she had the best and worst parents in the world.

Wobin believed that her purpose on earth was not only to devour frightening amounts of cafeteria poutine but also to make as much money as possible before she became a ghost. In movies, violent Japanese ghosts seemed to crawl everywhere using only their pale, insectoid arms, so she felt that she would do a fantastic job being hideous and scary, as her legs didn't even work when she was alive.

"It's, like, my destiny," she declared, looking at me with her favourite eye. Wobin had one thin, slanted eye that she liked very much, and a lopsided marble-sized one that ogled the floor.

At first, I had resented looking after Wobin, but I soon saw the benefits. I would push her innocently through the cafeteria lineup and sneak a slimy hotdog or wet taco into my hoodie, while Wobin, on cue, would start screaming and slurring as soon as she caught the eye of a terrified-looking cafeteria lady.

Admittedly, we made exceptional horror villains: Wobin said that with my bad skin I resembled a surly ogre with leprosy, and I told her that she looked like a demure vampire monkey. Together, we were the fortunate recipients of a dozen complimentary bacon burgers, sometimes three extra cheesy pizzas, or a tray of yesterday's Subway sandwiches—anything to make us leave as quickly as possible. Occasionally, we were sloppily bribed with buckets of lollipops and blue-and-white gummy strips that wound around our fingers like sugarcoated entrails. And after we had taken all we could carry, cackling to the wide-eyed cafeteria ladies that we would be back tomorrow at the same time, we would sit outside and divide our divine bounty.

We believed that we were repulsive and frightening and convinced ourselves that the world trembled at our twitchy, food-lifting fingers, that the cafeteria ladies were awed by our portentous appetites for greasy food. But mostly, I think, they felt sorry for us and let us get away with our ridiculous performance.

"Do people randomly come up to you and just give you money?" I asked Wobin once, when we were both feeling nauseated from overeating. I was supremely curious about how she always seemed to have excess cash, and I leaned in to hear her strangled reply.

"People give me money all the time," Wobin said proudly, "especially in churches. I usually visit three different ones on Sundays. But Christmas is the best time for me. You get random people coming up to you and giving you twenties. You don't know how much money I can make in this chair!"

"That's so great!" I said, feeling happier and a little less queasy. Although I did not envy Wobin's paralysis, I respected that she knew how to make money. I had been raised to believe that money was power, and here was Wobin, enticing me with the possibility that vulnerability could also be monetized—enhanced into power. If Wobin died tomorrow, or by the end of the week, I was determined to help her make at least 100 bucks, and I'd take a happy thirty-percent commission.

I thought about where we could go during lunch to meet the kinds of people who handed out stacks of glorious twenties; perhaps we could loiter outside a bank and pretend we were teenage beggars, instead of miserable privileged kids from the Poteau. There would be more chances that strangers had cash on them if I parked Wobin in front of an ATM. I would need to apply my future mortician skills by smearing dark makeup under our eyes, and Wobin would need to turn her brand-name clothes inside out. Hell, I could even give us both phony makeup bruises on our faces and arms, like we were freshly dead.

"Can you get us an early lunch on Friday?" I said, visualizing an empire of banks and sleek ATMs that we would monopolize and rule with our superior begging skills. I knew for certain that I would have received a high score in con artistry if the computer programming endorsed illegal activities.

"Hmmm," Wobin wheezed, shoving three oily chicken fingers into her mouth and offering me the one that she had dropped into her lap. "Can you finish all my socials homework and my essay for French? Just get me a C minus or a C and we have a deal."

I should have known my days of skipping school and gorging on cafeteria food were over when I stopped feeling anxious and paranoid. I should have known to always glance over my shoulder. Because whenever I wasn't worrying about whatever superficial calm the universe had deigned to bestow on me was when trouble came out of nowhere.

I was cheerfully shoving lukewarm nachos into my mouth, waiting for Wobin to finish what she called her Special Ed Death Class (to prepare her for an early purgatory), and got slimy cheese sauce up my nostrils when Demeter and her Titans jumped me. She was furious about the mandatory "vacation" we had both taken, and her overseas mafia parents did not like that the principal had scolded their do-nothing-wrong daughter. I didn't even have a chance to decently hit back—one against four. A chaotic, headachy, vomiting blur. The hallmark of my disempowerment.

I like to think that I punched someone with great enthusiasm, but when I lost my balance, someone, maybe sneaky Demeter, kicked me in the forehead. Curling up on the ground, I did my best not to cry, because only Woo-Woo people like my mother and grandmother wailed through their eyeballs. I gritted my teeth, bit my tongue, and thought of how I would not even scream if Demeter and her gang shattered my legs.

But a few ghostly tears began to leak out, which I prayed were snot. I could not afford to get possessed, to become hysterical and raw like my mother. Even though I knew that mental illness was a ghostly superstition, being vulnerable, and therefore weak, was not a state that I could indulge. When I would first become paralyzed in New York City, face down on the dirty sidewalk, I was so afraid to look vulnerable that I prayed no one would look at me. It was the Upper West Side, so everyone left me alone.

Nearly passing out from the exertion of squeezing in my tears, I ended up being sent home after a horrified teacher found me drooling in fetal position on the hallway floor.

Luckily, it is a universal truth that rich girls do not hit excessively hard. It's the petty middle-class ones that you have to watch out for.

It was also lucky that I had lost, because the next day the principal agreed to make the incident disappear from my permanent record, provided I took "time off to reflect." There were no witnesses, and he wasn't sure if I had started the fight given "the violent history between the girls," he said, looking flummoxed. But I think he felt sorry for me, and as a small, bald, egg-headed man, he looked as if he might have been bullied his entire life.

Was there anyone who wanted to help me, who actually could?

My parents were called in to speak to the principal and pick me up from school. My mother did not react, but I passively sulked while my father complained that he was losing money every minute that he was away from work. I kept my face like concrete, in case I betrayed any of my feelings.

"The principal talk too slow on purpose!" my father shouted, while my insides cringed. "One-hour meeting take three hour! He think we don't speak English or something?"

My dictator of a Russian piano tutor (a former head of the Moscow Conservatory and a Bolshevik), whom I saw twice a week, counselled me during a three-hour music session to start another fight as soon as I was allowed back.

"What the hell were you thinking? I heard from Mommy you got beat up today," she said in her phlegmy Russian accent, clearly miffed that I did not win. She had expected better of me and was disappointed that I hadn't given anyone a bloody nose or a hairline fracture. "Why did you not punch her? What if those idiot broke your finger and no more piano?"

She was proof enough that it wasn't only my family's culture that used rage to overcompensate for pain. But I wasn't looking for life lessons, or even piano ones.

"Shut up," I said, feeling monstrously ill. I hated losing, but looking weak and ungainly made me ache with weakness and worry. And back then, it was also in my nature to crudely dismiss her since she liked to give me advice, but our piano lesson was charged by the hour.

"I want to work on Debussy now."

Hey, where's Robin?" I asked my guidance counsellor one day when I was allowed back to school to pick up my homework assignments. I was planning on asking Wobin if she wanted to skip Special Ed Death Class and head to the mall to shovel down hot fudge sundaes from McDonald's.

"She's been transferred to a special needs school," the counsellor said, handing me a thick binder.

"Which school?" I asked, stunned.

"I don't know," the counsellor said, shrugging. "It's not in our district."

As I left the guidance office and slowly trudged to the mall's food court alone, I thought about Wobin. I had spent a month developing a superior con-artist partnership with Wheelchair Wobin and had not been entirely grateful for the skipped classes and free cafeteria food. But without me diligently finishing her homework, Wobin would eventually fall behind in her classes. What had I expected?

Since I did not know how to make friends, I did not realize Wobin had been the closest thing I had to one, though we were never friends in the typical sense. We did not hang out or speak outside of school; I did not even have her cell number or email address. All I knew was her class schedule, her preference for anything deep-fried, and that she owed me $7.50.

I was deeply disappointed that she was gone. And I was almost as sad that I had been sent back to the surreal emptiness of the Belcarra, where I was getting a first-rate education in dangerous Chinese ghosts.

Since my inappropriate behaviour in kindergarten, when I bashed other kids in the brain with books and chopped off braids with scissors, I would be on school number six and running out of institutions in the district. And who knew if there would ever be another scheming Wheelchair Wobin who just wanted to make money off strangers and gobble poutine with me?

Without my partner in crime, I felt truly empty, as if I had lost some desperate, less ugly part of myself. If I didn't have a future, it was nice knowing that someone else didn't have one too. Most of all, it was really nice knowing that someone else understood. Wobin and I had been singled out for our shittiness, selected by bad genes and computer programming. What sense did it make if we had been officially declared unfit for society and then punished for not being allowed to fit in?

How much Daddy pay you to be the Best Empty at school?" my father asked me, a few days after the fight with Demeter.

As a family, we would never discuss the fight but cryptically reference the events preceding it. This would just be another Wong counterintelligence secret, to be permanently destroyed and deleted from our database of woe.

"How much will you pay me to finish the school year?" I countered, stuffing down the sadness of having lost my first and only friend with the sudden realization that I could make some fast money from this awful situation.

"Two hundred," my father said.

"How about five hundred?"

"Three twenty. But you be little bit nice to Mommy and Sister."

"Three fifty. The sister is obviously extra."

"Fine," he said, handing over the contents of his wallet. "But if she WAHH and complain, you pay Daddy refund."

"Whatever," I said, rolling my eyes.

"No school mean you can practise piano and run around block three time every day," he said, sounding serious. "Counsellor and principal say that Lindsay need to be Best Empty, so next week, you must be Very Full."

"Sure," I said, knowing even then that I'd have to fake being Very Full, and I'd have to do it without a friend.

CHAPTER 7
YOUR FUTURE CALLING

While I was on my mandatory "vacation" from school for fighting, there was a funeral; a very distant relation had died of breast cancer. My mother pointed at her chest and said, "Chop, chop." She made a slicing motion, giggling shrilly. A joke that I didn't understand then but find uncomfortable now. Death, in all its forms, always devastated my mother's fragile mind.

This was why she went outside: she took awkward steps backwards, thrice around the cul-de-sac, bowing with her back towards the house, up up up the broad pebbled driveway of the Belcarra. Round and round my mother went: speed-walking in reverse, an umbrella over her head. I was used to my relations doing strange and inexplicable things, and tried to mind my own business.

But I needed to know whether my mother was just an average Woo-Woo: was she spouting Chinese superstitions or was it the never-diagnosed crazy inside her mouthing mumbo-jumbo? Our family constantly dismissed mental illness as "Western bullshit," making wicked fun of Poh-Poh's psychiatrist, who was supposedly a very distant cousin (no one really knew how he was related to us). The aunties always crowed, pleased with their own hilarity: "He love Poh-Poh so much he studied Poh-Poh in college! P is for Poh-Poh and phony PhD!"

In the mornings, I watched my mother perform what seemed to be this made-up ritual, huddling under a busted umbrella. Later, she would claim that this post-funeral rite had probably been invented by our seventeenth-century merchant ancestors; she was just improvising.

One day she called me out of the house to practise her ritual— just to be safe. She had returned from the funeral, closed casket, thank God, she said. She was terribly afraid of funeral services and dead bodies—she wouldn't go at all if it wasn't family. Since I didn't know the deceased, I had refused to attend the service and thought I was protected from "the ghosts."

"No, no, you have to participate too," she insisted. "You are very weak in the head and the ghosts can kill you!"

"How about you just walk for both of us?" I said, when I was finally crammed under her umbrella for a marathon of backwards walking. "You can lead the ghost parade; I'll cheerlead from my room."

"Do you want to have bad luck for your entire life? Do you see all the ghosts that I see? Awooooo! Awooooo!"

"I didn't go to the stupid funeral," I snarled after our first out-of-sync loop around the cul-de-sac. And wrenching her bulky purse away to pluck out her jangle of keys, too hot-headed to think clearly, too angry at myself for getting suspended, I went into the house and locked her out.

Ten minutes later, my father called me. He was worried that I was disrupting the rare peace of our household and felt inclined to side with my mother.

"Why are you calling me on the best day of my life?" I snapped at him sarcastically, checking caller ID on my cell before I answered.

"Why did you lock Mommy out?" he said, sounding exasperated. "She called me. She very, very mad. How come you don't pick up the phone when she call you? She say she go round and round house."

"Um, Mommy loves to walk in circles. I'm doing her a favour."

I was furious at my mother—for her inability to repress her fears, her Woo-Woo, all the vulnerable emotions that she'd asked me my whole life to bury inside. I didn't think she was a good mother. I wanted to punish her. I raged.

"How come we raise such a bitchy-bitch?" my father asked.

"No, I thought you guys raised me to be passive-aggressive. Goodbye!"

To avoid any emotional exertion, he would camp out at his firm for weeks. This was how he retained his robust mental health. "Twenty-four/seven-hour workday!" he had begun saying, panicking if someone in the family "acted up." "Bye-bye! Sorry! Too bad! Daddy's office is now closed."

It was true that he cared enough to make sure everyone was ensconced in the house (as long as we kept the screaming indoors), but he believed in a hands-off, laissez-faire approach to domestic bliss, either via phone, text message, or his favourite means: email. "Daddy is just like God," he would often boast. "I watch and tell you what to do from a distance."

Another phone call later, my father was now pretending to be an omnipotent entity, which was an ineffective child-bullying technique.

"Hello, hello," he yelled. "This is your future calling. I am calling with friendly prophecy. As your future, I am telling you that you are garbage. You are flipping burger at McDonald's because you locked Mommy out and since your parents have kicked you out, you are now a homeless at skid row. As Lindsay's future, I am calling to tell you that it SUCK living in a Dumpster and it's very hard work flipping burger—"

"Hey, do you want to hear my new nocturne?" I said, ignoring him. "I'm putting you on speakerphone."

I played half an arpeggio to impress him, but he had hung up on me.

A few minutes later, he phoned again and said, "Lindsay! I have lunch client in fifteen minute! I can't come home! Open door for Mommy! Your future is saying thank you in advance! Your future is very grateful! Your future is—"

My mother was now hitting the back windows with a gardening broom. The window frame quaked, the patio door shuddered, and she began to howl. I knew I had to open it before glass sprayed everywhere. I was doing a very dangerous thing—provoking my mother. It was like teasing a grizzly bear with a stomach ulcer, but I couldn't help it, because my heart really hurt.

And my heart wasn't going to be healed anytime soon; after all, my mother was not well, nor was she being treated. Because I did not have school in the morning, and to show that she had forgiven me for locking her out, my mother decided that we would drive all night. She jumped on my bed, stepped on my face, and ordered me into our hillbilly pickup truck. Of course, I screamed, begged, and cried fake tears, but she would not have any of it. She was in charge and had to let me know it. Because nothing my mother did was strange to me anymore, I soon stopped arguing. But I was still twitchy-eyed with resentment. I was furious at my mother's inability to control herself; her undiagnosed illness made me irritable like a tiger with a toothache.

At two a.m., she stopped at the twenty-four-hour casino in a highway's backside boondocks so she could play slots. I realized that this must be a really nice break for her, especially from the isolation and gloominess of the Belcarra. Exhausted and still furious, I had no choice but to wait in the parking lot. Gambling, like diabetes, lupus, and Parkinson's disease, was rock hard in our gene pool; if any of the aunties drove past a casino, we knew we might never see them again, their bank accounts drained. In Hong Kong, Gung-Gung had gambled away his household supply store and all the monthly cash his mother-in law sent over from in Canada, and a couple of great-uncles had gambled their entire savings after helping to build the continental railroad, so they could never return to China.

Fortunately and unfortunately, my mother's other compulsions drove her away from the slots. It was the battle of the two illnesses, and luckily, the less expensive one won. After four hours, our night drive finally terminated in a Starbucks parking lot, which was when my mother asked me if she should kill herself. Poh-Poh was always trying to commit suicide, so this announcement did not shock me. My mother was just a carbon copy of her mother. Also, wanting to kill oneself was a fact in our family, ugly and upsetting, yes, but truer than any sentiment I understood. And I knew her dying, my mother's choice to live or not, would depend directly on my answer.

"Will you miss me if I go bye-bye?" she said, as if inquiring about my day.

"Shut the fuck up," I said. "You are not allowed to die."

Seeming not to hear what I said, she continued: "I've made enough fucking food in the freezer to last until the end of the month. Then you will have to learn how to fucking cook. T&T Market does not have fresh meat, so you have to eat it as soon as you buy it."

But I did not want to think about frozen food or my mother killing herself, because it hurt too much, so instead, I thought about finding a high school that would register me ASAP, tomorrow, at eight a.m. I could not allow myself to feel slug-like sadness and despair, in case my brain or heart or stomach broke. I was afraid to be vulnerable and weak, like a one-eyed rabbit.

What I didn't know then was that my mother was desperately depressed and needed someone (like my father) to give a shit—in addition to intensive treatment. My mother needed an outsider, a certified psychiatrist to diagnose her phobias and talk her through severe mood swings. Without help, there was no hope for any of us, and I was terrified that I'd end up, broken and emotionally unmoored, like my mother and grandmother.

The only friend my mother had was my aunt Beautiful One, and all day long, they compared ghosts. If my mother claimed that she saw three benign ghosts at breakfast, Beautiful One argued that she had conversed with six malignant ones, and this unhealthy cycle would go on and on until someone, usually my mother, had a nervous breakdown.

My mother did not like us enough to stick around, but her grand obsessiveness would ensure that we would be well fed, at least for a month, ensuring that she had done her duty as a mother while she was part of our lives. It was perhaps a deformed version of motherhood, maybe even self-sacrifice to the point of death.

Eventually, as we sat uncomfortably, my mother attempted to lure me out of the truck and into the empty parking lot, brandishing a crinkly twenty-dollar bill. She must have still thought she could buy me like a grocery store transaction, which made me evaluate myself in dollars and cents (back then, my self-esteem plummeted and rose like the New York stock exchange).

"Go buy coffee," she pleaded weakly and began sobbing.

It was four a.m.; Starbucks was brightly lit but closed, the inverted chairs on tables. She quickly buckled up and keyed the engine on.

"No thanks," I said, knowing that she needed to get rid of me so she could go die. I was not going to let her off that easy, especially if she wanted to pay me only twenty dollars. Because I knew by the next morning she might change her mind, and what good would that be, when she was already dead, her eyes pecked out of her head by Canada geese? I didn't exactly like her in that moment, but I didn't hate her that much either. I just pitied her for crying, like I did with Demeter. Besides, she knew that I knew her plan, so she exploited her Chinese-mother bargaining tactics: "Okay then, how about forty? Fifty? Sixty. You love moolah."

Her animal-like begging me filled me with a bleak rage. I kicked the glove compartment, but my mother ignored me.

For forty, fifty, or even sixty dollars, I did not think I deserved to be dumped in the ghostly parking lot of a strip mall so she could die, but for $500, out of spite, I might have punished both of us and slogged home. I might have taken the two-hour grind up our eerie mountain path, plodding uneasily towards the murky, phantom-infested woods that surrounded the Belcarra. Walking home in the necrotic night might have been my personal test, an ungodly pilgrimage in my Hello Kitty pyjamas; for a moment, I could redeem myself for being subhuman, and my mother would not really die or disappear, because I had succeeded in my gruesome trials.

I felt strongly that she had failed at being maternal, someone who didn't scream obscenities at me and call me lazy and retarded. A grizzly bear was kinder to its cubs, and as a bad-tempered teenager, I had been forced to be my own mother and parent, only knowing how to solve issues with blunt force and violence.

"What the fuck is wrong with you?" my mother sobbed into the steering wheel. "Why are you just sitting there like a goddamn sack of rice?!"

I stared at her, amazed. What did she want me to do? Was I supposed to punch her between the eyes? The option of walking home sounded more appealing.

But it was also too chilly and too late. I was wearing tennis socks, not even flip-flops. Not dressed for any kind of redemption or punishment. And I knew that my mother was just delaying our life, postponing our exact same tomorrow, our same future.

I did not want this woman, my mother, to die.

Because a part of me had known all along that the Chinese mumbo-jumbo only exacerbated my mother's fearfulness. Hyperbolic medieval superstition did not adequately explain why we were parked in a vacant strip mall at four a.m., our pyjamas making us look like escapee mental patients. I also knew we were inhumanly alike, sharing sharpened pieces of the same sad ghost. The demonic fury that often possessed her leaped into me more often that I wanted it to. How else to explain why I could not control myself, why I lashed out, like a teenage crime lord, at my siblings and peers without fear of death or punishment. In this moment I began to view my mother through a cleaner, uncracked lens, to see her as someone that I could easily become if I did not chomp on my tongue and apply myself to rigorous social convention. Her way of being, existing, was the opposite of what I wanted. I hated her Woo-Wooness, her screaming, how she explicitly showed her feelings, while I buried mine.

"Hey, Lindsay!" she finally screamed when I did not respond to her unbreakable sadness. "You want Mommy or not? You want Poh-Poh? I guess you have no appreciation for me, huh?"

Seeing her as a hysterical mess stalled my momentous resentment for a second. Her trauma had manifested in all-night driving and all-night screaming. Like any fifteen-year-old, I liked my villains to be pure evil—my mothers to be one-dimensional monsters who wore last season's yoga clothes and my fathers to be unavailable, distant, three-headed horned beasts who took their instant coffee black.

Huddled in our pickup truck, I suddenly felt pity for my mother, and I didn't like it one bit.

Was I destined to become as batshit as my mother?

Jesus Christ, we even had the same boxy faces: skullish cheekbones and jack-o'-lantern dimples. If you looked closely, I knew that she had many admirable qualities: on her good days, she could be a proficient housewife/feeder who cooked three elaborate meals a day, folded the laundry, tended her peonies with neurotic fervour, and sliced our egg sandwiches into enviable triangles. My mother was also never dull, even if she went for weeks without shampooing her hair and wore the same soiled outfit for months: sweatpants and a sacky fleece pullover. Other Asian neighbourhood mothers wore Chanel or, if they were the Mainland Chinese wives of new-money billionaires, had terrible dental work with large piranha-yellow choppers. But my mother defied classification; she was a mash-up of West Coast yoga homeless.

So although she was proficient in many things, including being a formidable screamer, she had many household oddities. You might wonder why our off-white carpets were peculiarly grimy, or why eight months of soggy newspapers were stockpiled in the Belcarra's hallways, or why pieces of cardboard junk were accumulating on the kitchen counters. We were pack rats, the enthusiastic, obsessive immigrant kind, who were too paranoid to unpack, just in case the government decided to send us back.

To the world, my mother managed an exceptionally thriving immigrant family, who lived on a very desirable mountain, in a very sprawling house with three white garages, always with three or four new American cars. In some ways, she was the head of a proper middle-class family that seemed to do everything right.

And the worst part of this charade was admitting that this unstable creature sometimes accepted me, took me home and fed me three meals a day. That I could one day be unable to control my despair, like her. I could one day become this sad, yo-yoing woman. And thus, as a reminder, I was obligated to take my expected place beside her, in our unsmiling Christmas photo, in a house souring with sadness.

I resented her drama and manipulation, resented that I was taught to equate fucked-upness to something akin to love. It was hard holding out my love for her. She was a monster, yes, but she was also my mother, someone who needed me in this moment, just like when she was terrified, sleeping in my bed when I was six years old.

Instead, I blurted: "You better not kill yourself. You are just not allowed, or else."

CHAPTER 8
CHINESE HELL MONTH

Because she feared starving so much, my mother shopped three days a week at Costco, which meant that we hoarded food, and that eating was almost as essential as money. In our family, a large gift of cash was better than love, but a platinum credit card showed genuine affection. Food, however, was real currency. It was a symbol of our family's unusual makeup. In the Hong Kong slum of my mother's childhood, you could sell a whole person for enough rice to last one or two months (depending on how much you liked your children).

"Couldn't you just sell, like, parts of someone?" I asked my mother one day, several months after she had recovered from our all-night drive to Starbucks by sleeping three days straight. I was genuinely curious, and after being marooned with my mother in the car, I think part of me knew I could lose her. And I was getting bolder, more willing to say the craziest shit, even if it was cruel, to hold her attention. "I mean, what if you only wanted enough rice for two weeks? Like, couldn't you offer up one of your sister's legs, and then next week sell another sister's arm?"

"Oh my fucking God," my mother declared, sighing. "You really are retarded."

"No, seriously," I said, eyeing my sister and wondering how many pounds of rice she was worth and whether trading her in would earn me more time with my mother, who was clearly overwhelmed by three kids. Why did my mother have to be so traditional and have my brother? Why couldn't she just stop with me? Also, did the exchange go by the pound? And how did each party decide what was fair? Some children were bigger boned than others.

This collective obsession with starving meant that our basement, known as the food room, was basically a makeshift earthquake shelter or a post-apocalyptic zombie survival room for all your end-of-the-world needs. Shelves stocked with every type of pasta. Wheat crackers in obnoxious cardboard towers. Plastic bins became vending machines, spewing out every species of granola bar and rice noodle—fresh and stale—manically stockpiled together. I am not kidding when I say that we might buy six family-sized tubs of salsa, and then in the following weeks, my mother would desperately buy another three or four more.

"It's for emergencies," she insisted whenever I sniped at her for hoarding groceries. "See that shovel? We'll dig out the freezer and find water and frozen waffles."

If western North America did not plummet into the murky Pacific and we did not drown first, if the Belcarra did not topple backwards down the mountain in a mudslide, and if we survived all the terrible afterquakes, the autopsy reports would show that a family of five found shelter but were poisoned by trying to survive on spoiled goods. A nationwide warning would be issued: *Update your emergency rations. Look at what happened to those Wongs—they never checked the expiry date. Hadn't the idiots heard of botulism?*

But every August was Chinese Hell Month, also known by Buddhist monks as the Hungry Ghost Festival, which only fuelled my mother's neurotic worry about ghosts and starvation. Chinese Hell Month proved that my family couldn't escape the judgment of our ancestors, who came rushing to our house for an overextended visit, so we were supposed to leave out packaged food for our hungry ghosts. Fortunately, we had a year-round food room with countless varieties, which meant we could supposedly please all our dead visitors from last year to the Tang dynasty. In our family, it was believed that those who had abundant food had tremendous wealth and power. Food could make anyone, including monsters, grateful and happy, so if we fed the ghosts, we could prevent possessions and unnatural deaths.

Unfortunately, it was just before Hell Month when news of Gung-Gung's dying spread, and it was thought that all the hungry ghosts leaving hell were responsible. My grandfather was a long-time sufferer of Parkinson's disease, and the aunties believed his death was long overdue. Besides, they said, he was paralyzed from the waist down and strapped to a wheelchair, so what else could he possibly do? The best solution, the family had agreed, was to find a convenient date for everyone so that he could kick the bucket.

"He's a bad man," my mother explained to my siblings and me, always furious whenever someone mentioned him. "So it's going to take him many tries to die, not peaceful. He lived in the gambling house and he lost *all* of our money and brought home other women to laugh at Poh-Poh. So now it really sucks to be him."

Before his mind went fuzzy, Gung-Gung used to say he didn't "give a shit" about Poh-Poh and pretended that she didn't exist.

Over the years, the convulsions in Gung-Gung's limbs had worsened as his muscles gradually atrophied. It began when he would accidentally catapult his chopsticks across the room. He could be sipping tea or sawing steak, and his miniature Chinese teacup or knife would suddenly spring forward to twirl mockingly on the linoleum floor. "Watch out!" he had to learn to holler in English as his muscles suddenly went berserk and his arms spasmed and pitched whatever utensil he was holding.

In his semi-functional years, as he slumped in his wheelchair, Grandpa became a robot timed to sporadically assassinate his family—he could really turn on you. Then one day his muscles finally stopped quivering, though his feet, which were stuffed into fat woolly ski socks, still shuddered like quaky continents banging into one other: *thuck, thuck thuck.* But it still looked like he was going to sideways punt you. Sometimes Gung-Gung's fingers would tremble like they were trying to pounce in a tremulous staccato on the piano or, depending on your point of view, like he very much wanted to claw out an eye or two. It was always an interesting and dangerous experience to be in the same room as him.

Despite Parkinson's disease and myriad other genetic afflictions, mental illness was our family's inborn cancer—we would eventually learn that we could not run away from ourselves.

A few days before Chinese Hell Month, I got "possessed." My mother was sure it was because we hadn't left the ghosts enough food, even though they couldn't really eat and it was supposed to be a symbolic gesture. Also, because I constantly ridiculed her about rituals, and she seemed frightened that she couldn't make me her capable conspirator against her spirits anymore. By now, my siblings and father had stopped speaking to her, responding only with savvy silence or a spare "Shut up." Because my siblings and I took her illness personally, not understanding it, we followed our father's example and took any opportunity to dismiss her. Retribution, no matter how petty, I felt at sixteen, was real power. This also meant that if our mother forfeited the terms of our acquaintanceship, she'd be completely ostracized in our home, her ranting attributed to just another moaning ghost.

It had been much too hot to stay indoors, and my siblings wanted cheeseburgers, no more steamed fish on rice, which was what we had most nights. We drove the five minutes to a local restaurant on the mountain, and my mother and I gulped down Bellinis to celebrate the upcoming Chinese Halloween/Chinese Hell Month. Beer-drinking age in our household was nine, because my parents had been raised in flea-infested villages in Hong Kong, where homemade rice alcohol was often safer to drink than well water. But this was my first Bellini, which I thought tasted like toilet cleaner and fruit punch. Family dinner in public, rare, and usually only on Chinese holidays to save money, was always strange, since we really did not know how to communicate civilly. This was quickly done, lest any of us should admit to having fun. No one spoke, and the purpose of dining together in public seemed to be a competition of whoever could be the quietest and quickest eater. Really, we had nothing to say to one another.

Later that evening, my father decided to splurge on a movie for us (we went to the movies once a year for blockbuster action films), and while we were standing in line to purchase our tickets at the Poteau's only movie theatre, "the ghosts got me" and suddenly I was struck blind. Blood emptied from my head as if I had been flipped upside down, and my vision flickered in and out. The room spun. I staggered to the right and bumped into walls and rammed into a life-sized cardboard cut-out of Shrek. I mowed down a few more movie characters.

I heard my mother screaming, "She's possessed! Help! Help! Ohmygod, help!"

It happened so quickly that there was no time to be scared. No time to be afraid of the Woo-Woo ghosts, no time to realize that I was no longer in possession of my seizing body. Zombielike, I was staggering around in the dark with my arms in front of me. I could hear people shouting, and swiftly, I was toppling over and smacking my head on the carpet of the lobby. My muscles slackened, and there was piss pouring down my legs and soaking my denim skirt a darker hue. People were shouting even louder, and everything went tarry black.

Then I was abruptly waking up on the floor. The theatre manager had arranged maybe twenty standing movie posters—an impressive circus ring—to hide my unintended solo act. It was supposed to give me some privacy, but now I was on display. Most people on Pot Mountain went to the theatre on Friday, since there was nothing else to do, and they were all crowding and staring. I recognized the neighbours and a few kids I disliked, who snapped pictures of me with their cellphones. I was the Poteau's opening entertainment before they watched Hollywood blockbusters on the big screen. Slumped in a contortionist's pose, my left arm snagged behind my back; my entire body was freakishly paralyzed. As if my limbs were anaesthetized.

"Don't move," the manager instructed me urgently. "You've been unconscious for six minutes. The ambulance is on its way."

This made me a little angry that I had been reduced to a cinematic preview. At sixteen, I thought I might really be dying, but I didn't feel too bad about it. Dying seemed temporary and brief, like getting a booster shot for measles, or even getting punched in the face. Besides, if I died now, I wouldn't have to write college entrance exams in senior year. If I died now, I would not have to worry about Chinese Hell Month and would find out if my ancestors would welcome a semi-skeptic and half-believer. Mostly, I think, as a teenager, I felt that death was not permanent or final, as I'd return as a ghost with abundant powers. Wasn't my family always going on about the power of the undead?

The theatre manager was still arranging the silver movie poster stands at least a foot apart, so people could still see me.

"Stop doing that," I slurred at him. Even dying and dizzy, I was still abrasive, a result of my father's lifelong lesson to never reveal any weakness. I was also humiliated that strangers had seen me in such a weakened state. "Hey, put the posters closer together. You're doing it all wrong."

I was still soaking in my pond of pee—it seemed like an hour, but it had only been twenty-five minutes. And then I blacked out again, and the paramedics took a blood sample, pricking my index finger with what looked like a dagger or a thermometer. My stomach churned and cramped. The older, kinder female paramedic rushed me to the bathroom because I insisted I needed to go, but it was much too late and I shat myself. The paramedics, who were incredibly slow-moving in real life, strapped me onto a stretcher and someone propped the movie theatre doors open. I was so groggy I did not care anymore. My mother was jogging enthusiastically beside the lurching stretcher, asking me how many ghosts were housed inside me and if possession hurt at all. She spoke in rapid besieged Cantonese, so the paramedics could not understand. I did not need an interrogation right now, but she was not the kind to ask how you were feeling.

"What's it like being possessed?" my mother yelled again, as the stretcher bounced up and down a few movie theatre entrance steps. The trip to the ambulance was uncomfortable and dawdling; luckily, I was not an emergency, because the paramedics had parked underground and couldn't remember where their vehicle was. They argued for a bit, while I tried to move my legs without a lot of luck.

"Am I talking to Lindsay or a ghost?" my mother persisted, looking fascinated. "I'm Lindsay's mommy. Hello! Hello?"

"Go home," I mumbled, furious that she was only concerned about the ghosts instead of my well-being. Like anyone and anything else, I was secondary to her obsession, what I didn't realize then belonged to her cultural superstitions and her mental illness but had only attributed to pure selfishness. "I really need you to get me a change of clothes," I said.

"Oh, I already sent Daddy and your sister to get your underwear and pants. You know, you smell like shit! Did you poo your pants?"

Before I was clumsily loaded into the ambulance like a package, my mother fiercely argued with the paramedics that she should travel in the back with me, so we could talk in detail about what had happened. I was relieved when I was suddenly plunging into swirly blackness again, a rabbit hole in front of me getting deeper and darker at nauseous velocity. I would not be expected to jabber with her, thank God—she could annoy the ambulance driver instead. But I wouldn't put it past her to maintain a one-sided dialogue with me even as I gladly passed out. She was panicking about ghosts instead of my health, so I did not want my mother in my conscious space, here, now. I didn't want her to pursue me into my pause-button blackness, my own intermission from life. I resented myself for being so vulnerable and weak, especially in public. And I could not bear for both my parents to criticize me for passing out.

What I most wanted from my mother was silence, especially if she wasn't going to ask me how I was feeling. It took a dramatic possession in a movie theatre to be worthy of her attention, and then I didn't want it if I was going to be accused of having a mental deficiency.

And even though I would have loudly told everyone that I most definitely resented my mother at this point, this wasn't completely true—she was like a shaggy mole or a bad facial feature that you were born with and had to make peace with or surgically remove. But in this situation, she was a starving mosquito.

In the emergency room, the other paramedic, a junior in college, argued with the triage nurse, who was upset that I had drunk a cocktail underage and wanted to phone a social worker.

"Dude, she only had *one* drink with her parents," he said, exasperated and perplexed. "Come on!"

The nurse did not call social services, maybe because she glimpsed my mother, a cliché serious-looking Asian woman. To outsiders, my mother must have looked uptight and terrifyingly accountable; because she was going out for dinner, she was wearing red lipstick, an expensive milk-coloured blouse instead of her usual yoga pants and housecoat. She looked like she shopped at department stores and was clopping along in hoof-like heels.

The ER doctor said I was probably having a bizarre allergic reaction to the alcohol, but he didn't put it in his report for legal reasons. "I'm going to say you're allergic to the calamari you ate, okay? It was probably fried in peanut oil and you're highly allergic to peanuts, right? Say yes, okay?"

As the doctor checked under my hospital gown, I got my period, which stained the hospital sheet and made me cringe. "I need a tampon," I said.

"Serves you right!" my mother bellowed in English, which so shocked the physician that he did not know what to say. I had offended the ghosts, which meant that my ancestors were punishing me.

"I bet you didn't even bring your tampons, did you?" she ranted on, as if possessed. She had transformed into a much livelier version of herself. This was how she normally acted at home, so I didn't bother replying. "So fucking irresponsible. So fucking retarded. I do not know why you are so fucking stupid! What the fuck is wrong with your head? I should just sell you on fucking eBay!"

For my mother, who was so disappointed that she hadn't gotten to meet my ghosts, which meant that she had failed in her duty to protect me from demonic possession, and who also had no clue how she sounded, this was a regular diatribe that did not make me flinch or feel too bad about myself. But the doctor, this *lo-fahn* outsider, stared at us, a muddle of alarm and shock and pity flickering like shadows over his features. I looked away because I suddenly felt embarrassed. There was something seriously wrong with us, which I could sense but didn't wholly understand. It was the first time that my mother had lost control in front of a stranger unprovoked, unless someone budged in front of her in the supermarket lineup. I could tell that she did not care, or did not even realize, that she was screaming. Behind her anger was terror. It was all a projection to seem strong. I still didn't quite get that as a teenager.

It was also the first time she had slipped up and sputtered the wrong, explosive language when she didn't mean to, but she was so obsessed with fixing me, with trying to be good ghost-fighting mother, nothing else mattered.

"I'll get you a sanitary napkin," the doctor quickly offered, trying to interrupt her shrieking. He turned to my mother, shooing her out. "Mrs Wong, can I talk to my patient for a second? You can wait outside."

"Why?" my mother yelled, folding her arms in refusal.

"Is everything okay at home?" the doctor asked me, looking worried and ignoring my mother, who stood at the edge of the bed. "You can tell me if you took any drugs. Maybe a friend, or say, a close family member, like a parent, might have something that you thought was candy or medicine?"

"I didn't take anything," I replied, confused. Why the hell was he asking? Did I look like I was dying? Was the diagnosis some kind of cancer? Maybe he had glimpsed something soft and cadaverous in me, a tumour the size of an obese adolescent spectre.

"Are you sure?" he asked me, while my mother looked at both of us, baffled. "I promise you won't get in trouble."

"Can I have my pad now?" I said, because I was bleeding like a pig in a Chinese butcher shop through the crinkly paper gown onto the gurney. I wondered if I had misunderstood his question, because he was still looking at me strangely. Why didn't he want my mother in the room?

The doctor finally handed me a pad as thick as a pillow. "Tell your mother you're going to be fine. You should probably rest for the next few days." And he closed the blue curtain and left.

It occurred to me later that the doctor must have never heard such extreme Chinese-style scolding before. I wondered how my mother's unhappy machine-gun blasts sounded to an outsider. I guessed that the doctor thought there was more to my "bad food" story and my mother wasn't who she seemed to be. He had no idea that her DNA was made from small and faulty atomic bombs. What I now believe to be her undiagnosed personality disorder.

When my mother left the room to call my father, in the small private bathroom I ripped the pad out of its pale pink wrapper and started to think about disappearing from the Poteau. I thought that I would very much like to be invisible, but if I couldn't, I might be able to hide away for a while. I was embarrassed that I could not have a softer, more malleable mother but felt that I was suddenly more mature and worldly and cynical. Blacking out from alcohol and being loaded into an ambulance heralded a new sensibility. I just needed my own un-Woo-Woo space.

I was becoming light-headed and just wanted to knock myself out for another four to six minutes. But I saw something strange in the mirror: my face had become a bloated moon, the colour of rotten milk, and there were two abnormal red pebbles floating on the surface. Under the sickly, fulgent lights, I saw that the red rocks were my pupils. Suddenly, I was so afraid of myself. I looked sly and horrendous. If I hadn't been possessed at the theatre, I certainly looked unearthly now. I thought sarcastically that shitting myself in public had somehow provided me with self-esteem and a fresh perspective. Surely, my fainting curse was a sign that I was becoming partly Poh-Poh and partly my mother. Was this how the Woo-Woo happened? First, an earth-shaking warning? Losing your eyesight and control of your intestines? But how could I continue to keep the ghosts away?

In that sickening moment, I felt a sense of hopelessness eclipsing me. A souring, vomit-like desperation and lack of control came over my body, in a reality that was not my parallel unconsciousness. *Fuck, fuck, fuck!* This was the most Woo-Woo I had ever been. I shut my eyes and prayed that my new demonic image would fade. It did not.

Later, when we checked out of the emergency room, my mother fearfully complained that I was still very much possessed because I hadn't been respectful of the hungry ghosts.

"But I'm not fucking possessed," I yelled at her, irritated but unsure of myself. "I'm fucking fine, okay?"

When we got home, I was sent to my room, because it was going to be Hell Month soon, and was told I could not come out. We could not go around spreading to other family members what my father jokingly called "Lindsay's exorcist," to deal with the anxious repercussions of the incident. According to seventeenth-century Chinese Buddhist teachings, when monks exorcised the ghosts from the "possessed," if the afflicted fainted and shat, they had been purified. But my mother thought it was quite the opposite—that a ghost had tried to teach me a valuable life lesson: respect the magnificent undead and get stronger in the head. My public possession made my parents stop arguing with each other, as they focused on scolding me for my weakened state. I disagreed with both interpretations, arguing that I had an adverse reaction to an alcoholic beverage.

In fact, it would turn out that I was deathly allergic to champagne and peaches.

More importantly, it was a foreshadowing of what was to come in my first week in New York City. A power outage inside my brain.

If you asked me then, I would have said that being possessed by a badly behaved Woo-Woo had been quite literally like taking a very humiliating and incredibly public shit. Yet in my gloomy, collapsing chest, I worried that my mother was right, and I did not know how to keep our Woo-Woo ghosts away. If my mother hadn't been so proud, I'd have fallen at the varicose veins on her knees and begged her to make me sane, which would have meant ceaseless visits to the Buddhist temple to burn hell notes (tiny papier-mâché versions of fake money, sometimes even postcard images of prostitutes and Viagra, sold at Chinatown grocery shops) to appease our ancestors in the afterlife.

What if I was in the very early stages of Woo-Woo too? Was there a remedy to reverse the small damage? Or was it a one-time deal, a nasty scolding from the universe to listen to my mother's people?

By the middle of August, the entire family was required to shelter indoors for Hell Month. No one was permitted in or out of the Belcarra, not even to water the plants. My mother worried that we would all get possessed and act like Poh-Poh if we dared crack open the front doors or even a window—an underhanded ghost might flutter into our brains, like mad cow disease.

Normally, I'd make a snide remark or roll my teenage eyeballs, but I said nothing this time, which seemed to satisfy my mother.

Gung-Gung suffered three mini heart attacks the week we declared ourselves hermits, which ended our self-imposed quarantine. The paramedics had pronounced Gung-Gung dead during his second heart attack and zipped him up into a cheerful orange body bag, but he began to jerk his legs a bit and moan—another false alarm. They had to unzip him and take him out, and then zip him back in and out for a third time that week. And I think everyone, including the ambulance workers, was getting a bit tired of what our family called his "flakiness."

We could not handle any imminent death in our family, so we had to evacuate the country. We had to go on mandatory vacation. Essentially, a Chinese family functions like a matriarchal dictatorship—if the richest auntie says we must evacuate, the others must follow.

The truth was that our family was too afraid to be left behind to handle Gung-Gung's upcoming death and pay for any health costs. Also, my mother said that she was very worried, because after my fainting in the theatre, she felt that I was especially vulnerable to demonic possession. Gung-Gung dying and me suddenly losing consciousness was surely a double omen that our immediate family was in cataclysmic danger. I did not realize then that this was the only way she knew how to protect me.

So all the RVs were hitched to trucks and vans, a travelling band of caravans. Most of the extended family headed to Burnaby Hospital. My father pulled into the drop-off zone and my mother charged inside to say "a three-minute goodbye" to Gung-Gung, who was dying for the fourth or fifth time.

Because of my dizzy, debilitated state, my mother told me to stay in the pickup truck and not "let any ghost in." I sighed softly so she wouldn't hear me. I wanted her to acknowledge that I was a human being, not a puppet, like Poh-Poh, who everyone believed housed evil entities permanently.

Like all the aunties, we would cross the border to look for safety in the biggest American grocery store we could find. Because Walmart was everywhere, it was decided that it was a food centre that all the ghosts from hell would instantly recognize. The dead chasing us would love the selection of junk food, which was much better than Canada's.

Thank God the Walmart Supercenter in Bellingham was open twenty-four/seven. The aunties decided to camp out at the various Walmarts in the towns across Washington and Oregon States. My aunt Beautiful One's family was one of the more imaginative ones and was going camping beside Disneyland. They asked me if I wanted to tag along, but I was still quite afraid of Uncle E.T., and I worried about him making me run laps in a sunny Anaheim parking lot.

"Feel better, Lindsay," Auntie Beautiful One said on speakerphone. "I heard from your mom that you fainted."

"A ghost got her because she was weak!" my mother interjected. "Why are you telling her to feel better? It's out of her control."

I thought my aunt's response, like the doctor's in the ER, to be normal when discussing someone's malady, in contrast to my mother's sharp shrieking. And I bitterly wished my mother could react more like Beautiful One, who may not have been maternal, but she seemed concerned about my well-being. Unlike my mother, Beautiful One did not blame my medical emergency on my personal shortcomings. Was this how average people handled sickness? And why was my mother so convinced it was my fault?

"Oh, Quiet Snow," Auntie Beautiful One finally said, sighing. But she did not speak further of the fainting, because Beautiful One was often afraid of angering her older sister. Instead she asked, "What are we going to do about dad dying?"

"Save ourselves from ghosts!" my mother declared, as if there was no other possibility.

To protect ourselves from the undead, while allowing me to convalesce, my mother's first pick was Costco, but Walmart welcomed loyal overnight camper-customers. The Wongs were going to take refuge in the Walmart parking lot until we thought Gung-Gung was dead and the hell gates were closed, but we had to remember to turn off our cellphones in case the hospital called with bad news. We were ill-equipped for tragedy and disaster, and this was what we always did to evade our spectacular real-life problems—we ran away. If you ever asked my father if anything was wrong, he always said, without giving a straightforward, sincere answer, "What the fuck you talking about? Everything okay except I have dumb kid and not enough money!"

In previous summers, we had vacationed for two weeks at Seattle Premium Outlets and then spent another week at Oregon's Woodburn Premium Outlets with Auntie Beautiful One's family.

"Do you want to sleep in our trailer tonight?" Beautiful One would often ask me, sounding enthusiastic. "We can have a sleepover!"

Before I could say no because of Uncle E.T.'s presence, my mother would shake her head and pinch my arm. It was her usual way of speaking for me. "Lindsay, you don't know yet if they have ghost in their trailer!" she said, looking scared. Normally I'd have argued, but I did not want to have a sleepover.

This silencing, of course, irked me, but Beautiful One and I said nothing because my mother was in charge. It was sometimes better to let her be the only grown-up, her phobias the supreme queen mother in all decision-making. Whereas my mother held jurisdiction over ghosts and prepared meals in the camper, Beautiful One ordered in fried chicken and fed her children tubs of Neapolitan ice cream. While camping, I preferred my auntie's way of mothering. No one was ever shamed at the dinner table for being fat or lazy or retarded.

And I wondered if our constant fear, which escalated whenever we tried to flee, was a symptom of our mental illness.

August was RV season at Walmart. The boxy trailers and commercial trucks, the Winnebagos cozying side by side—a camping season fairground. A trailer park suburbia. Parked at the back of the lot for modest privacy, our trailer hid out in concrete accommodations. At night, truck stomachs growled with indigestible thunder, so it was almost impossible to sleep as they lurched in beside us.

Despite still feeling woozy and exhausted from the incident at the theatre, I felt a sharp sense of relief in the parking lot, as if I had narrowly escaped some grotesque shadow life, which now seemed to be far away and barely existing. In many ways, the Walmart/McDonald's parking lot was healthier than our sweaty house. Not only did I have the freedom of an entire supercentre and more than 300 parking stalls, but I could not complain about stewing in this foreign, sultry aroma: car exhaust and tropical blasts from a deep potato fryer. None of the Wongs had showered in a week, and no brand of deodorant was compatible with cars and fast food and summer. I was a souring french fry, a putrid McNugget. The RV required a trailer park hookup so we had no electricity, no running water.

However, I was still secretly worried that the incident at the theatre meant that there was something wrong, mentally, with me. My mother constantly fussed over me during mealtimes, while my father read his newspaper. "How is Lindsay's ghost?" she said, sounding anxious. "Is it still inside you?"

"Shut up," I said, but she continued trying to communicate with my ghosts. Her reminders only echoed the sharp pounding beginning to pulsate inside my head, which gradually lessened.

That summer before senior year, for eleven days, I could be

seen in my pyjamas, greasy hair gone stiff on my scalp, pushing a shopping cart in the junk food aisle at least twice a day. In this way, left to myself, I could also begin to plan and plot and dream. I could pretend that I wasn't trapped in a much larger and more fluorescent version of my mother's food room. Hell, I was unsupervised and free, and the store was so bright at night that it seemed like the Woo-Woo could not exist here. It was as if my mysterious ailment had never happened. Was this what insanity was like? A black crack in the brain that deepened with age and rage and fear?

Only when I ran out of clean clothes did I leave the fantasy food aisles and disappear into the clothing department to purchase temporary ones, cheap cotton panties in plastic packs. Polyester bras and rainbow-coloured shorts to be used once and chucked away, all for $9.99. Our family flung our grubby laundry into the garbage can under the McDonald's happy golden arches once or twice a day. This was luxury living—a way to pretend that we had escaped our troubles.

I like to think that being away from home gave us hope that we could one day become unafraid. For instance, the Wongs were briefly relieved of darkness, where the shopping carts could be our life rafts into simulated happiness.

At Walmart, we tried to become the very best of families, verbally abusing each other once every few days.

"Why are you getting so bald like chicken egg?" my father shouted once, half-heartedly, at my mother, who asked him why he was getting so fat and old.

But could we outrun our mental illness? Could we actually outmanoeuvre our ghosts?

At first, believing in the brightly lit promise of American supermarkets, I wanted to think we could. But then my mother began to obsess about the ghosts waiting for her when we returned home. Near the end of our asylum, she stopped sleeping again, blasted the radio and TV infomercials all night, the volume at the highest level, keeping us all up in the one-room RV with long monologues.

"Why can't we just live here?" she moaned again and again. "I don't want to go back."

"Don't be retarded," my father said, putting his headphones on. "I have to go to work and make money."

"Lindsay needs to stay here," my mother yelled, using me as an excuse, since Hell Month would soon officially be over. "See! She's cured now! No more ghost, right? Lindsay, Lindsay, tell Daddy that you need to live here or the ghost will come back."

Groaning, I pretended to sleep.

"Lindsay? Lindsay?" my mother shouted across the room, while a stranger in an adjacent trailer (the walls were not soundproof) screamed, "Shut up! Oh my God! It's four a.m.! Don't you people ever shut the fuck up?!"

But as usual, my mother did not care. She persisted: "Tell Daddy you are only safe here, okay? You just can't go back home, okay?"

Exhausted and afraid that I would one day, like my mother, not be able to control myself, I resisted screaming at her and pulled the covers over my head. But one thing I did know for certain was that even if I wanted to tell anyone about my summer vacations in a parking lot, no one would believe me anyway.

CHAPTER 9
FUN-FUN'S IGLOO

Strangely enough, after the Walmart vacation, our family drama plateaued to a point of semi-normalcy, or at least the sense that I could survive, study enough, maybe even graduate high school. During that year, my siblings and I were nearly grown and no longer involved in multiple extracurricular activities, so my unmedicated mother seemed relaxed and less bothered. And I was able to hope for the future—college.

But nothing ever stays the same. After my seizure-like episode in the movie theatre, I began to wonder if the problem was really weirdo me. So during the summer after senior year, when I found myself face down on a tiled, space-white floor, I was feverish and nervous and terrified. There was nothing scarier than waking up in a *Star Trek* living room and thinking that you were trapped in a high-end appliance.

I was immobilized by some deadly anxiety, and the medical whiteness of the room did not help. I could not remember where I was. Sleek white walls and the cold white floor made me feel as if I inhabited a vast storage freezer in Antarctica that had been scrubbed antiseptic clean. The room was freezing in a chic autopsy kind of way, cadaver-cold with a hostile post-mortem decor.

I suddenly understood what had happened. I had been killed when I wasn't paying attention. Someone had murdered me without my knowing, which explained why I couldn't flex my toes or twist my tired rigor-mortis neck.

My vision was hot and blurry. I began to panic. Then I remembered I was legally blind without my glasses, which were near me on the floor.

Suddenly, a shaft of sunlight burned into my bare arm, and I remembered everything else with giddy relief: senior year was finally over, and I was inhabiting a soulless igloo in desperate, sunny Honolulu. Someone's sterile apartment on the twenty-third floor.

I had been taking over-the-counter sleeping pills so I would not have to think anymore, three to four a day. I heard my cellphone ring and groggily picked up. My mother was calling, worried and panicked.

"Did the ghost or alien get you?" she asked. "If they did, you must tell them to fuck off, okay?"

Predictably, with my erratic academic performance, by the end of high school I had not earned enough credits to graduate, but my guidance counsellor, with pixelated pity morphing in her wet, exhausted eyes, thought it was best to just assign me the missing few.

"Good luck, Lindsay," she had said, sighing the first syllable of my name. We both knew that it was not worth arguing with me over two measly goddamn credits.

The problem with being mostly home-schooled that year, because of my vehement insistence on not attending classes with Demeter and her gang, was that there was no dull-eyed, puritanical teacher to set up due dates. I had not failed biology because I was especially dim-witted or sloppy, but because I had allowed the textbooks to suffocate in their plastic-wrapped casings for the entire school year. Luckily, colleges in British Columbia in 2005 emphasized entrance examinations, which meant that my parents could hire tutors to help me pass.

After high school, everyone in our family was required to attend UBC, the University of British Columbia—or the University of Billion Chinese—because it was the second-best school in the country. With our disturbing and unfocused Woo-Woo genes, it was no surprise that we could only be second-best model minorities. If you belonged to my mother's side of the family, UBC was the only Canadian Ivy League you were allowed to apply to (it was close to home and you could save a bundle on dormitory fees).

I was "too retarded to be George Bush or the Donald Trump or even simple doctor," so my father expected me to major in music, but I had adamantly refused to audition.

That was why I had come to Honolulu. To flee, to escape—I was legitimately, literally scared shitless (anxiety-induced diarrhea and vomiting) when I thought about the Armageddon that was going to be college. I had been so micromanaged my whole life that I didn't know what to do with the imminent semi-freedom; ironically, that same fear sent me all the way to Hawaii.

I was suffering from fear of the Woo-Woo, which some sly part of me still felt could shiv me in the shower. Realistically, I knew that this would not happen. But it was my momentous fear of any change or transition, coupled with the expectation that I was going to fail spectacularly and be kicked out within a month, that made me dangerous. In retrospect, I did not think of post-secondary education as a privilege but rather as another shit-filled familial obligation, one that I would dismiss.

Two weeks before, without telling anyone, I had booked a cheap ticket with my emergency credit card, gifted to me by my father for any ghost-related catastrophes—my mother had insisted everyone in our family have funds (e.g., if you saw a ghost at school and needed to cab home immediately). Without any luggage, I took a taxi to the

airport, flew non-stop to Honolulu, and thought I could stay until I
ran out of money. I had $5,000 in cash and my emergency credit card.

The Honolulu igloo on the twenty-third floor belonged to an Asian
Poteau mother who wanted me to be friends with her spazzy,
ridiculous teenager, whose English name was Fun-Fun, so she offered
to put me up in her Hawaiian vacation home. It was just some inherent
Asian networking scheme: the underhanded, global kind that connects
the richest, most book-smart, or simply the most helpful (dumb but
good for a quick aristocratic marriage) Chinese sons and daughters
across the world.

At school, Fun-Fun, a Honger (a bossy FOB), who dyed her stringy
black hair Einstein white and wore alien-green contacts over her shocked,
enormous pupils, had told a story about her great-auntie's impending
death, and I had snorted, demanding, "Why are you telling me this?" I
did not know I was being insensitive, and that my response was socially
offensive. All the Wongs spoke like this. I thought her story had no
point; none of us listening even knew her great-auntie in Hong Kong.
So it surprised me that Fun-Fun did not want to be friends afterwards.

Of course, as an adult I realized that my interactions with Fun-Fun,
and everyone else, were bright and cruel and toxic, a bleakly radioactive
orange, except I was the only one who couldn't see it.

In Honolulu, I don't believe I ever exchanged a truce-like "Hi"
with white-haired Fun-Fun and her thin, beautiful, multicoloured-hair
Hongers. She was their sulky leader, the ice princess and polar-bear
ruler of the apartment, and she viewed me as you would a grotesque
spider that needed to be stomped and obliterated. Poor Fun-Fun had
no choice but to obey her mother's overseas orders and let me in.

She and her friends were not terrible people, but I was suffering
from deep social anxiety and a sense that I was an unavoidable failure,

an awful cocktail of nature versus nurture. During that period of my life, I could not have run far enough from my surroundings and myself.

When I got there, Fun-Fun and I grunted twice at each other and that was about it. Afraid to annoy her further, I found a gritty beach blanket in a closet and went to bed on the floor. I did not want to interact with her specific sect of Hong Kong royalty, girls who all suffered from cranky, unmitigated bitchiness. In truth, her ladies-in-waiting couldn't care less that I shared their living quarters, but I was suspicious and terrified.

Afraid of their well-adjustedness and of being identified as abnormal, I crept around the apartment like a cockroach. I was not myself at all: my bad habit of scratching my skin raw culminated in being afraid to use the bathroom. I had not had a bowel movement in twelve days, and I could fill the entire Pacific Ocean. My paranoia of being heard, of taking up space in an overtly conspicuous way, prevented me from functioning. I could not speak. I could not eat. I could not bear to use the toilet in case I was caught and blamed.

Instead, I curled up in a corner of the floor and convinced myself that I was better off asleep.

When I was conscious again, I was tucked beside the dishwasher, sheltering half underneath the sink. I was groggy and nauseated; my throat felt as if I were choking on a napkin. But I was afraid to get up and use the faucet. What if they heard me *drink?* I remembered Fun-Fun and her friends, dripping sand and salt water all over the kitchen floor, sunburnt pink from the beach, snickering girlishly. Like a peckish menagerie of exotic birds, their fashionable Honger heads were the blurry colours of the rainbow, all of them staring down at me. But oh so groggy, I had muttered a petulant "Go away" and promptly gone back to sleep.

"Freak," Fun-Fun had drawled in Cantonese, even though I had done my best to stay out of her way. I could not have made myself less visible.

Suddenly, I was a sick, grotesque blur, touching my stomach where my moneybelt was. The cash I had earned from hockey, piano, and family members. Oh God. My moneybelt had been stripped off me. It had disappeared. Gone!

I gagged, from the starchy dryness in my mouth and the coppery bile of disbelief. I decided that someone, or someones, from Fun-Fun's clique must have taken my moneybelt. Was that what they were snickering about? There was no one else in the apartment. It must have bulged under my clothing, an obvious giveaway. All $5,000 of it.

I decided that it was their thinness and normalcy that had allowed them to treat others this way. Filled with shame at my own fatness, I decided Fun-Fun's FOBs would have to pay.

With too much melatonin and chemicals in my blood, I drifted furiously back to sleep.

And because I was embarrassed, I did what my mother and grandmother always did: responded to fear by masking it with spurts of extreme anger. Later that night, when no one was home, I lashed out. The effects of the sleeping pills were wearing off. It took me ten minutes to find my glasses, which I had forgotten were nestled near my head. Another half hour to find my chalk-coloured moneybelt thrown under the white leather couch. Luckily, it still had my passport and credit cards.

Feeling like a centipede amid the luxury of my surroundings, I could no longer repress my envy and resentment. I seethed. Couldn't the other girls see my heartache? In a glacial rage, I raided closets and pitched accessories off the balcony. Clunky designer handbags somersaulted like baby bodies; the clothes and scarves became soundless fabric ghosts. No one was home, so I tossed whatever I could find into Honolulu's empty black street for anyone to take. I screamed in aggravation as the belongings eventually landed like heaped rubbish. Then I ransacked the bedrooms. I threw crisp bed sheets and flighty down pillows. I smashed a grinning glass statue of all-knowing Buddha with someone's unfussy wedge sandal and felt so much better about myself.

This was my shame, all seventeen years of it. And it was emptying out of my pores. It was wonderful and toxic when I became a less sane tornado of myself. It was an outlet of rank emotional expression, especially when my culture and family forbade me to have feelings.

Like my mother and my grandmother, I was a by-product of my culture, history, and volatile upbringing. And I did not want to think about my actions. I just wanted Fun-Fun and her friends to understand my neon-coloured pain.

As I yelled and littered the street below with pillows and stolen offerings, I felt relieved. My slow-cooking anxiety had been dense, black, and explosive. And even though, deep down, I was often ashamed of my rage, and wanted to be less afraid, less extreme, I told myself that I had been born Attila the Hun. I could feel rage in my fingertips and in the enamel of all my scuzzy, unbrushed teeth—it often made me do things that I would regret later.

It was ten p.m., and I was still not myself when Fun-Fun and her herd returned home from a day at the shops. I don't know what I expected, but I had not thought about the consequences.

"What the fuck is your problem?" Fun-Fun screamed at me when she saw what I had done. Clothes and glass made a frightening mosaic on the floor. "You're such a freak! Get the fuck out of my house, you fucking bitch!"

And when I saw her face, greasy from tears, I knew I had

misinterpreted the situation, like I always did. I had gone too far. "Sorry" was not in my Wong vocabulary, and I did not know what to do when I had caused someone emotional distress.

But as an automatic, self-protective reaction, I was ready for a hair-jerking, eye-gashing fight. Because I was terrified of losing face, and because I was terrified of being out on the street, I shoved Fun-Fun with feral instinct, but she called out to her friend for help, a robust high school basketball jock, and I had to be carried out of the building, kicking and screaming. I swear they could hear me howling all the way back home in Canada. Like a hungry ghost. *Let me goooooooo! Nowwwwwwww!*

After wandering the streets until two a.m., cranky and afraid, I found a twenty-four-hour Denny's. I was lost, fearful, and furious, having been dropped in a strange place. And now I could feel the ungodly stillness of the diner in the early morning as I slid into a red vinyl booth, which squeaked and stuck to my perspiring thighs. I still had my ghost-emergency credit cards, but I thought that I would just dine and dash—just in case my father was checking his VISA account online. He would have been furious if he saw the un-supernatural charges, and I could not risk it.

For a moment, my mother's food room seemed almost preferable. Our scummy kitchen, where my meals were laboured over with neurotic worry, was dull and routine. The Belcarra no longer seemed ominous or unbearable but much safer than Hawaii, because I knew exactly what to expect.

I did not want to think anymore, so I ordered my fried eggs bleeding into volcanic black toast, which I wanted to believe would cure most of my discomfort. But a few older American women marched up to me and demanded, "Where are your parents?" I supposed they assumed I was young and lost; with my baby-fat face, I was often mistaken for a middle schooler.

"Don't you know Honolulu is a dangerous place?" one of the elderly women asked me (she couldn't have been more than fifty, but I thought she was ancient). "This is a big city!" she continued. "Why are you out wandering by yourself?"

"Oh," I said, a little surprised by her reaction. "My parents are at home. I'm actually on vacation."

"By yourself?" the old woman asked, looking skeptical.

"Um, yeah," I said. Their shocked expressions had me wondering if she was particularly hard of hearing or I had just said the wrong thing.

I wished I had pretended that I didn't speak English so they would go away. They both looked incredibly worried as I ignored more questions. And then the other woman handed me twenty dollars. Twenty whole dollars! For doing absolutely nothing! I was pleased. The outside world was not cheap, and now I had free money for just sitting in a diner.

It would take me years to understand that these hovering women could see right through me; they weren't absolute idiots, but the quickest way to handle me was to give me cash like my father—anything to make the problem go away, whatever change they could spare from their flush, touristy wallets. In hindsight, it is almost comical that my father reacted to me like I was a homeless beggar in our day-to-day interactions, but like him, in those days I believed cash could cure any malfunction of the heart.

After the women left, I decided that to make even more money, I would need to appear as if I were desperate, confused, and crying. Back then, I saw them, and every single person, as intricate puzzle pieces to be cautiously positioned into my grand, spastic narratives and dirty, absurdist schemes. I was not allowed to snivel at home, and

I didn't know how to sob on demand. If my mother or father caught my siblings or me crying, we got an enormous smack on the crown of our head with an open hand or blunt wooden spoon, depending on the parent's mood. This smack was supposed to distract us from whatever emotional turmoil we were afflicted with and knock the ghost right out of our ears. Of course, in my experience, it never seemed to work. I was more distressed after being hit.

So I tried to jab my eyes with my fingers to make them look scary and bloodshot so that strangers might think I was in terrible distress and give me even more money. I was furious that my parents had deprived me of such a crucial life skill. A girl who knew how to cry most often got her way, and who knew how long I might be wandering around. So I did my best to make myself cry with my dry pointer finger, but all I gave myself was sore eyeballs and what would later turn out to be mild conjunctivitis.

In Honolulu, I was far from my family and I imagined them all suffering without me. It was August again (Hell Month) and they had no air conditioning; maybe they had gone to Walmart and were having so much fun they had forgotten I existed. The thought made me very happy; they had been mostly unappreciative of me. At Denny's, I could pretend to myself that I was a fearless, independent person who had figured out how to make money off concerned strangers. Maybe I had even discovered my true vocation. Getting kicked out of the apartment could be a thrilling adventure. All I wanted in running to Hawaii in the first place was to be on my own for a while and flourish among the healthy and the living—forget toxic Chinese ghosts.

After I finished my breakfast at Denny's (I made sure I ate twenty dollars' worth of food), public transportation tested my abilities as a teenage explorer. I was a suburban princess, used to my parents chauffeuring me everywhere I went. I had never taken the bus before, and I didn't even know its exotic destination. But everyone else was getting on, so I thought I should too. The bus was like an old-fashioned trolley, with red tasseled ropes hanging precariously on its open sides. It was unbearable and crowded, and I couldn't understand how real people suffered this daily. The bus was a horrid invention because it did not even take credit cards. Maybe because of my violently pink eyes, a Japanese tourist couple randomly handed me some dollar bills.

Really, I didn't even need to try to look pitiable. I was dead-eyed and dirty. I was still wearing the grimy skort that I had arrived in and a T-shirt that I had taken randomly from someone's closet at Fun-Fun's apartment. I had not showered in nearly two weeks, so my scalp was intensely itchy and I could not stop scratching. All the tourists appeared to be blooming and glowing in their floral Hawaiian outfits. They wore happy hotbeds of tropical flora, their own private gardens stretched across backs and broad backsides. By my family's criteria, Americans were fat. At home, and on the Poteau, I was made to feel like an obese Chinese girl, but I was suddenly average weight in Honolulu. This was a revelation! On my mountain, in my Fake Asia, I had never seen girls heavier than a size two, so this meant that I could afford to eat more. It was liberating.

The brightness of the sun depressed me as we lurched along the touristy streets that looked like a grown-up's Disneyland, expensively clean and palm-treed. But suddenly, there was a screech and a bang; a white rental sedan slammed into the trolley's exposed sides, and I flew across two seats, crashed headfirst, and cracked my kneecap upon emergency landing. Like a gunned-down bird, a deluded turkey attempting flight. I could not find my glasses.

Luckily, the Japanese couple who had paid my fare found them at the front of the bus. The frames were crushed, twisted, and lopsided.

I did not stay to wait for the paramedics because I did not know that I should go to the hospital with the others who had been injured; instead, I fled the crash site in a daze. I was running away again, and by now, I knew that no one would ever stop me, even if I wanted them to. Everything seemed brighter and, unfortunately, much louder; my neck and head were squeezing tight, and I swore I had injured my brain because certain areas of it felt raw, as if enthusiastically tenderized by a steak cleaver. There was a bombastic ringing in my ears: a high G or C (it varied). I would have a permanent neck injury from the crash, but I was too young and naïve to think about seeking medical attention. I began to experience a strange floating sensation, like I was skydiving inside my own corneas—a lesser version of the vertigo I would later suffer in New York City.

I decided that it was time to leave Honolulu and, limping, hailed a cab to the airport. I did not have any cash and shrugged mutely when the driver screamed obscenities at me for not paying. He may have thought that he could frighten me, but I had grown up with my mother, and "Fuck you, bitch!" sometimes meant "Thank you" or "How are you?"

"Shut up," I told the driver as unfeelingly as possible, and hopped out of his cab.

At the airport, I bought a stand-by ticket to Hongcouver with my emergency credit card and waited in a frantic daze.

I checked the messages on my cellphone. "Daddy has many ghost inside him!" My mother had filled the mailbox with the same message, sounding as if she were the answering machine voice. In my ringing eardrums, her voice crackled and dinged with achy electricity: "I'm going to fly over there and pick you up right now!"

But I did not think either of my parents had flown on a plane since immigrating, and if she hadn't come by now, she was in her food room or sandwiched in the abundant aisles of Walmart or Costco.

"I'm coming home," I announced to her on the phone when I was in the boarding area.

She had picked up on the first ring.

Hey, why are you so fucking dirty?" my mother exclaimed, as I slid into the passenger seat at the international pickup zone. She turned on the interior car light to get a better look and reached across to rap my forehead as if checking for any ghosts, but I pulled away.

I had transformed, and she knew it.

"It's none of your business," I snarled, ready for another hair-pulling, jaw-shattering fight.

For a moment, I thought I saw concern in her eyes, but it could have been the flickering airport lights on her pencilled eyebrows imitating dainty distress lines. Then my mother's usual face was back. I worried that I was beginning to see things that weren't there. What if the Woo-Woo was here in our car? Oh God, what if I was Woo-Woo and this was a hallucination?

I didn't know how I felt about my mother being concerned for me, because it was so new. My ordeal made me want something familiar, even automated screaming from a family member. I like to think that my mother understood the monstrous fear that had pursued me on my round-trip from Hongcouver to Honolulu.

There was something about being away from the Belcarra that made life at home much clearer. As if I had been wearing anamorphic, distorting goggles my entire life, and I could truly see now that she was genuinely worried about me, even if she refused to ever say it. As an adult, I understand that she was too preoccupied with her ghosts to be a mother and a human; she was a grieving, shell-shocked victim of her illness. In the car I could see that my mother and I both looked different, half-submerged by compact shadows and eerie streetlights. We both seemed a little less proud and much less malevolent, though we were both still afraid of ourselves, of what we were inherently capable of. Almost as if we could become possessed by being too honest with each other and ourselves.

In the strange buttery light, her everyday ferocity had been replaced by heartbreaking terror, and my new face looked vulnerable instead of deceitful. I saw that we were small and insignificant, sitting as ramrod straight as our car seats allowed, like crash test dummies, preparing for absolute catastrophe. There was a brittle newness to her, despite the harsh smattering of police-style questions that followed.

"Why is there a big hole?" my mother asked, a bit perplexed. "Whose T-shirt is that? I didn't buy it for you, and it's not one of your cousin's. Did you sleep in a Dumpster or something?"

I ignored her and got out of the car, slammed the door, and briefly thought about going back inside the airport, but my knee was fat and globular, a black alien planet stacked on another bruised moon. No walking for me. I ended up collapsing into the back seat to avoid her invasive questions, curling up in an awkward, perpendicular position. Trying to bring my legs closer to my body, I accidentally whumped my injured knee against the back of the driver's seat and yelped. I was freezing in my skimpy T-shirt, even though it was late August, but I was too proud to ask her to turn up the heat.

"So dirty," my mother said, turning to stare at me. "Make sure you take a shower when you get home, or we're all going to get fleas or fucking flesh-eating disease. Do you want to stop at McDonald's?

Burger King? Taco Bell? Oh, I know, Dairy Queen. You like ice cream. You have my permission to have six large sundaes, okay?"

It made me a little sad that my mother thought she could cure me with helpings of soft serve and hot fudge. And it made me sadder still that ice cream would not help, and that she did not know how to help me. My mother thought she could cure me by letting me eat fast food, by allowing me to become heftier and therefore happier; this was a blaring, red-light emergency, so I could eat whatever I wanted. If a twenty-four-hour, all-you-can-eat buffet existed in Hongcouver, she'd have driven us there in an instant; my fatty ghosts would be drawn to the buffet's lukewarm food under the floating heat lamps and leave me alone. She wanted to appease my hungry ghosts. This was all she knew how to do. What I really needed was extra-strength laxatives, Metamucil, and a dozen bran muffins.

All joking aside, I needed her to tell me that I was not going to die, that I was safe from danger in our car. But I knew that she couldn't. She still didn't have the right words for the situation. Feeding me was her version of normalcy, of parental kindness—when her mental illness was not flaring up. Would our lives, our entire relationship, be different and far less antagonistic if she behaved like this every day?

But I could not think of what could have been or what could be better. I was almost done with my childhood, and all possibilities hurt too much.

"I told Daddy you were possessed again," she muttered when I did not say anything. "But you know him. He's screwed in the fucking head. You seem fine. Not too possessed. That's good."

For once, I understood that she was a little off and did not push the interrogation any further. I suppose other parents would have panicked and phoned the police or, if we were more Westernized, insisted on family therapy ASAP. But like all Wong crises, even messy end-of-the-world ones, this one was taken with little overt discomfort—perhaps some inner confusion and anxiety, but that would be the extent of it.

In the blackness of the car, I felt that I had been born of the extreme nothingness that haunted my mother, a cyclonic unhappiness that was sad and terrorizing and perpetual. I had tried to leave it all behind in Honolulu. As if it could stay there among the pineapples and floury, cake-batter beaches.

In the car, my mother and I settled into a calm, inconsolable silence, the kind that made us too afraid to ask questions, and I think we both felt an appalling willingness, a compassionate virus-like alliance to begin anew. She had no one, and I had no one too, and she was better than speaking to the yellowing carpets in my bedroom.

CHAPTER 10
REPLACEMENT KID

As soon as Auntie Beautiful One heard the news that my father had gone quite Woo-Woo (he had bought one of those fat-faced Labradors to replace me when I absconded to Honolulu and spent his days in bed wailing about his failure to reproduce above-average offspring, etc.), she invited me to stay at her house for a few days until he felt better. The truth was, he seemed to take my failings personally, for he felt that his immigration to Canada and sacrifices should have made his children first-rate professionals of his own choosing.

In our Chinese family, it was absolute lunacy to buy a large animal unless it was for eating, and first-born kids did not fail at basic college-level piano: these were absolute truths, in which my father wholly believed. Beautiful One wanted to help us, she said, because it was her duty as a good Christian and most benevolent relative. So my mother, saying that she wanted a break from her "retarded kid," said that I could stay over for a day or two, just in case Beautiful One's house was haunted—there had been that incident a few Lunar New Years ago when an auntie was half certain that there was a ghost trapped in the wallpaper of their basement bathroom. Besides, everyone knew that Beautiful One always found this kind of family drama exhilarating and was especially hurt if you did not consult her first if someone required open-heart surgery or was considering painting their kitchen a darker shade. All the aunties agreed that it would have been unseemly to deprive Beautiful One of her only fun.

"I always knew your daddy was crazy," Beautiful One whispered to me, giggling, when she came a few days later to pick me up in her truck. She could never be serious and did not care much for my father because she felt he was too opinionated, and my father was still complaining that she was gossipy and insane. I refused to believe that Auntie Beautiful One could be off-kilter, so as usual, I excused her behaviour as "quirky." After all, she had a full-time job and managed several businesses, much more responsibility than my father, so how could she be like Poh-Poh?

"Look at him!" she squealed, sounding as if she was enjoying the situation immensely.

My father, who had once been as terrifying as the Headless Horseman, was crawling on the floor, picking up yellow dog hair to knit a sweater for himself. It seemed as if he had lost his mind, but it felt like a grown man's tantrum. My disappearance to Honolulu had caused him to react as if he were four years old, demanding attention.

"He's just not normal!" she exclaimed, and I could not help but wordlessly, if not heart-flinchingly, agree—this was proof that the Woo-Woo could be contagious, and my father had caught our black magic curse.

"Woof!" he said, and then ignored her.

Beautiful One kept laughing at him, and us, which imbued me with a profuse cobweb-like shame, as it made me feel that we were too far gone to be saved. She had looked so pleased with the extent of this family melodrama, had dressed up for it as if she were going to a matinee opera at the supermarket: diamond earrings, bright red lipstick, sneakers, and grungy low-rise jeans. I did not think much of any of this, for this was typical behaviour that back then I considered "normal."

"How is my favourite niece!" she finally asked, turning to scrutinize me. "I'm so glad that you can keep me company! We'll go shopping, and I'll take you to my hairdresser, okay? You don't want to look like you're from the SPCA."

"Um, it's okay," I said, uncomfortable with the attention. But I was also secretly pleased that someone wanted something better for me, and that I was worthy of this superficial transformation. "You really don't have to do anything."

"Why not? I don't understand why you want to look so homeless all the time. I mean, just because your mother dresses like a bum, I don't see why you have to too. Your entire family looks like they're camping in the woods. Remember, we're the only sane ones in the family, okay?"

I believe now that Auntie Beautiful One was already in the slow-cooking stages of her breakdown: how else to explain the fly-swatting pantomiming of her hands, the spurts of bird-like giggles? Still reeling from Honolulu, I refused to recognize it then; she might have already been infected. But I had to believe my aunt's reassurance to continue to survive. The Woo-Woo could not come for both of us.

In her own slightly crass, haphazard way Beautiful One was trying to be kind to me. We drove back to her house and dropped off my overnight bags, and Beautiful One had a special outing planned. Normally, I wasn't doted on or told that I deserved much better, except sometimes on my childhood camping trips with Beautiful One. I knew what my aunt said was mostly flattery, but it was a nice change from screaming. When my mother took me shopping, she often had panic attacks from the Woo-Woo, which pursued us to the mall, and at stores, she told me that I looked fat, never mind what I wore. And even though my cousin Flowery Face, who was now eleven, had begged to come along, her mother refused, because busy auntie just wanted to spend some quality time with her favourite niece. After all these years, she was still frequently, carelessly, cruel to her daughter, like my mother was to me.

"Please?" Flowery Face had begged at the staircase. "Please! Can I come with you guys? *Please?* I promise to be good!"

But while Flowery Face ran desperately upstairs to grab her jacket and shoes, Beautiful One shushed me and hurried me along, sneaking me into her car and driving speedily away, like we were two nasty preteen girls abandoning an awkward friend. I felt uncomfortable because Auntie Beautiful One was supposed to be a grown-up, a mother of three, not a trivial adolescent with flawless makeup. It was too reminiscent of our trailer vacation to Osoyoos.

"I just want to spend time with you," Beautiful One told me as we drove, flipping her long black hair.

She must have been so lonely in her marriage, so she had latched onto me, like the girlish ghost of a slaughtered maiden, auditioning me for both mentee and confidante. Like all the adults in my life, she was present but not quite all there, which meant that she was searching desperately for someone to like, if not appreciate, her—something that I also needed. Although I did not know that she needed someone to like her or that even *I* wanted an adult to like me then. I felt special that she had chosen me, and I much preferred her company to my mother's—she was still the only grown-up who did not call me retarded to my face. She seemed to believe that I could be different from the rest of our family and wanted to teach me to maintain an exterior persona that was both distinct and separate from the one I had inherited.

When we had spent our summer vacation in Osoyoos, I had wanted, desperately, to believe that Beautiful One thought that our fates were intertwined, because she was successful and driven—it was as if someone wholly believed in adolescent me. Most importantly, both of us had been willing to sympathize with each other's bullshitty, arcane ailments ("A flu, you say? That really sucks!") We never accused each other of having multiple demons. With no other role model, I thought Beautiful One was the personification of how a person should be.

After a while, Beautiful One continued sadly: "Lindsay, you're the only one who kind of understands me, and you're the only one who says nice things to me. Your mother screams at me and so does E.T. Flowery Face just isn't you: she doesn't listen to me enough to deserve a shopping spree at the mall."

"Oh," I said, feeling unsettled and a little sorry for poor Flowery Face, whose mother had left her behind once again. This would not bode well for their future relationship.

"So I want you to tell me all the wonderful things about myself," Beautiful One chirped, checking her heavy makeup in the rear-view mirror; her wispy tattooed eyebrows needed retouching. "Tell me why I'm your favourite aunt. I just need you to do this for me, okay? You have a lot of time before we get there."

So I repeated what I had once told her in Osoyoos, that she was the smartest and most talented and most beautiful one in our family. As she drove and fixed her hair, I was beginning to feel troubled by her, but I ignored the feeling; she was just unpredictable. But then again, she was beautiful—and I wanted to be too.

At the mall, Beautiful One took me to the food court, where one of her chain Vietnamese restaurants was, and let me order whatever I wanted (I gobbled eight extra-large plates of lemongrass chicken that tasted like salty citronella bug spray; the gristly grey meat hugging all the gaps in my teeth like waxy dental floss). And then she coaxed me to cut my hair so I looked orderly and neat.

After I had been fed and groomed, she bought me a bridesmaid's dress that was seventy percent off (she bought herself a matching one too). Unfortunately, the dress did not flatter me, and I looked like a magenta wheelbarrow, a pig in polyester, a bloated five-two, size-fourteen fruit roll-up. I could hear my mother's voice waterfalling inside my mind; she would have said that I was a girly sumo wrestler who could crush you with her floppy and terrifying gut.

"It's okay," I told Beautiful One, self-conscious and embarrassed but secretly pleased with the attention. "I don't need this dress."

"Don't be stupid!" she said, trying to sound wise and generous but failing. "This is what you should wear every day. Just think of it as a costume. You have to show the world who you should be, instead of who you are. Your job is to fit in. Don't you want people to like you, Lindsay?

"Your mother and I used to be Chinese trailer trash, but look at how far we've come! You just have to go to UBC for our family's sake, okay? I had the best time of my life there!"

Then Auntie Beautiful One, who neglected to mention that she had gotten knocked up in her junior year, slipped me 150 bucks, like she was fatally embarrassed for me and didn't want anyone in the suburban mall to see. She was the only adult in my life who believed that I could fit in, even if she herself didn't know how. I did not see it then, but all the makeup, the ill-fitting clothes, were false and terrible bravado for what she didn't know was inside her: insecurity and desperation and hope that someone would one day acknowledge this ache to be noticed. To be liked.

And in some ways, I knew exactly what she meant: I wore the Woo-Woo in my hand-me-downs and in my stringy, uncut hair. Like I had already given up, accepted my parents' foggy, half-living state. Like I was less lively than anything scheming and supernatural. Beautiful One was trying to help me in the only way she knew how: by grooming my outsides so that my insides wouldn't show. Even when she was completely insane, she would still worry about her looks before attempting to jump off the Ironworkers Memorial Bridge, because she understood that she was on the world's stage.

Even one of my paternal aunties in New York claimed that she had seen Beautiful One on TV: "She so pretty of course she make the news. Beautiful people have nothing to do all day, which is why they like to have jump."

Soon I realized that my Hawaii debacle had ruined me, made me mopey and more off-putting. After a bad case of *scratch-scratch-motherfucking!* head lice, by the end of summer, I had done nothing but create quarter-sized bald spots on my scalp. I watched black bears gorge on the viscous juice of Japanese pears gloomily budding in our backyard. I watched West Coast rains lash into the coppice of trees, the white pears catapulting into textured grass. I watched black bears somersault on the lawn like cute suburban children, gnawing fruit all day, holding it with their scalpel-like claws.

Things were not improving, but I had gotten so used to it I could not imagine anything worse or better.

So I walked around like I was brain-damaged, IQ minus 100 billion. Call it formidable adolescent defeat or paralyzing fear or even half-hearted depression, but my adventure to Honolulu had put me into this state. Like I had been suddenly lobotomized in my sleep. I couldn't function. Couldn't sleep. Could only mindlessly eat.

That summer, while I blossomed into Jabba the Hutt and our mountain flooded relentlessly, I thought about my father. How Beautiful One had seen us in our soiled state of disrepair. How she had laughed at us, in a mean but relieved way. *Ha-ha-ha! I am glad that I am not you!*

Her mocking only reinforced what I knew all along: we were so insane that a member of our tribe could laugh at us, like we were Poh-Poh attacking a kitchen appliance.

Meanwhile, the shitty foundations of the Belcarra were half-submerged and everyone on the Poteau thought the entire mountain would have to evacuate. Emergency preparations were well underway. I wondered if they would have to helicopter us to safety if the damned monsoons swirled higher. The basement swamped tirelessly, and the grumbly faucets sputtered hot, gelatinous mud. And there were water quakes at night, which tilted and shifted our house so that the walls popped and cracked open in thin jagged wounds. I became convinced our house and others on the cul-de-sac would whirl downhill into squelchy messiness, smashing black conifers into unrecognizable bits. All summer, the rains and the ghastly winds pounded the roof, and when I woke up in the late afternoons, the trees in our greenbelt had been shredded and their massacred limbs had been guttered in grassy funeral mounds.

I became afraid to leave the house because I thought I was not equipped to handle the outside world. I finally understood why my parents rarely left the safety of our fenced-off aquarium, and why they only vacationed at the outlet mall in their RV. It was dangerous outside our cesspool of a fish tank; it was better to be surrounded by familiar shrubbery and live inside the rotting, fortified castle of the Woo than be vulnerable in the world. You could certainly try, but you would end up frantic and desperate, like Poh-Poh and my mother.

"Lindsay, what are we going to do about Dad?" my little sister asked me one day. She was fourteen and troubled by our father's behaviour. For a week, he had been moaning and moping around the house, like one of my mother's ghosts, as if to show us that he could also act Woo-Woo.

Destitution didn't seem to worry my sister, but I was more concerned with practical matters—who would pay for our massive food bills if our father couldn't work anymore?

"We could sell the furniture," I suggested. I wasn't being helpful, but I couldn't give her the satisfaction of knowing how anxious and sad, and therefore weak, I was. "But we don't have any furniture, so I guess Mom and Make Lots of Money have to go if he doesn't want to support any of us anymore. Think anyone will buy them on eBay?"

"Don't joke," my sister snapped, her eyes bulging, fright twisting her face into something strange and unpretty and caterpillar-like. We had always ignored each other, and this was our longest conversation ever. It would define our tense, unsisterly relationship to the present day. "This is serious, Lindsay. When are you going to grow up and start thinking about other people? Dad's gone crazy and he might go suicidal, like they always do!"

"Good luck with that," I said. "You like helping people who obviously cannot be helped. I think he's faking it."

"Unlike you, I'm not a fucking psycho who thinks the world revolves around her. Why are you such a bitch?"

"The difference is you actually think our parents are okay," I said. I was jealous of her normalcy, her ability to thrive socially and scholastically. Because she was considerably smarter and thinner than me, in this household, it meant that she was left alone and ignored. She had her teenybopper's Japanese anime and her phone book stacks of grey and white manga, her brainy middle-child obsessions with the advanced science club at school. I had potato chips and sarcasm, which I mistook for bona fide wit.

"They ignore you, but they can't stand me because I got the dumb Poh-Poh genes," I said to her. "You can be a saint if you want, but no one here is going to appreciate you."

"You shouldn't have come back," she snapped, tearing up. Her irises looked soggy and infected by an alien pink virus; in truth, she been crying for days. "How come you didn't just stay wherever the hell you went?"

"Better go psychoanalyze Dad, just in case he suddenly decides to kill himself while he's out walking the dog and you're wasting time talking to me. If you hurry, you can catch him."

Then my sister did the unexpected (there was too much wildness in us, e.g., hockey, in our blood); she punched me in the gut. (Did I deserve it? Okay, maybe.) *Oooof.* It hurt like a motherfucker. Fearing my retaliation, she locked herself in her bathroom and refused to come out. Miserably, I took my typhooning futility out on my little brother—anyone and everyone was a reasonable target.

This was the moment the furious continental rift that had been wedged between us since early childhood unmistakably exposed itself, forcing us to acknowledge that we were a very different species. Me, L. Rex: beast-like, squat, and furry, and her: cute and gazelle-thin. Like a messy divorce, she would take my brother with her, and he too refused to speak to me for many years. As long as both siblings died of old age and I wasn't connected to their downfalls in any way, I told myself that I was perfectly fine with pretending that they did not exist. Since we were all averse to apology, chained together by childhood trauma and faulty DNA, I felt that it was simply better this way. But I wish I had been more understanding in our squabble, sarcastic without being excessively cruel. Unlike me, she was so outwardly calm, untouched by the Woo-Woo, no strange tics or behavioural issues. The reason for her normalcy, I believe, was her fierce refusal to be governed by anything except her rational belief in science. Her encyclopedic obsession with facts.

Usually, my sister would ignore our Woo-Woo situation, lock herself in her bedroom with her Xbox, and declare herself separate from our defective family unit. I could have threatened to kick down the bathroom door and bullied her into feeling better (I'd *never* apologize—what kind of sissy big sister would I have been?). In those days, I knew that my greatest talent was making my family suffer, and I had been born the eldest for that very reason. As the first-born, I believe that my parents targeted me with higher expectations. In a way, my siblings were treated better because they weren't held to such high hopes and aspirations, which as children and then as surly adolescents and teenagers we did not understand.

As Deep Thinker cried, I desperately wanted her to let our parents handle their own shitty Woo-Woo-ness. Why should my siblings and I have to micromanage their craziness?

"Sucks to be you," I finally said to my sister through the bathroom door, only realizing too late that my tone sounded exactly like my mother. I flinched, but it was too late to retract my words.

Because I had not signed up for a music audition at UBC, my father, his spitefulness exacerbating his many melodramatic tendencies, eventually dropped hints about *my* suicide, while having dinner in his pyjamas.

"Why you suck so much, huh?" he asked me, sounding hurt. If we were in a Victorian-era stage drama, he might have pretended to faint. Instead, he scratched his enormous belly, gnawed on steamed chicken feet, and burped.

"Why doesn't Retarded Lindsay just hurry up and kill herself?" he said in his meanest voice, forgetting that he was supposed to be imitating one of my mother's breakdowns. "It will be good for everyone. No one likes a stinky truck who take up too much room at dinner table."

I said nothing. His question made me unhappy that I had failed at my temporary escape, and for a moment, I worried that my parents were right about my disorderly retardedness. Was I especially thick and stupid? It was true that I didn't catch on so quick at school, so maybe I was born with an extraordinarily low IQ. If I were smarter, maybe the Honolulu cure would have worked, and I would have known how to navigate the outside world and mitigate its freakish tsunami of disasters. But I was only good at one damn thing so far: I could manage the Woo-Woo, refusing to let it bother me on the outside, even when it could be swelling inside me, like an obsidian kidney stone.

Cuckoo was in my blood.

And it was waiting to be released.

But my mother became angry: her eyes squinted and disappeared into her white, clam-like forehead, while her mouth got larger, like it had swallowed up her face. She looked like a mollusk that had been pried open for its gritty, disgusting pearl. My father seemed to have crossed a line, broken something twisted and flimsy inside her, maybe even gutted her yellowing Styrofoam heart, because this was the first time I heard her defend me. This was one of the only times I thought there was some grimy, unspeakable hope for her. That I felt that I could possibly forgive her one day.

"If you want to die, just go right ahead!" she yelled at my

father, which bewildered me; I never thought she'd take my side. "No one's stopping you!" she said. "But don't tell Lindsay to kill herself! She's weak in the fucking head. She's so retarded she might actually listen to you! You want her to die in the house and give us bad luck?"

"What's wrong with that?" my father asked, as if he didn't know the answer. He folded his arms and looked bewildered. "I have two other kids already and now I have Doggy, so that makes perfect three! I am so sad Retarded Lindsay fail at piano!"

"Lindsay's a stupid piece of shit, but don't fucking tell her to kill herself. She hasn't done anything to you!"

"I'm just telling Retarded Lindsay the truth!" he screamed, making his new dog bark. "None of you can handle the truth! Can Retarded Lindsay please go die now, thank you very much. Daddy appreciate it. How about early birthday present to me?"

"Ummm, Lindsay is standing right here," I said, but they ignored me as if I were already one of my mother's ghosts. "I'm right in front of you. Jesus, you can't have a discussion about me killing myself without my input. God, what the fuck is wrong with you? You want to know why I'm a fucking mess? You raised me! I'm exactly like you!"

It was the first time that I had confronted them, and it shocked me: my ugly smidgeon of boldness was a terrifying revelation; instead of snarkily avoiding the subject altogether, my all-serious brashness had sucked out all the air from inside me, and around me, and it suddenly felt like I, and everyone around me, was deflating. Shrinking.

I had been the first person to point out our unhappy circumstances, and for a second, I like to think my family could see the bewildered hurt splotched and mirrored on all our real faces. Here were the Belcarra's scuzzy, peeling walls and the stacks of raggedy newspapers and messy spires of expired dry goods.

As always, our makeshift illusion was so strong that reality would always be a mirage, and instead of seeing our misery and their junkyard milieu, my parents could only see their aspiring perfection. Things were not skewed—nothing was tenuously out of place. I had not broken our disaffected disenchantment, had not really blasted away the webby illusion fogging up our frontal lobes with my AK-47 flash of wordy and excruciating shrapnel—maybe just dented our steely supervillain shields for a minute—*kapow!* I like to think that my parents, for that unsavoury millisecond, saw that this wonderful immigrant family inhabited a chaotic jungle that had to be kept hidden from the outside world.

But our myopic pursuit of the American dream was so powerful—the heavy, mythic curtain sliding over our eyeballs like a dollar-store mosquito net. So after a moment of intense and choking quiet, they ignored my outburst. I supposed that it was the best way to maintain such a toxic enchantment, an invisible, odourless gas that poisoned and deluded us. It was like I had never uttered the damning words at all. Like I had never been there at all.

For what seemed an eternity, I listened to them viciously bicker about why I should or should not kill myself—obvious pros and cons—which might last for a few days if no one else in the family decided to have a psychotic occurrence. Their quarrelling did not bother me—at least, I managed to convince myself that I did not think they really meant it. And besides, I told myself, they needed something a little controversial to argue about. Domestic topics and extended family gossip were scarce that week. But if I was honest, it affected me on a much darker and subterranean level than I would ever admit. A malevolent kind of inner keloid scar that would manifest in crippling shyness throughout adulthood. A fear that every short-lived anti-social thought was foreshadowing psychosis. In New York, with the severe vertigo, I couldn't help but believe that I was too lost, too far gone down my family's rabbit-hole madness to be saved.

After I devoured a family-sized bag of Doritos and licked the chemical cheese debris off my fingers, I felt considerably better. Inside this household, there was nothing junk food couldn't cure. It settled my nerves and refocused my stifled sadness. In the end, I agreed with my mother: Why should I listen to a man who had bought a dog to replace me?

"Okay, fine," I eventually said to my father, furious and a little sulky. I enrolled at the University of Billion Chinese in the fall as a general arts student. For once in my life, not that I'd ever admit it, he would be right.

The first month of college was like anaphylactic shock. I pretended not to speak English when approached by toothy, smiling strangers. I did not know how to interact with my eager peers or professors. Choking from severe social anxiety, I stared at the ground, scratching my arms raw. The Belcarra may have taught me that I was stupid, but I had inherited my mother's and my grandmother's obsessive tendencies—and like ice hockey, college essays and exams took discipline. To avoid having to socialize, I hurled myself at my studies. Believing that my IQ was possibly fossilized by now, I read every assigned college textbook, like, fourteen or fifteen or sixteen times. I scared the shit out of myself when I got 100 percent on an art history midterm. And 98 percent in music history, 95 percent in women's studies.

These achievements forced me to see a startling change in myself, or at least in what or who I could be, a hopeful glimpse of someone or something less angry, less fearful, less deadbeat. Was this the type of student my father had always wanted me to be? I had a suspicion he must have thought that I could be above average when he screamed at me to be the "Best Empty." At the University of Billion Chinese, that year saw the start of burgeoning self-esteem and, dare I say, scholastic pride.

That year also saw the formation of a new self, perhaps normalcy. Whenever I saw Fun-Fun and her gang of high school girls on campus or around the Poteau, we avoided one another and pretended that we had no previous acquaintanceship. One of the older girls, C.C., had been kicked out of their crowd because of gossip mongering and jealousy from the others. Exceptionally tall and swanlike, she had been a fashion model in Singapore. High school cliques did not seem to matter as much at the University of a Billion Chinese, so C.C. shocked me by inviting me to her house on the Poteau after music history one day and showing me her Tupperware of designer makeup and three closets crammed with expensive clothes. For eighteen years, I had never been inside another Poteau McMansion and was astonished when the gardener greeted me and the housekeeper ushered me inside, curtseying and asking me what I would like to eat. The inside of C.C.'s house was decorated like an eighteenth-century pastoral English estate.

Was this how normal Chinese people lived? Like George III, the mad king?

"Here, Lindsay, you can have these," C.C. said, grabbing a mountain of clothes that she didn't want anymore. "They're much better than the ones you have on."

I was wearing an oversized sparkly sweatshirt that read, *JJJ DA*

LUCK IZ IN DA CLUB, a neon flowing peasant skirt, and chunky leopard-print platform sneakers. Unshowered for weeks, my hair smelled like stale vegetable oil. Even though I was now in college, I still had no sense of personal hygiene or acceptable physical presentation.

"I'll do your makeup," C.C. offered, pointing to a stool beside her vanity. "Then we're going out for drinks."

From Auntie Beautiful One's early attempts that summer, I recognized this as a gesture of friendship, or at least, girlish friendliness. Letting someone give you clothes and paint your face was some sort of centuries-old bonding ritual. Unsure how to respond, I sat on the proffered stool, mute and anxious but hoping that I could pretend to be someone wholly different if I just transformed my outer self. With combed hair and matching clothes for once, would I finally embody the best superficial traits of Beautiful One?

CHAPTER 11
THE SUICIDED

Before my cousin's wedding, the family said that poor Auntie Beautiful One had gotten herself possessed. By that I mean she had never been so loopy before. Sure, she had her moments of paralyzing sadness and ghoulish uncertainty, but didn't everybody? One day she said her brain suddenly "detached" from her body, and her arms started swinging like a deranged weathervane. Then her foot tap-tap-tapped a jazzy quickstep, as she quaked like a mechanical mummy before doing a possessed person's pirouette.

"My brain can't control my body anymore!" she sang when we saw her. She said that God was now chit-chatting exclusively with her floating cortex.

For months, Beautiful One had been gnawing and sucking on the same Costco-sized bag of almonds before spitting them out. Starving herself into a size smaller than zero, crooning that God wanted her to DIE, motherfuckers, why couldn't she just die-die-die?

"I'm being killed!" she screamed at us. "I can't swallow anything!" Hunched over her kitchen table, she spat out nutty purée.

She was a thriving franchise queen, recently opening three new and different Vietnamese restaurants in and around Vancouver, but had dialled everyone to broadcast that all nourishment would kill us and we'd better quit eating at once.

"Shut the fuck up!" everyone in our family had said, which was our way of being supportive. "Just eat and you'll be okay."

But I was horrified, because Auntie Beautiful One had once been the sanest relative I knew. Despite her moments of sadness, my aunt had always appeared mostly outgoing and normal, a role model who seemed cheerfully unhindered by ghosts. How could she have ended up this way—unable to control herself, like my mother and grandmother?

I felt betrayed that she had gone completely insane without consulting me. After all, we had trusted each other, liked each other enough to arrange annual shopping trips to Seattle when our families no longer had time to go camping. She had tried to be an older sister to me, if not a typical mother, that one time after I had gotten back from Honolulu.

I still cannot believe that I had ignored all her symptoms, but I had been unwilling to consider Beautiful One's escalating depression, because it meant that my standard for normalcy wasn't as normal as I had thought it was.

But it was also not surprising that someone in my family wanted to kill herself. In our family, you had to be vigilant twenty-four hours a day because you could become "possessed" anytime, anywhere—particularly in a private bathroom. The Woo-Woo loved it there, my mother said. Showering was terrifically dangerous. So was taking too long on the toilet. Every kid in our family knew creepy-crawlies could jump us when we were alone, which was why my mother insisted on chaperoning my siblings and me to the bathroom anytime she could, even as adults. Auntie Beautiful One, the littler cousins whispered, had violated a sacred spirit code: she had hogged the bathroom in the hours it took to slather on her makeup and been accosted by a zealously vain Chinese ghost. It's not like I believed any of this crap of course, I told myself, but being home was always like entering a parallel universe, where certain rules had to be acknowledged and maintained.

"Lindsay, you should leave the door open when you pee," my mother said, sounding concerned. "It's not safe anymore. The ghosts are acting up."

I had finished exams only five hours before, and now we were fighting about my risky bathroom habits. During the academic year, I spent three days a week in a private hotel room on campus and then bussed back to the Belcarra, since my parents were paying for my tuition and living expenses. Despite my parents' faults, the Bank of Mom and Dad was always open, which I took for granted. There I was, back in the land of the Woo-Woo, where my mother and her demons were in charge. I was twenty years old and had just finished junior year, and I would not pee supervised, especially because of an invisible threat.

"No way," I snapped, no longer bothering to hide my irritation but then doubting myself for arguing with her. "I'm not leaving the door open. What about my privacy? Jesus Christ. Are you fucking insane? No, don't fucking answer that."

"Do you want me to come with you?" my mother persisted, looking worried. "The ghosts are scared of me."

I ignored her and thought about poor Auntie Beautiful One in her kitchen with her humongous bag of nuts and wondered if she was doing okay.

Later that night, right before my cousin's wedding, there was a turning point in the youngest auntie's downward plummet. At forty-two years old, poor Beautiful One was fully manic but perhaps more uncertain and desperate, spewing musical suicide warnings on our answering machine.

"Gooooodbyeee?" she trilled sadly. "Goodbyeeeee? La-la-la? I'm leaving nooooow? Goodbyeee! Hahaha!"

"Get over yourself," my mother snarled at the recording, refusing to pick up. "Lindsay, listen to that piece of shit!"

I said I did not want to listen to the piece of shit that had once been my aunt, but my mother insisted it was good for me. "You need to understand what selfish is! What if you grow up to be a bitch?"

I mimicked her, snidely spitting back her gibberish, and she looked wounded, like she did whenever I challenged her. For a second, I considered whether I was being irrational and nasty, but our exchange would sour my entire evening, as I thought I had overcome my frightening insecurity—if our insanity was so catching, and Auntie Beautiful One had been so easily infected, how long did I have left?

My mother snatched a beer from the refrigerator and went to check the baby monitors that she had planted in the hallways and bedrooms (she had gotten so scared of the Woo-Woo that she had resorted to this, worried that she would miss a supernatural noise and fearing my late-night abduction by mystical monsters and America's most wanted).

"Lindsay," she said desperately, swigging from her bottle and glaring at the monitor's anxious static, "why don't you fucking believe me about the ghosts?"

Auntie Beautiful One's death would have to wait. My cousin's $150,000 three day wedding with designer tuxedos and tailored Chinese emperor-inspired robes would not be cancelled on account of someone in the family having a shitty ghost encounter. Auntie had plenty of chances to off herself and she hadn't bothered, I had cruelly thought and then regretted. She was my aunt, and I had looked up to her. Overwhelmed, I was behaving too much like my mother.

And like my mother, I was going to pretend that she would soon get better.

At least 1,500 people had been invited to my oldest auntie's monstrous McMansion, and my brother and sister, who had been avoiding me for months, were probably already getting wasted at the basement bar with our father. Because we were afraid to acknowledge our illness, we were all trying to protect ourselves by denying that Beautiful One had a serious problem. Before going to the bar, I went to pet my auntie's dogs that had been let loose to roam in the dining room and backyard.

For the wedding banquet, my mother and one of the older aunts had announced themselves the Chosen, which meant that they were supposed to be the Lucky Aunties, i.e., snide middle-aged women who had amassed some wealth via smart marriages and had been competent at procreating sons. They had selected themselves to bless the bride. I guess they were supposed to be magical boy-producing priestesses, because everyone treated the Chosen like royalty, handing them cash in fat red envelopes while bowing. I felt sorry for the bride, who seemed genuinely nice; she did not deserve to have my mother follow her around like the maid of honour on her wedding day. Luckily, newly possessed Beautiful One had not bothered to attend the festivities. Otherwise, the bride would have cancelled the wedding.

For the past few days, I had been trying to avoid Poh-Poh, who had finally arrived at the banquet. She had forgotten to put on pantyhose and instead wore dirty soccer socks with sneakers.

Some grandmothers are just too hard to love. Really, old Poh-Poh was still a ghoulish nightmare, as she enjoyed hitting her grandchildren at parties. Whereas other grannies might demand a phony hug or shoo you away with bribes of money, Poh-Poh was the violent kind who did not like girls and would not hesitate to beat you with her metal walking stick, pretending that she mistook you for a sobering hallucination. Over the years, we had learned that it was best to ignore her. She herself had been beaten for being born a girl, and she thought that this was what you were supposed to do whenever you saw one of your female progeny wandering around at a social gathering.

As soon as Poh-Poh was settled in the sitting room, she chased my aunt's Scottish terrier with a pair of orange kiddie scissors. At seventy-five, she was still as sprightly as she had been when she had stayed with us that summer I was thirteen. Poh-Poh, told by her family not to take her antipsychotic drugs, was enacting her surround-sound delusions. She was grabbing fistfuls of the old doggy's white hair and yanking on his tail, screaming that it affected her eyesight. His tail had to go. Chop, chop.

"I have to cut it!" she yelled, making snipping motions with her scissors. With her white popping eyes, she looked very much like a rabid toad.

We had all tried speaking normally to her, but only tremendous yelling and waving our arms could make her lose interest in whatever she was doing.

"Don't even try it," I said, upset because I liked this dog. "Sit down!"

Moaning, Poh-Poh covered her eyes and slunk to the floor, her bony legs splayed out from her pink dress suit. She peeked over her clawed hands, which had become deformed when she was a little girl, hauling firewood and planting twisty yams like corpses, as Japanese bombs ravaged the sky. In her fancy wedding clothes, she was still lost, a feral woman who had no concept of reality or chronological time. For my grandmother, it would always be 1941 every day of her life, and her enemy, Japanese prime minister Fumimaro Konoe, was plotting an attack.

"I can't see anymore!" Poh-Poh screamed at me, frantic. "I really can't see!"

"Take your hands off your face," I snapped, a little unnerved. "And don't touch the dog. He's not yours. Do you even know who I am?"

Poh-Poh jerked her head no, said she had absolutely no idea, she had no grandchildren (there were nineteen of us scattered through the noisy, sweating house). But this was considered normal. After all, Poh-Poh, too weak to fight the spirits, was allowed to be perpetually possessed because she had survived a major invasion.

It was always frightening and heartbreaking to see that the woman, who had never received proper psychiatric treatment, did not understand that she was safe, the war had been won.

The banquet was still being prepared, so I wandered around the kitchen, where a second cousin, who only ever spoke to me when everyone else under age twenty-five was preoccupied, asked me if I wanted to smoke some "pretty okay weed." Like every Hongcouver cousin of mine, she was pale and dainty, another skeletal peony in outlet Prada.

Earlier, our hair had been curled and sculpted by the same family stylist who had transformed all my cousins' heads into prissy botanical gardens. But on me, the seaweed tresses looked matronly, especially with my clunky purple glasses, and the overall effect was, everyone said, well, highly disturbing. It sent mixed messages: Was I a wannabe hipster or a dowdy grandmother? "It's Sir Elton John's mother," someone witty had quipped, but they said something like this at every family gathering while I flipped them the finger.

As expected, our generation was still competing inhumanely with each other.

"Let's go upstairs," I said to my cousin, who would be my ally for the next ten or twelve minutes. I tried not to feel ungainly next to her in my mall-bought dress. I did not have money for last season's Prada; my immediate family had already lost the competition.

On our way to the balcony, we passed another distant cousin I'd never talked to, some chubby wannabe gangster with pimples—who would turn out to be an actual gangster, buckling a bulletproof vest over his black tuxedo, telling everyone he was, like, totally scared of dying that night. I thought that he was being unnecessarily paranoid. This was a wedding between my engineer cousin and a gushing Filipino kindergarten teacher—but with a family as disturbed and large and diverse as ours, it was not surprising that we produced either delusional professionals or extra-phobic criminals. I chose to ignore this crazy, scared cousin who couldn't stop babbling about dying.

"Is he more related to you or me?" I said, and my cousin, who always had a few grams of weed on her, made a funny face and the cuckoo sign around her earlobe.

A few months later, I heard that our acne-scarred gangster cousin had his arms chopped off by a rival gang member, some asshole clumsily wielding a machete, and now, his poor mother had to spoon-feed him oxtail soup. I do not know if this was completely true, as he probably only had one appendage hacked off (the Chan clan tended to exaggerate). And the anecdote soon got turned into an exhilarating parable about attending an Ivy League college and not becoming an inconvenience to the family. The distant cousin—an obvious dummy—was thought to be inconsiderate for getting himself disabled, and now he couldn't be relied on to provide for his aging parents. He had dishonoured the Chan family name, which was nearly as upsetting as getting possessed.

"Jesus," an auntie, the mother of the groom, proclaimed loudly, as suddenly everyone in the room was bobbing their mechanical heads, bowing at an embarrassed bride and her gossiping entourage; my cousin and I tried to quickly bypass the gaggle of crotchety women on the marble staircase, most of them dressed in identical Vegas-gold cheongsams. "We moved to Canada so our kids could do sex and make baby with the Filipino? Back in Hong Kong we could own maybe five or six of these people."

"It's because these days our kids want to be politically correct," I heard my mother say; she was vicious when she was bored and even more inhuman now, too worried about her favourite sister to be nice. She also did not care to acknowledge the Filipina bride, who was standing right beside her, teary-eyed. "Fuck," she continued, "I don't want to be here, do you? This is a shitty time for a wedding. Beautiful One isn't here."

"Lindsay!" the mother of the groom exclaimed, and I bowed because I was supposed to. It'd be rude if I did not acknowledge her, though I was tempted to pretend that I couldn't hear her. "You look abnormally large tonight," she announced. "Have you had your thyroid checked? Obese is not attractive for someone so young."

"Okay, Auntie," I said, pretending to agree with her but cringing inwardly, and she was so pleased with my answer that she handed me fifty bucks. I had gained ten pounds the previous semester, and I was now a gossipy size 14. But this was the oldest and richest auntie, who thought fifty dollars was fifty cents, and she made sure everyone on the staircase could see our imperial exchange.

If Beautiful One had bothered to show up, she would not have been outdone: it was Chinese custom to exhibit the gluttony of wealth at extravagant social events, and she'd have handed out brittle twenties to every single wedding guest to make sure that she was the most beloved Chan queen. Unlike my mother, who was considered "too middle class" (i.e., cheap and poor), my aunties used showy displays of money to feel better about themselves and to momentarily forget about their negligent childhoods of Third-World poverty.

"Fuck," I said, after the entourage had found someone else to pick on. I averted my eyes.

And my cousin quickly lied, sensing a bleak insecurity in me, which made my round face blaze like an apocalyptic sun. "You're not fat," she said. "Seriously, Lindsay, you look fine. She's just saying it because she has nothing else to talk about. They invent shit all the time."

Nothing good has ever happened when a pig has been barbecued and ushered in on a tray, double front doors propped open, five pallbearers from the butcher's conveying the wide-eyed carcass, still shocked. Tummy hollowed out, skin like a fitted cape, dyed shocking sienna. One of the uncles hacked the animal into bite-sized snacks with an executioner's axe. Another uncle yanked out the pig's underbelly, a metal rib cage inserted to uphold its crispy contour. Extra-large trays of pan-fried strings, tangled noodles with mussels and clams, for 1,500 lip-smacking wedding guests. A final feast to celebrate the bride and indulge in fatty flesh, a status symbol of all good-luck things.

After the pig had been carved up, Uncle E.T. reported Auntie Beautiful One missing by phone. Beautiful One, in a lively display of mania, had stomped over to the oldest auntie's house. With a steak knife, she made a half-hearted effort to slit her wrists on the clean-cut lawn. Beautiful One had thought enthusiastically about dying in her own bathroom but later said that God wanted her to expire in front of all "the losers who didn't believe." Besides, her kids kept hammering on the door to pee.

The oldest auntie's house, the suburban banquet venue, was incredibly tacky and monstrous, with show-off marble staircases and ghostly colonnades. Under the raucous laughter and the nervous erhu, the crucial string instrument of classical Chinese opera, chatty carnivores fed on the succulent carcass that occupied most of the butcher's dining table. There was bad Korean boy band karaoke to help the guests digest their gluttonous meal. Most of them did not know about my aunt's performance on the lawn. And when everyone began their drunken karaoke, I worried that my father, who had been avoiding my mother's relatives at the bar, guzzling at least a dozen beers and a bottle of wine, would launch into his eardrum-gashing rendition of "House of the Rising Sun." In all fairness, I was a little drunk and stoned myself.

However, most of the family saw Beautiful One's attempted suicide, text messages beeping helpfully on our cellphones. *Beautiful One missing! SOS! SOS!*

My mother charged into the stately basement bathroom that had a gold-plated toilet and bidet so she would not have to watch her sister die.

"Is she dead?" she asked me. I had followed her, perhaps unwittingly sensing that the bathroom would be an effective place to temporarily hide.

"Does it matter?" I finally said, wondering when our hosts would bring out dessert. I was starving; anxiety always made me think about my stomach, as if I could cure myself with a plate of expensive cakes. Feeling passive-aggressive in addition to scared shitless for Beautiful One, I said: "I thought you said you didn't care about your sister."

"It's bad luck to die at a wedding," she said, becoming an email auto-reply when it involved her feelings. "Did you call nine-one-one?"

"I'm sure somebody already did."

"Shut the fucking door," she said.

She began to cry, collapsing on the edge of the toilet seat, allowing the spidered hem of her cocktail dress to sag into the bowl.

"Lindsay, I said close the fucking door. I don't want anyone to see."

My mother did not like to cry, in case there were ghosts around who wanted to possess her. Witnessing her cry was always an exceptional and uncomfortable and judgmental experience, much like one of our family members marrying someone not-Chinese.

"It's not your fault, you know," I said, trying to be kind.

"Close the door."

"It's not like you killed her, you know," I said, trying to sound composed.

I thought that being realistic in this situation was much better than trying to be pleasant—my mother would be too distraught to remember a gentler tone or semi-friendly phrase, but a week or a month or a year later, she'd remember my unwavering practicality. She appreciated pragmatic and uncompromising behaviour in any tragedy, from broken dishes to car crashes. Unwittingly, I still craved a little of her approval, especially in these terrible moments, and needed her to understand why she had given birth to me, even if it was just to recognize that eldest children are always the most useful in an emergency.

Over the years, my mother had shrunk sideways and inwards, becoming a scary, skeletal chicken-woman and even more foul-tempered in her day-to-day interactions. Her up-and-down moods were still hazardous, but I could not even be sure I knew this strange witchy creature perched on the toilet seat, cakey black circles under her eyes, her dress wrinkled and looking very much like a bad costume. Her hair had been carefully poofed by a stylist in the morning, but now I saw all the patchy bald spots in her imposing curtain of curls, which had become loose and unravelled. There was a frightening paper-thinness to her scalp that she could only hide temporarily—her animated Medusa head had wilted, almost comically. In this moment, I was embarrassed more than usual for my mother.

Yet this was certainly not my mother bawling in front of me. I had never witnessed my goofy-haired, manga-looking mother blubber over anyone except herself, and I thought she was headed for a cerebral crash. Her sudden transformation totally unnerved me. Tough, self-assured, tactlessly mulish, my mother was never touchy-feely. She was unequivocally, 100 percent a tough Chinese mother when she was not obsessed with her poltergeists and phantoms. The woman in the bathroom, however, was steeping her fuchsia dress in toilet water and bawling smeared mascara tears over someone living; she was a weirdo doppelgänger from an alternate dimension.

One thing I did know was that Auntie "acting up" was a family disaster because it involved evil ghosts, but attempted suicide did not count as a noteworthy crisis anymore. It was a basic side effect of possession. There was always someone in the family who abruptly wanted to off themselves, but they never succeeded. I did not blame these sad people for having had enough—it was tiresome work always protecting yourself from an unseen ghost-enemy.

Although I was secretly worried and nauseated about Auntie Beautiful One, I was quite certain that she would not die—because everyone in our family always talked about self-extermination as if they were casually commenting on dinner. A rejection from a top-tier college, a late mortgage payment, failed basement renovations—all the customary suburban bullshit, the failings of the immigrant American dream—and someone was yelling for a cocktail of household bleach. My mother's people were a twitchy-eyed theatrical tribe, inventors of jittery hysteria. No one in our family would ever admit it, but it was incredibly exhausting and distressing to believe that you could be attacked any hour of the day. It was like building a tornado shelter on the West Coast when everyone knew that our undoing would be a 9.8 magnitude earthquake. We were a product of untreated mental illness that had escalated for generations.

"Will you go upstairs and check?" my mother finally wailed at me, plucking at her hair.

"There's no point crying if you don't know," I said, in what I believed was my most supportive tone.

"I didn't pick up the phone," she said, fumbling for the toilet paper. "Lindsay, I didn't pick up the phone when she called. I told her to shut the fuck up when she cried."

"There's nothing you can do about it now," I said, confident that the situation would improve—no one had ever died before.

But she cried harder; my reassurances did not appear to be helping.

Perhaps it was time to call a cab to go home, but I would probably have to wait at least an hour for a driver to locate this backwoods suburb of Hongcouver. Unhappily, I headed upstairs to watch our evening's surprise entertainment.

I did not recognize my aunt; she was so desperate-looking. A caricature of her former self, wilted and unpolished without her usual plastered movie-star makeup. My heart sank.

Jerking her head up, sticking her tongue out, Beautiful One was handcuffed to the door of a police car. A cerise housecoat barely covered her thighs, and she wore the tatty sneakers of her teenage son.

"Shut up!" a cop yelled. Perhaps she had been uncooperative. I would have been pissed at the cop if I hadn't been so stunned.

Bending over, Beautiful One complained about her abdomen and began to moan quietly about her hunger. "You see, sir, I can't keep my food down. Sir, will you please buy me some McDonald's? Please? Can we go to McDonald's? Mickey D's?"

Suddenly, my aunt shifted tactics and began to thrash and twitch against the car door: "Don't you see that God wants me to die? Don't you know I can leave my body if I try hard enough? Just watch me, *watch me*. I'm dying, you see? I've just left my body! Because God wants me to!"

The death of that mouth-watering piggy was supposed to symbolize the joyous conclusion of the wedding ceremony, but it was upstaged by our flamboyant auntie's live finale. I was morbidly fascinated by the incident, but it was over so quick I could not be sure what had happened.

On the lawn, my auntie wiggled her tongue again, then hollered, "Congratulations" at the blessed bride and groom, who did not even know she was there. If she died, Chinese superstition meant postponing the wedding's pig banquet and transporting the guests home to defer bad luck. I had never seen a human being expire in front of me before, and for a moment I wondered what it would be like, whether it would be difficult to describe to my death-obsessed mother. I wondered if Beautiful One would take a gratuitous amount of time to bleed out; if she would perish with her mouth open, like our lucky pig on the dining room table. But since the cops had handcuffed Beautiful One, it probably meant she didn't dig deep enough with that steak knife, probably just a melodramatic scratch.

Fuck Beautiful One, I thought angrily, almost meaning it, *for causing such a fuss.* I was suddenly furious at her for acting up, for taking her delusion too far, as if she had a choice. *Why are you doing this?* I wanted to scream at her and shake her, even though I knew it would not help. *I thought you were different from everyone else.*

I could not bear to watch anymore, so I quickly scurried to the basement, grabbing another beer from the bar on the way to the bathroom. I wanted to puke.

"She suicided then?" my mother asked, puzzled, her English suddenly going strange and more accented because she was frazzled. She wanted an instant report.

I took a seat on the edge of the bathtub, pulling my polyester cocktail dress over my legs. She did not care that I was drunk or high, or perhaps she never noticed. Alcohol and drugs were not supernatural issues, so she would have felt that she had no jurisdiction or opinion over my condition. I felt irrationally calm, and then suddenly annoyed that our family couldn't have a normal wedding—Beautiful One, who had an instinct for centre stage, could not have waited until the next day to kill herself. I was furious that our brand of "normal behaviour" was causing a stupendous uneasiness. It was like a brain aneurism had transformed everyone from loud-mouthed lionesses to comatose livestock.

"Nah, she's not dead," I slurred, more intoxicated than I had thought I was, and then sighed at the absurdity of the question. Melodrama always made me meaner and considerably less tolerant. It was a defence mechanism that inflated me like a pus-filled pimple. I easily became the most obnoxious person in the room.

"She 'attempted' suicide," I said, correcting my mother's grammar. "Not 'committed.' You can't 'suicided.'"

"Lindsay, I'm positive suicide is a verb. We learned it in ESL class."

"Auntie Beautiful One's okay. They're taking her to the hospital."

"They should press charges. She has to learn to control herself.

I mean, *fuck her.* Did anyone else cry? Can you ask someone else about 'suicided'?"

But all the aunties and uncles had immediately driven over to see Beautiful One's kids, who cried and cried and thought she was dead because my mother's generation insisted that "she suicided."

"Your mother suicided," I imagined an uncle whispering conspiratorially to my cousins, as he genuinely grappled to conjugate the "verb" because he had a limited facility with Canada's official languages, French and English. "Kids," I imagined him saying, "she suicided at your auntie's house by slitting her wrists. Aiya!"

Much later, someone rented a movie to entertain Beautiful One's kids, who were thirteen, sixteen, and nineteen. An auntie stuck *Little Miss Sunshine* into the DVD player, but Steve Carell's character tried to "suicide himself" in the opening credits. Beautiful One's three teenagers wailed again, the television had to be shut off, the DVD returned, unwatchable.

My memory of the wedding banquet was a chaotic, headachy blur; suddenly nauseated, I vomited on a cakey lace flower arrangement before happily blacking out. My parents later complained about hauling me unconscious to their car. At 150 pounds, I was not a dainty, drooling princess but, my family said, a chunky, slobbering mule. When I woke up in my bedroom, still in my sticky cocktail gown, the incident was over, I was still unwell, and my mother was fiercely muted, serving breakfast at noon: blueberry pancakes, a goopy cauldron of peasant congee, and a tray of flowering wontons. Here she was, cooking since five a.m.—like she usually did, using food to conceal our clan's imperfections. The starchy, sweet smells saturated the entire house and barely masked her terrific fear. You could tell how upset she was by the amount of food she had prepared.

"Beautiful One isn't dead," she mumbled flatly, and went to

pucker more chalky wonton skins, even though she had made 200 already. A while later, she said, in the same scary, desperate tone because she loved her sister, "Beautiful One isn't dead, right?"

Our auntie's mental problems had been contained—"Which fucker called the police?" she would ask later. For weeks afterwards, my mother eagerly collected her bounty of fresh sympathy flowers, a few overly kind Hallmark cards from apprehensive neighbours (supermarket strangers), because she liked to tell people her youngest sister "suddenly suicided." "I'm *so* sorry," people whispered, and offered her a sincere squeeze. I could tell that they genuinely felt sorry for us, while my mother pretended that she didn't know the difference between suicide and suicided. More than anyone, she needed their comfort, because our family couldn't give it to her.

And after a while, I began to pity her. As usual, she blamed herself, saying that she did not understand what she had done wrong to cause her sister's possession. I almost blamed her for Beautiful One's downfall, but I realized that I was old enough to be my own person. If I had phoned her in the months leading up to the wedding, our conversation might have told me that something was amiss. I had no excuse. I had been busy with alcohol and college papers and examinations. I felt that I had failed my auntie because I was the only one in our family who didn't believe that exorcisms and medieval superstitions could cure hallucinations.

After the wedding banquet, I spent my summer in bed with a miserable little baggie of weed. A joint made me even more petrified and gave me terrific eye-popping insomnia, so most days, I was as resplendent as a member of the walking dead. I didn't know what else to do with myself to forget about the wedding and the raw kryptonite shock of Auntie Beautiful One's suicide attempt. I did not question what the incident at the wedding meant, thinking that maybe it was an isolated occurrence, a quick and dirty plea for some tender affection—at least that was what I told myself. Secretly, I was terrified that I was going batty too. In my semi-comatose, high-strung state, I was obsessed with the end of the world. I couldn't help but concern myself with what ifs, as my nerves were so rickety in this house that I imagined the world collapsing with its shabby continental scaffolding. I couldn't trust Europe not to collide with Asia, and what if the United States decided to fall off Canada? Would we sink because we were no longer buoyant and balanced? My room sometimes spun, and I was scared all the time, listening to my own sweaty heart palpitations pound out SOS in wonky Morse code. Under the stickiness of unwashed sheets, I gnashed my teeth, terrified to leave my room.

As usual, I believed my mother to be the main cause of my paranoia, more potent than any strain of marijuana or tumultuous stress from Beautiful One's "suicided." For the next week, my mother often visited me at three or four in the morning, saying that we should run around outside until dawn to exorcise the ghosts that were chasing me.

Leaping into my bed, as she did when I was six years old, she stepped on my insomniac face.

"Hey, Lindsay, wake up! We need to hurry! Fuck! The ghosts are already here!"

"Ughhhh," I said, and swatted her toes off my lips and nose.

I was already fragile and terrified, and I knew if we did not do this, if we ignored her gifted premonitions, we'd have to talk all night, so I agreed. Beautiful One's decline had traumatized my mother, and she reacted to it by literally barking and charging around like a howling chihuahua.

In hindsight, it is astonishing that we survived with so little care and attention, though our behaviour only exacerbated my mother's spastic condition, and mine as well. The first week that I moved to New York, when I began feeling faint and vertiginous and could not sleep, I often thought of my mother, and how if she were present in my shared student apartment, she'd make me run up and down the entire island of Manhattan. "This is the only way!" she would insist, trying to be devoted and helpful.

Not believing in boundaries or privacy, my mother would often punt open the bathroom door while I was inserting a tampon or articulate a gloomy sermon about Chinese demons while I was trying to have a bowel movement. Her fear strangling her heart and brain, she'd smash the lock on the doorknob while I was showering to check if a wayward phantom was floating among our flimsy floral curtains, if a shy spectre was lurking in a bubble bath (everyone knew that Chinese ghosts were the mousy colour of water with some resemblance to a former person).

After the wedding, my father, looking horrified, said, "No more wedding for Mommy from now on," before disappearing from the house with his dog.

He was right, as her downward descent into madness mimicked Auntie Beautiful One's. And my future too seemed as if it could be the exact replica of all the women in my family.

"AHHHHHHHHH!" my mother would howl, seeming ready to tackle any hefty spirit, but what she really meant was, like everyone else in the family, "I'm afraid! Don't leave me alone!"

I still could not wholly comprehend her terrors then, so I'd scream at her, and she would complain that I thought I was invincible. She could not bear it if I were to become possessed and meant her protectiveness to be a peculiar expression of affection. Tenderness did not exist in our family, but duty and safekeeping were priorities, like lavish weddings and overeating.

"Oh, come on," I said, knowing that I could not convince her otherwise, while fighting a terrific urge to chuck my loofah at her. "The ghosts won't get me."

"But I think I saw one float across your eyelids," she said. She still assumed that everything, including a funny-sounding sneeze or hiccup, was cursed and mystical.

"That was probably the light," I said.

It was probably more frightening to be ambushed in the bathroom by my mother than to encounter a real ghost. At home, things were usually uncomfortable and chaotic, and I could not spend four months of summer trying to avoid the damned supernatural.

If I had a fantastic mental breakdown, my family would spend thousands of dollars exorcising the scary Woo-Woo out of me—this was what we did, loyally wrote cheques to bribe away our problems. Yet after Beautiful One's breakdown, I was beginning to feel afraid that there was something truly deformed inside me, and all summer, I felt as if I were being electroshocked by worry. With my mother jumping out at me from hallways and staircases, it was like living inside a haunted house at a wacky carnival—an apocalyptic heart attack waiting for me every time I ventured outside my bedroom. I could feel myself sinking slowly into my own brain.

CHAPTER 12
"JUMP, BITCH, JUMP!"

I don't want to go to the hospital," Auntie Beautiful One sang after she tried to slit her wrists (just a barely-there scratch, the family complained).

It was the middle of the summer, and consumed by a daytime, vampire-like terror, I would not leave my bed until a family intervention was ordered for Beautiful One. She had been released from the emergency room, but there had been no change in her condition. It had been almost a week since my cousin's wedding, and I was worried and nervous as we (all eight families, i.e., seventy very frightened people) congregated in my aunt's living room. Even after everyone took turns yelling at her for what our family called "shitty behaviour," Beautiful One, her face blank, was not cured.

"I'm dying, okay?" Beautiful One shrilled at us in response.

My heart sank, for I knew she did not recognize herself at all. This was not the woman who had, many years ago on our family camping trip, once assured me that she was different from every Woo-Woo we knew. And as she yelled, she resembled both Poh-Poh and my mother, her face contorted into a mask of paralyzing fear.

She yelled: "I can't eat because it just comes out anyway. My brain is sooooo alive. Do you know how powerful it is? Do you know how powerful I am? But my body is dying. Dyiiing!!"

If we looked back at her month of screaming and spitting nuts at the kitchen table, the incident at my cousin's wedding should not have been surprising. If our family had been less occupied by ghosts and paid a little attention to her sadness and her distance from reality, her breakdown may have been prevented. Yet, realistically, we could only have saved her if someone (non–superstition believing) had spiked her coffee with Benadryl, clubbed her on the forehead, and then chucked her into the back of a psychiatrist-bound taxi. Yet I knew that no one would trust an outsider, God forbid a medical professional, to diagnose Auntie Beautiful One, when we all thought willpower and exorcism could rid her of the ghosts.

After all these years, Beautiful One had officially gone Woo-Woo, and only my father was pleased. He had always suspected that his sister-in-law did not have much of a brain.

"She just realize now she Woo-Woo?" he said, amazed. "Wow, took long enough. See, no one listen to me when I say the woman is fucking nuts! She so Woo-Woo she think all food, even just ONE apple can kill her! Karma is fucking great."

Uncle E.T., horrified by his wife's "self-cause" mental collapse, decided that she was more hopeless and futile than "the global warning." Prioritizing his self-preservation more than anything, he ran off to Hongcouver Island.

After her attempted suicide, with the rest of my family (minus E.T.), I watched in absolute horror as Auntie Beautiful One tumbled to the floor because she said that God liked to zap her with his electrical finger. She'd be walking to the kitchen and then an almighty poke would throw her to the ground. The vicious buzzing noise inside her brain made Beautiful One think she wasn't a real person anymore, just another machine. Zap, zap, zap—she said God's finger sounded like an electric flytrap. I wondered what it felt like to be fried in the electrical circuit of your robotic nerves, a quick current smacking your fat mechanical heart. He zapped Beautiful One the Automaton, and then he pinched her battery-volted butt.

This was Beautiful One, head thrown back, hands clasped in maniacal prayer, crying for our help, the volume of her terror and confusion amplified to the highest level.

"Shut the fuck up," everyone said, when she threatened to die and die and die again.

As always, on Westwood Poteau, if you weren't the kind to have a breakdown, there was nothing to do except indulge in the constant buffet of cannabis. There was soft, sugary cocaine and Skittle-sized pills of ecstasy to be had from any suburban drug-growing neighbour, if you wanted them. There was also the lengthy two-hour commute into the city, but I didn't know how to drive. I also wasn't sure what one was supposed to do in civilization. After years of intensive piano practice, I had no hobbies or interests. The Chinese cliques on the Poteau were scared of me because I had happily bashed a ringette stick *and* a golf club into Demeter's knees in high school, so there were no invitations to what I imagine were barbecues and sailing, but I told myself I didn't mind. I was used to it.

That summer after junior year, I bloomed into a bovine stoner with bountiful food and marijuana, and I was getting fatter and slower and nastier by the day. The family-sized tubs of ice cream and entire apple pies combined with pepperoni pizzas added marbled fat to my stomach and thighs. My father didn't care—I could eat as much as I wanted, as long as I was getting all As in college. I felt smug with how hefty I was getting, as if I could get back at my family and suffocate them with my 165 pounds of sirloin steak bulk.

And while I shovelled food into my mouth, Beautiful One was

refusing all sustenance, afraid that eating would poison her. Yet her impending death made her even more obsessed with her looks, as if her beauty could be preserved by suddenly dying.

"You know I'm pretty, right?" she often repeated, shrilled, and obsessed, during her manic episodes. "Everyone thinks I'm twenty years younger than I am!"

My mother was too preoccupied with Beautiful One's intensifying madness to stop my eating (it seemed that they screamed about suicide on speakerphone for four to six hours every day). I promised myself that I would stop binge eating and become productive again by September, once school began.

Then one day, C.C. called, which surprised me, because I thought our acquaintanceship had an end-of-semester expiry date, like a carton of fat-free milk. It was a relief when she (someone "normal") phoned, as I could not bear to listen to anyone, even if they were very convincing, cry about becoming a ghost.

"What are you up to, my favourite freak?" C.C. drawled, lazy and glamorous at the same time. I had forgotten how direct C.C. could be. I envied her easy charm—how people seemed to want to be around her even if she wasn't always very nice.

"Want to go to Europe next week?" she said.

"Why?" I said, instantly suspicious. "What's in Europe?"

"I don't know, like, countries, I guess. There's going to be food. Plural."

"There's food plural in Canada," I pointed out. "It's a First World country."

"There's going to be different food," she promised me. "Lots of different food. Oh, for Christ's sake, just come. I don't care if you eat the entire time we're there."

C.C. had a venture-capitalist uncle who wanted to pay for

a month in Europe—she was a year above me and had already finished her degree at the University of Billion Chinese, and this was a graduation present for his dearest niece. I was surprised that she wanted to take me, but I guessed that she was bored and wanted a summer project.

I did not want to think of Beautiful One and be reminded of the wedding anymore, and I couldn't afford to be choosy, so I decided that I had nothing to lose. C.C. had unwittingly offered me a timely break from the chaotic aftermath of the wedding. Was it selfish of me to want to leave? It would be a real vacation away from the Woo-Woo.

"You have to find a new hobby," I instructed my mother, when I told her I was leaving for Europe. "I'm not available anymore. You can try the Chinese community centre. Lots of great old people there. They'd love to listen to you talk about dying."

She and I fought about the trip, about me terminating my summer employment as her weak-headed, fucked-up offspring. She argued about how Europe was the most intensely haunted locale in the world, how London, Edinburgh, Dublin, and Paris were practically unlivable because of all the unfortunate people slaughtered in their convoluted wars.

"You know the ghosts are all angry there!" she protested weakly. "Don't you know Canada is safest? Why are you leaving a country with very little wars? You'll end up like a dead bitch in a Dumpster," she cried in warning, saying anything to make me stay with her, anything to frighten me. "Something fucked is going to happen, and I know it's going to happen to you. You can't leave the house! You're too weak in the head! I'll pay you five hundred dollars if you stay! One thousand? Two thousand? What about the ghosts, Lindsay?"

For once, I did not have to listen to her, for I did not need her money. C.C. was offering free four-star hotel accommodations and fine dining. And this financial freedom gave me a quasi-rebellious power. One that forced my mother to gawk at me, speechless.

"I'll buy you a souvenir!" I yelled at her, pleased to escape her neurosis and ecstatic that I wouldn't have to worry about Beautiful One anymore.

In Paris, a member of the Moroccan royal family had lent C.C. one of their dusty, unused apartments. It was almost three weeks of glorious, unimaginable fun: bottomless beer, boys, butter-filled cakes, and crepes.

But then I received a cryptic email (the only family news and lecture) from my father, who assumed that I was an avid reader of the *Vancouver Sun*. It seemed that some overachieving distant relative was always in the news, because we were Asian. Otherwise, no one would have cared if a second cousin was "up and coming," or if a grand-uncle's Chinese opera fundraiser for BC's children's hospital was "a screeching success." This was 2008, and ethnic newcomers usually took turns on the front page with epic world disasters and local hit and runs.

If my father had bothered to contact me, it meant that the Poteau had vanished, or there was some exciting news about his sister-in-law.

July 1, 2008
From: bestengineerincanada@shawlink.net
To: lindsaywong608@hotmail.com
L:
Don't mention to people that it's your aunt who tied up traffic for hours, a lot of people missed the

firework and other important things and they will curse you. Keep quiet.

Mommy is very upset. We will DISCUSS when you come home

Have you finished Rhode essay yet? I don't think you'll get MFA so don't be hopeful because you will be flipping burger.

I've already paid your VISA. Don't worry so much, relax. Enjoy Paris. But don't eat too much because you will get FATTER. L Mommy say you like to binge on sweet things such as cake and pie which is disgusting.

Say thankyou and hello to your friend. Don't chew with mouth open.

Confucius Gentleman Engineering Ltd

My mother was still hurt and miserable at my absence. And I ignored my father's customary digs about my random and assorted graduate school applications because I did not yet know what I wanted to do after my final year of college. Since I earned straight As in university, my father did not antagonize me as much as before. I had finally succeeded in becoming someone he could brag about, and my reward was still sarcasm but mixed with sly pride and sometimes a generous financial aid package. After all, the new and academically improved Lindsay had been selected to represent UBC on their shortlist for the Rhodes Scholarship. (I didn't know what the hell a Rhodes Scholarship was until I received the invitational email from the committee and sat through the four-hour information session, but I wanted to take advantage of any beautiful moneymaking opportunities that came my way.)

I sent back a pithy, fast-tempered reply: *What the fuck???!!!!!!!!!*

It seemed that all our problems stemmed from my mother's side, whose family crest should have featured a bottle of home-brewed rice wine (drinking) and a deck of cards (gambling) stacked inside an orange life preserver (an affinity for suicide). If my father knew how to cook, he always joked, he might have considered leaving her. But truthfully, my mother, who did not know how to pay bills or use the internet, would fall apart without him. My father was a traditionalist, and I think he saw himself as a martyr. I can only guess what our lives would have been like if he had ever decided to buy someone younger and better-looking from a catalogue in China. Yet despite his frequent mocking, I think he might have secretly loved his wife. Although emotionally distant and frequently absent from home, my father never officially abandoned us and continued to manage our finances.

I wanted to ignore his email, and I think I would have. But this was about Beautiful One, who had, until the wedding, been the person I had looked up to most. And I thought that if this Woo-Woo emergency could happen to her, it could easily happen to me. It went against every fibre and disgusting instinct of my being not to deny what was in front of me, but I fought through my fat, unequivocal terror and reread his email, long after I had replied.

While waiting to hear from my father, I Googled the news.

BEYOND THE CALL: VANCOUVER POLICE MAGAZINE
Just past noon, police saw a woman who was visibly distraught standing on the sidewalk mid-span on the bridge. When they approached her, she climbed over the railing. She perched precariously on three parallel cables, reaching up and behind her to hold on with one free hand. There was nothing beneath her. If she released her grip, she would fall to her certain death.

VANCOUVER (NEWS1130)—*The Ironworkers Memorial Bridge remains closed in both directions to a police incident that started just after 1 pm. And it's impacting traffic in Vancouver, North Vancouver and West Vancouver.*

TransLink is rerouting buses that normally head over the bridge to instead provide access to Seabus and using Lions Gate Bridge. SeaBus is now at full capacity. With drivers forced to use the 3 lanes of the Lions Gate Bridge, traffic along Georgia St. through downtown Vancouver is gridlocked.

Was Beautiful One the distraught woman on the bridge on Canada Day? This could not be true: Beautiful One was not allowed to be Woo-Woo on one of the major bridges in BC. We just didn't flaunt our mental infection that way. But then again, Beautiful One was an exhibitionist, the family would say.

There were conflicting anecdotes from bloggers and commentators. And the newspapers couldn't decide if the bridge had been closed for six or eight hours (I averaged seven), and then decided that most of it was bullshit and inflated speculation anyway.

I saw the pictures, she was standing in the middle of the bridge, not on the side ready to jump. She obviously was looking for attention. Someone who is serious about committing suicide would not pick a busy bridge in a big city on Canada day. The police should have tackled her ... or shot her with a tranquilizer. Some one should figure out the economic cost of her actions and send her a bill. But then again what's the point she probably can't afford it anyway. Now our tax dollars are going to pay for a selfish, idiotic, attention whore's medical bills.

We actually felt sorry for the jumper, we were sitting back and

relaxing on the side of the road for 8 and a half hours, we pulled up some
chairs and were just watching the road rage. I have awesome pictures
of her swinging on the cable. What made us mad was when the police
told us that she tried the same thing earlier in the morning and they
released her!! What is that all about?

I chewed my nails and gulped down three beers for breakfast.
Suicide usually left me unfazed, but the fact that it was national news
made it more tangible and less like an episode in a parallel universe.
It was as if my secret life, inescapable, had collided headfirst with the
normalcy of a European vacation for college girls. I could no longer
pretend that I had not been born of heart-quaking generational tragedy.

The Woo-Woo's Chosen did not have mental breakdowns in public,
especially on public holidays. This was certainly new. We always went
quietly back to our houses, put on our frumpy pastel housecoats, and
then went hopelessly, incurably insane. As if by hiding our sickness,
slamming it away, we could pretend that it did not exist outside of
our family's private sphere and Hongcouver's closed-door Chinese
community. What was once secret to me seemed suddenly explosive:
shameful and filthy. I shuddered with this knowledge. I could not bear
to think of Beautiful One, who I felt symbolized my very sanity, alone
and crazed and desperate, preparing for a final jump.

I shut off my laptop while C.C., in last night's clubbing clothes, rose
from the *mtarba,* the living room's Moroccan silk couch, and asked
me what the hell was wrong.

"I don't talk about myself with strangers," I snapped at my only friend,
who had taken a chance on me, invited me on vacation, painstakingly
civilized me in girlhood matters, like personal hygiene and socially
correct politeness. Understandably, she looked quite taken aback.

Because C.C. insisted that there was no mental illness in her family, I had latched onto her like a confused tick. I wore her hand-me-downs and adopted her opinions, her pragmatic rich-person politics, in the hope of appearing "normal." I was determined to become C.C., if not a lesser, more invisible version, by the end of my European escape. In my mind then, any person who wasn't afraid of ghosts and travelled beyond the local shopping mall was sane. But communicating with my family had suddenly turned me into my father. Like him, I became unflinchingly nasty when overwhelmed and burdened by family drama. Surrounded by Moroccan luxury in a Parisian flat, I suddenly resented C.C. for her seemingly perfect life.

"Why the hell are you asking me this question for?" I snarled in humiliation. "Guess you have nothing else to think about."

Ignoring C.C.'s attempts to talk to me, I escaped to the fancy outdoor café downstairs, where I ate six crepes, two hot fudge sundaes in flimsy champagne flutes, and three girlishly pink gelatos, and sampled every stifled fruit pastry, meringue tart, and slice of caramelized praline pie that was offered (at least fifteen or sixteen delicacies in one piggish sitting). C.C. had followed me to the café, but I ignored her. I ate obsessively, because I couldn't stop, and I wasn't the one who was paying.

But everything that pooled and clamped onto my tongue tasted wrong and disloyal. No matter how much I ate, I did not feel like myself, and there was a queasiness, which could only be caused by the Woo-Woo and made me feel as if I were waiting to skydive off a crashing mini plane with no parachute.

I knew that Beautiful One was the distraught woman on the Ironworkers Memorial Bridge, the Canada Day bridge jumper, and I didn't know if she was dead. And here I had genuinely thought that I could delay the Woo-Woo by hiding out in a delusional fairy tale, pretending to be a carefree McPrincess who shopped, dined in sit-down restaurants, and had a rich friend. Someone who did not have to worry about a family member who may have died a nine-hour time difference away. Someone who did not have to worry about becoming insane. For I had been retreating into a fluorescent fantasy where I would not have to deal with the lunacy and acid-inducing heartbreak that was my family.

"Lindsay?" C.C. asked, looking worried, as she picked at her sludgy gelato.

And I was immediately ashamed that I told her to fuck off. This was right before I puked on the café's sidewalk, sick splashing over our pedicured feet.

"Have a great life," I told her sadly, knowing that I could not pretend to be her anymore. "Sorry you wasted time and money on me."

Finally, back home on the mountain three days later, my father asked me if I had absorbed the entire European continent's annual supply of butter.

"Your face will make Buddha jealous," he said, forgetting that he was supposed to be nice to me because I was now his second-favourite kid, right after the dog. "I just knew we should have sent you reminder not to eat every day. Only eat every second day. But I see you have no fucking control."

"Shut up," I said, angry and fed up. All I wanted was a dozen supersized cheeseburgers from McDonald's, which I had truly missed in Europe. C.C. had never taken me to the fast-food chain, choosing four-star restaurants and touristy cafés instead. I did not want another passive-aggressive fight with my father. "If you want to complain about me, you're supposed to address them to the dog."

"But you just make Daddy so mad," he said, sighing. "You always do something so retarded that I cannot understand."

"How's Beautiful One?" I asked, grateful to change the subject. It was convenient for me that someone in our extended family was insane—it put my father in a very good mood.

"That fucker," my mother said.

Then she went to bed with an unrefrigerated six-pack of beer, and no one could get her to do anything else. So shocked was my mother at the bridge incident, because she could not fathom losing her favourite sister, that she was acting distant and more brittle than usual. When I arrived home from Paris, it seemed like she would be spending the next few days with the bedroom door closed.

"Is Mom, like, really, really upset?" I said, peering around the kitchen, which was dirtier than usual and stacked with old newspapers and last week's garbage.

"How the fuck should I know?" my father said, shrugging. "All she do is sleeping and screaming on the phone for twenty-four hours."

Neither my father nor I understood how to properly decipher emotions. And my mother's screaming was not foreign behaviour.

"But I have to tell you that it serve Beautiful One right." And my father narrated, gleefully, what he knew. Early on Canada Day, she had gone missing. The entire family had split up into small search parties around ten a.m., eager to scour Burnaby's Central Park in case she had been viciously murdered on one of her nocturnal jogs. While I was becoming "a beast" (obese) in Europe, he explained, she had taken to late-night runs in the park every night for hours and hours. Sometimes, she stayed out all night and came home, ecstatic and transformed, at seven or eight in the morning.

My father said that the family had brought heavy-duty garbage bags in case they found her chopped up parts—they all felt it was better to be prepared. But then, when an apologetic police officer phoned in the late afternoon, they had all been relieved and ordered the largest, most economical Domino's pizza party combo to watch the news like everyone else in Hongcouver. You had to admit, the family said, it was exciting that there was a close relative on the local news. One rich uncle, who felt constantly bored by suburban life, had found this incident to be the most fun that he had all year.

Beautiful One, crazed and blubbering histrionic tears, obviously beyond family intervention, was now locked up in the psychiatric ward at Burnaby Hospital. Newspapers and radio talk shows had reported rabidly on BC's best bridge jumper.

"It serve your auntie right," my father repeated cheerfully, and then went to watch TV, like nothing had happened. I think he felt validated that, for once, my mother's family had to acknowledge their illness, and being generally insensitive, he took the opportunity to gloat openly about Beautiful One's downfall.

"The cops said I was the best bridge jumper ever," Beautiful One squealed to me on the phone when I called her that week to see if she was doing better.

Normally, I'd be too afraid to phone my auntie and would rely instead on second-hand news via my mother or father. But being away from my family for a month had prompted a change in me—whether better or grotesque, it allowed me to experience a strange sensation. Was it regret? Was it bruising reality? In gloomy Hongcouver, perhaps because I was fully immersed in our spiralling drama, I often refused to believe I was suffocating in so much sadness. But in Paris, peeking in from the outside, I was able to begrudgingly accept the horror as real life instead of make-believe. Perhaps because the suicide attempt was on the news, disassociating was now impossible for me.

On the phone, it felt terrifying to talk to a manic Beautiful One, but she was thrilled to brag to her "absolute best and favourite niece," which was what she always said, but now she sounded like a recording of her former self.

Our conversation sickened me. This is what I learned:

Poor Beautiful One, completely delusional and communing with an insistent God inside her brain, had squatted on the observatory deck of the vast Ironworkers Memorial Bridge and then tottered on three parallel cables, gripping a cable behind and above her with just one hand. Beautiful One said that she became a big-shot superhero, whooping, as she swung-swung-swung. I imagined Beautiful One, weighing less than ninety pounds, on a major bridge that spanned 1,292 metres across Burrard Inlet, her legs flailing in a convulsive Wonder Woman cancan.

She had stopped traffic on a crucial part of the Trans-Canada Highway, which families needed to traverse for their Canada Day vacations and picnics and late-night fireworks. But Beautiful One had only cared about swinging and swinging (all that attention!)—she was glad that there was no suicide barrier.

"What are you doing?" a police officer first asked her around noon.

"I'm admiring the beautiful view. It's such a wonderful day, you know?"

He watched Beautiful One (she was used to people admiring her), so she began to snap pictures with her BlackBerry. The officer might have thought that she was homeless, armed with only a stolen phone, because she hadn't showered or changed her clothes for a month or so. When her phone ran out of batteries, she wanted more attention from the concerned officer. She threatened to jump.

"I'm very, very clever," she trilled at me over the phone. She sounded so pleased and exuberant as she reported the incident: "Don't you think that I am clever to get attention by jumping? I'm probably the smartest one in this whole family!"

For six, seven, or eight hours, depending on which talk show or blog or newspaper you followed, negotiators from the emergency response team, the marine unit, and the coast guard wheedled: "Ma'am, please! *Ma'am!* Please listen! Ma'am! Ma'am! Ma'am!"

Beautiful One said that she was thrilled to shut down three cities in the Lower Mainland and overjoyed to control the lives of the usual 200,000 commuters, not even counting the additional numbers of those unfortunate families on their way to the Canada Day fireworks. It was the only time in her life when she had so much power. She had even cornered a squad of emergency response workers as her personal hostages to play Mad Hatter word games. This was the best day of her life.

"Why don't you come down, ma'am?" the officers said. "You must be very thirsty."

"But there's lots of water down there, sir. Hahaha! What's wrong with the water down there? There's enough to drink for everyone! We can all share!"

"Jump, bitch, jump!" heat-stroked strangers in cars and raging motorcyclists had screamed.

I imagined most of them dehydrated or just desperate to pee, trapped in traffic in the smothering metropolitan heat. While kids complained of thirst, a few of the elderly fainted, so no one had any sympathy for the unhinged woman. But it was the first time Beautiful One felt so respected and truly happy. She needed the public's unadorned esteem, the SWAT team's inexhaustible attention—all because she could not get any from her own damned family.

"I don't care if my kids kill themselves because I killed myself," she had announced when suicide negotiators warned her about the dangers associated with bridge jumping—"Think of your daughters! Your son!"

"Why would you think I cared?" she said flippantly. Yet I think she was trying to distance herself—or her callousness meant that extreme psychosis had amplified every unkind personality trait that she possessed.

Flowery Face, who was thirteen, had been put on the phone to plead with her mother to come down, but that didn't help. "Don't die," my cousin begged, because her older siblings were too afraid to talk to Beautiful One just in case she jumped mid-call. Uncle E.T. was still "on vacation" and could not be reached.

"Do you think I give a fuck what you think?" Beautiful One had snapped.

I think she felt exasperated by life, bruised by the chilling indifference from a family as insensitive and internally crushing as ours. She must have been truly fed up and sick when she told her daughter: "You're better off without me. You don't need me anymore. You should be very happy for me when I die. Bye."

Joyously, Beautiful One swung back and forth on the steel cables until two constables distracted her ("Look over there!") and someone snatched her Q-tip arms. On cue, the emergency response team, leaping out of their black van with safety harnesses secured, plunged behind her and snagged my screaming auntie around the waist.

"I have the most amazing balancing skills," she bragged to me in an animated little girl's voice. And then she repeated herself.

Our one-sided phone conversation had lasted almost a whole hour, and I could feel my stomach lurch, a hard, choking bubble, a blister of remorse, forming in my throat. But I could not hang up, because it was like watching a car fall off a cliff. I had never had so much one-on-one time with tragedy, except with my mother, and I wanted to see where it led. I had grown up with my mother, whose bouts of madness were extreme, yes, but expected—yet Beautiful

One's breakdown seemed confusing and unbelievable, as if our family insanity could multiply and spread at random. I needed to understand why my aunt had gone insane, and whether by sheer magical thinking there had been a choice or action that could have prevented her madness. I should not have been so shocked, but I had never wanted to believe that Beautiful One could be so troubled and traumatized by her own childhood of poverty and neglect. She was as damaged as my mother, but I never saw it because I did not live with her. For why else would a grown woman sometimes confide in an adolescent on a family camping trip?

"Oh, Lindsay," Auntie Beautiful One sang, sighing. "I can balance without my hands and I can perform in a circus act, like the Cirque du Soleil. They said I was the best bridge jumper in BC! And I'm very clever. I'm so smart I told them there's water down there when they asked me if I needed water! You should be very happy when I die! Don't you understand that this is good for me? That dying is the best decision I ever made."

The family would always wonder if she really meant to jump, or if it was just the Woo-Woo talking. Love and affection, being similar to dirty, repressed stage-four cancer among our tight-knit clan, were never expressed, if they did exist, because of our ghosts, so this was the absolute best it would ever get for poor Auntie, who just wanted to feel adored and cherished for once. Being the best bridge jumper in BC made her feel like a celebrity on reality TV.

"I understand, Auntie," I lied, half singing the words (at this point, she would not acknowledge a reply if it wasn't musical).

Since no rational explanation was forthcoming, I finally hung up. I felt uncomfortable with the swift, plummeting trajectory of our conversation. Also, I felt an ounce of intense guilt. And I thought there might be a clue to the iPod shuffle of Beautiful One's brain.

I wondered if the bridge-jumping incident could have been prevented. I kept wondering: If Beautiful One had been given proper psychiatric attention, if she had been checked into a private hospital for treatment right after the wedding, would things have spiralled so completely out of control? Would her firecracker psychosis have spun into the pitiless territory of absolute madness? Was our family mostly at fault for the incident on Canada Day? Was *I* at fault?

The answer to my irrational blame mongering, despite my oscillating internal confusion, was maybe eighty/twenty, but only if you factored in culture and superstition, counted missing Uncle E.T., and divided the total by the other seven aunties and uncles. But culpability is easy to assign to other people. Because my family was not profound or stupid enough to consign guilt to ourselves, it was much easier to fault Auntie Beautiful One's lack of determination. Or, as in my case, horrible luck and genetics.

In hindsight, I believe that I initially took Beautiful One's decision to jump as a bratty but personal one. That she tried to jump not only pissed me off but also broke some amazing resolve or crass, elementary belief system in me. At the time, I did not recognize it or understand what was happening to me. I just thought that I was having a simple if fiendish gallbladder attack, not a crabby emotional reaction. I deluded myself into thinking that I did not know why I was reacting so abnormally.

I felt betrayed in an outsized, abstract way that I could not explain. Like my mother, I couldn't help but take her psychosis personally.

Two weeks after the Canada Day bridge-jumping incident, Uncle E.T., who had driven back from his runaway vacation on Hongcouver Island when he heard about his infamous holiday stuntwoman wife, supposedly begged the doctors to please, please, please, put the goddamn Woo-Woo in electroshock therapy and then perform a prompt lobotomy—at least, that's what Beautiful One claimed, though I wasn't sure if it was mostly her delusion. Like everyone else in our family, he was horrified and saddened by his wife's actions, but he could not show it (our ghosts were always waiting).

At Burnaby Hospital, Beautiful One enjoyed the psychiatric ward immensely, because she could sing all day to the other patients. Unlike our family, everyone in the psych ward liked her take on unconventional musical theatre—most of the patients sang back to her, she said. And Beautiful One became close friends with a patient with bipolar disorder and a crack addiction, who would later always call her house to ask for money. Beautiful One preferred the ward and its residents to her own uninspiring children. For supposed stellar behaviour (despite proudly admitting to finding a way to unscrew her bedroom window), she was given frequent day passes to visit the outside universe, but she was reluctant to leave the psychiatric ward and her stimulating new friends (they were staging a revolt, like *One Flew Over the Cuckoo's Nest,* she said).

"But I have a chess appointment with Mister X," she would always wail whenever my mother invited her out for cheap Tuesday dim sum.

"Isn't that the fucking homeless bum who keeps peeing in your shoes?" my mother asked over the speakerphone.

"Yes," Beautiful One admitted, "but he has an intellect almost as amazing and grandiose as mine."

When she was allowed home on a day pass for good behaviour, she printed out internet comments about the Canada Day bridge-jumping incident and stuck them to the refrigerator. She trilled her favourite comments over the phone, screeching at everyone to listen when she read the wittier ones.

"To seaaaa or not to seaaa," she quoted, tittering, *hehehehe*, asking me what I thought. The internet comments were cruel, yes, but they gave her a formidable sense of purpose:

> *Posted 01 July 2008 – 06:03 PM*
> *The female dog should just jump and let thousands of people get on with their lives on a holiday evening.*
>
> *I'm trying to feel sympathy for the "distraught woman," but if you really were distraught, you'd just end it at home somewhere. Pulling sh!t on a major bridge during the afternoon of a national holiday is just a stunt to get attention.*
> *Happy Canada Day.*
>
> *I really don't think she wanted to kill herself, if you want to kill yourself, you can't be stopped, and it would be fairly quick. Maybe she wanted attention? I don't know why people say they want to die, but then just stand there, i've seen on this tv.*
> *I hope this chick is proud. And you know what really sucks? I heard she didn't even jump.*

Beautiful One said that she was extremely proud of all the commotion she had caused—it seemed that nearly everyone trapped in traffic wanted to personally push BC's best potential bridge jumper off the Ironworkers Memorial Bridge. The public's anger was the reason the police and government reassigned Beautiful One to an at-risk age group. The public would be more sympathetic to a senior citizen, so a press rumour spread that on Canada Day an old woman was in a severe economic crisis. With no money, no employment, no housing to speak of, why shouldn't she jump?

This of course had made Beautiful One extremely upset, because reporters and journalists had called her "an elderly woman."

"Elderly?!" she had shrieked, and I couldn't help but laugh in a sharp, uncomfortable way. Beautiful One was not old. "An elderly woman?" she said, wounded. "I'm only forty-two!" Beautiful One had been so frantic when she read the newspapers that the nurses had thought she needed to be sedated.

And she resented the anonymity; she wanted to be known for her famous balancing feat. *Vancouver Magazine* had lumped her in with "one of the dozen or more people who leap from Metro Vancouver bridges each year," which meant God had lied—she wasn't so special after all.

Police officers even invented a nine-year-old son (in real life, my cousin was nineteen) to gain public compassion for the potential bridge jumper. "We gave that lady another chance at life," Inspector Chapman said. "We gave her a chance to go home to her family and her nine-year-old son. We saved her life."

But Beautiful One was not grateful; she displayed only un-adulterated anger. "But I'm pretty!" she screamed, as if that was all that mattered, howling into the phone like a cartoon coyote. "You don't understand! Like, I'm *really* pretty! Why didn't they say that? Didn't anyone notice?"

And Beautiful One planned to do it all over again—perhaps Labour Day, perhaps Remembrance Day—just to prove to the media that this bridge-jumping diva was spry and young, "not oooooooold!" She basked in the vindictive outpouring of online attention, and I wondered why she couldn't just be happy with our family's criticism of her public behaviour.

"Why are you so fucking pathetic?" my mother, shrunken and terrified, had screamed at her sister any chance she got.

Yelling multiple fuck-yous at the demon(s) inside Beautiful One somehow made ugly, abstract things, like our fear and sadness, much easier to manage.

Something in me crumbled and broke the day I saw Auntie Beautiful One post-breakdown. Paris had made me soft, fattened me with pounds of butter and refined sugar, and then destroyed all my sinewy defences. Cute little pastries and melt-in-your-mouth gelato had mutated me into a corporeal globe of convulsive nerves and jittery human emotions.

Back in Hongcouver, I missed the carefreeness of Europe, the straightforwardness of food and shopping and C.C.'s friendship. Most of all, I missed knowing someone who wasn't constantly stuffed with personal misery.

When I saw Auntie Beautiful One, I suddenly felt as desperate as my mother when she had cried in the basement bathroom at my cousin's wedding. I could not control the terror and sadness spiralling inside me and felt undisciplined and utterly wrong.

Nearly a month after her Woo-Woo on the bridge, Beautiful One didn't seem to recognize anyone. The hospital had declared her mentally fit enough to be a part-time resident, but she was still vacant and restless. It seemed that she only cared about shuffling around her house when I visited. According to our Chinese superstitions, the Beautiful One family were considered contagious, and they were not allowed in anyone's houses for the next month or so, until their "bad luck" had dissipated. They were in special quarantine, but my mother had risked sending me over so I could check on her sister for her. I didn't know what medications she was on, but I assumed that she was on a zombifying brew of antipsychotics. Her eyes didn't seem to flutter anymore, and she spoke in a flat, sloppy monotone. Her voice sounded masculine and machine-like, as if an oversized butterfly were trapped in her throat.

Auntie Beautiful One was no longer manic, but with her filthy clothes that were too loose and her mangled hair sticking up, she looked as if she had rolled out of a coffin. She had been transformed into a sullen corpse from a horror movie. Her eyes were black and dead and a little sandy. She couldn't be convinced to brush her teeth; she believed that toothpaste had been specifically designed to kill her.

"I am the smartest one in this whole family," Beautiful One had rasped at me in greeting. "I have discovered that you have to be careful of toothpaste. You see, I am so clever that I know there's poison in it, and we can all die. Pick up this tube and tell me you can feel the stinging in your arm, right? If you can feel the pain, it means there's poison in it."

This seemed like the most deranged thing that Beautiful One had ever said, which convinced me that she was too far gone for anyone's non-medical expertise.

I didn't know what to say to Beautiful One. And the situation got worse when she stopped her frantic pacing and mumbling and tried to give me some money. She opened her wallet, but there was only a ten-dollar bill left. She looked so confused and dejected. Grunting, she tried to make me take the ten dollars, but I couldn't accept it from this ghost of my former auntie. Beautiful One had been replaced by someone or something else entirely. I wanted to cry, but I couldn't. Years of hockey practice and emotion-resistance training from my father made me ashamed to show my sadness. Instead, I pretended to be nonchalant and unaffected.

"Take money, Lindsay," Unbeautiful One rasped, stuffing the bill into the front pocket of my hoodie.

L ife at the Belcarra had reached a sludgy, perverse sameness, so it took visiting Beautiful One's mental hospital of a household to realize that I was actually living in one. It is safe to say that my visit made me realize I had to leave Hongcouver ASAP. It is hard to know that you're living in absolute shit until someone else invites you over and proudly shows you the insides of their even grubbier, even shittier, even more bug-infested surroundings. From my new perspective, I could see the impenetrable monstrosity of the Woo-Woo in Beautiful One and her proud, decadent squalor. I was also terrified that what had happened to Beautiful One could happen to me overnight. There had to be a reason, even if slight, why she always said we were so alike on our family camping trips, even if I could not visualize any concrete similarities myself. For I still did not believe that I could be smart or self-sufficient. Until recently, I had more in common with my father and a garbage can. But had she seen a potential for normalcy and talent in me? Or was she simply deluding herself? I wanted her uncanny ability to make money, certainly, but at what cost? Was the Woo-Woo an ineluctable punishment for the female descendants of Poh-Poh? A cosmic curse that only affected the conventionally beautiful and money-grubbing?

On the exterior, Beautiful One's house was grander and larger and more sumptuous than ours, with its creeping black gate that hugged and spiked the property like a barbed-wire entanglement inspired by the rococo period and trench warfare. But what was more important was hidden inside its filthy interior. It was like looking at a mirage of a terrible yet beautiful palace that transformed into a derelict graveyard upon closer inspection. Our house, though dusty and unkempt, had not reached this stage of Woo-Woo.

"The bitch is fucking nuts!" Beautiful One's son announced as he opened the door from the garage, which was also his bedroom (my cousin was living in his BMW to avoid his mother). My cousin seemed not to notice or care that Beautiful One had started doing frantic laps on a sticky floor that had not been cleaned in weeks. Where was their housekeeper? Had she quit and no one noticed? My cousin also didn't seem to care that the furnace blasted thirty degrees Celsius even though it was summer.

"How long has she been walking in circles?" I asked him, horrified.

"Well, she's been hiding in the goddamn broom closet," my cousin said, shrugging. "She built a little fort out of black garbage bags. Thinks she's safe from God in there." He then mumbled that he had an upcoming examination for business school that he had to study for in the backseat of his car.

This was a typical exchange in our family; no one understood how they were supposed to feel, or why they should experience certain soul-crushing emotions. My cousin was certainly grieving, and he would have screamed and cried had he been allowed to show his godawful despair. But he could not risk a demonic possession right before a final exam.

Why does my mother like you better than me?" Flowery Face asked me as I grudgingly followed her into an even stickier and grimier kitchen.

A month's collection of dirty dishes was heaped on the counters; chemical-coloured takeout containers from their Vietnamese food franchises volcanoed on the stovetop and table. The only fresh food was a mammoth bag of semi-extinct apples from the Dark Ages—black and putrid. Flowery Face stopped and offered me one; I declined, but she started eating a soft wet apple, chunks of its necrotic flesh falling onto the carpet. She looked like a tired, gluttonous zombie. Poor Flowery Face, who was dressed in too-tight clothing that made her look twenty-eight; her false lashes were practically melting off her face.

Flowery Face and I had spent many major childhood vacations camping together in the interior of BC and, of course, at American outlet malls, but I hadn't seen her since our family's annual twelve-course Christmas banquet. She had seemed less haggard then, more childish and buoyant.

"Here's twenty dollars," I said. It was all that I had in my bag, but I gave it to her because, being nervous and cowardly, I needed her to shut up about her mother.

F.F. took my money, but she still wanted to know the answer to her terrible, treacherous question. Twenty bucks was not enough to silence her. It was like trying to cure stomach cancer with a tummy tuck. Like my father, in any difficult situation, I had been hoping that suffering could be measured in dollars and cents. This was all I knew how to do; I could not have fathomed anything else back then if it had knocked out all my teeth and shattered a very important bone. I did not have the emotional vocabulary to articulate how devastated I was. How my anger at Beautiful One was like mistaking specialty hot sauce for ketchup at a restaurant—no one's fault but my own—and how this mistake burned me with terror and helplessness. I stood still, hoping that this moment of gross uncertainty would be over soon.

"Lindsay, I had to try to talk her off the bridge," Flowery Face ranted instead, chucking the apple corpse onto the sofa like a used tissue. "It should have been you telling her not to. Why weren't you here? On the bridge she laughed at me, okay! She didn't even listen to what I had to say. I kept crying and telling her not to. What kind of mom does that?"

"I wouldn't be able to talk her down," I said, trying not to stammer.

I thought about how, many years ago, Beautiful One had taken me shopping and reassured me that I was going to turn out exactly like her. Because we were alike, she always said, talented and brilliant and capable of rational thinking. Was I supposed to do the same thing for Flowery Face now? I could have told her that we were special, that we did not need to worry about turning into our mothers, because I had already given her all the money that I had. Unfortunately, I did not know how to lie to her. It felt too disloyal, too cruel. So, quickly, I changed the subject instead: "Has everyone in our family been giving you lots of money?"

"Yes, they all feel really shitty, so I made six hundred dollars yesterday. Oh, except Uncle Ugly One. He's so cheap."

"Asshole," I said with emphasis, hoping that I was showing enough moral support.

"Lindsay, just tell me the truth: How come my mom doesn't like me? Why wouldn't she listen to me on the bridge?"

"I don't know," I lied, looking past her at the gilded wood carving of Jesus's last supper behind her in the foyer. I pretended to be interested in the infinitesimal details, but my stomach and head and heart hurt.

Eventually, I looked at Flowery Face. I wanted to tell her that her mother's madness was not her fault, but in that moment I was too afraid, because I believed that words were sickly incantations. Offering reassurance, even if it was an insecure whisper, meant that the worst could possibly come true. It would be like looking into the mirror and calling for the indomitable Bloody Mary three times. And because you were a member of this family, it meant that she would certainly pay you a violent visit. Bloody Mary only existed for certain people—like us.

"You could probably have talked her off the bridge!" Flowery Face insisted again, her face crumpling. "My mom loves you! She used to talk about you all the time, you know. No offence, but why does she even like you? You're not that great."

"Maybe you just didn't cry hard enough when you were talking to her on the bridge," I suggested. But I was feeling nauseated and guilty. I was not surprised that I was worthy of so much conversational time in the Beautiful One household, because my cousins and I were expected to compete aggressively with each other. It was considered important family news if someone gained five pounds or suffered from acid reflux.

"Ohmygod, Lindsay," my cousin said. "Tell me what I should do."

"Well, tell her she's beautiful and that we all love and forgive her. Tell her it was shit reporting and that she can sue. And everyone thought she was amazing at balancing. Tell her whatever she wants to hear."

"But that's bullshit!" Flowery Face screamed. "People fucking hate us! They call her names online, and they all say she should die."

"Listen, your mom only wants to hear good things, and that's what I'm going to tell her. You do want her to get better, right?"

"I think someone should have just pushed her off the bridge," Flowery Face said, sniffling.

I looked up from the dirt-packed floor that I had been examining for grungy wood bugs and tried to see if there was Woo-Woo in my cousin's pupils. Out of the corner of my eye, I saw their dog, some designer-purse rat, shit in a corner and hungrily huff up its dry, pebbly turds. At least someone was tidying up after themselves in this house.

"Well, it would have saved a lot of time and money if someone did," I said, trying not to be too serious. But she didn't find my joke particularly funny.

As a person disconnected from my feelings and severed from any semblance of self-worth, I did not understand that my cousin and I were experiencing what was generally known as trauma and loss.

"Out of curiosity, would you do it, though?" I asked Flowery Face, forgetting that she was just an impressionable teen.

"I think I could," Flowery Face said. "I just hate my mom so much."

"You're not supposed to like your mother. Welcome to our family."

"Hey, wanna watch *Hannah Montana* and smoke some weed?" she suddenly said, brightening.

"I have to go in, like, five minutes," I lied, making what I hoped was a frowny face even though I felt relieved to leave Beautiful One's oppressive habitat. "I have to go to the grocery store," I added when she did not respond.

"Thanks for stopping by," Flowery Face finally mumbled. "Lindsay, I'm really glad you're my cousin."

"I know," I said, and I wanted very much to invite her to stay with us at the Belcarra, which wasn't much better, but at least it wasn't a tomb-like prison that smelled of gross, perfumed death in its various stages of decomposition.

But I had to leave. I realized I had to leave the graveyard suburbs of Hongcouver with frightening urgency. Otherwise, it would just be me and Flowery Face—bad pot and worse television and constipating psychosis.

"Enjoy your drugs," I eventually called out to my cousin. But she was too absorbed in her singing show on the Disney Channel to take any notice of my leaving, and it made me remember that she was just a lost, broken kid.

Before I turned to go, I remembered that I had the ten dollars that Beautiful One had given me, so I left the money for Flowery Face on the kitchen table, near the bag of black apples.

It wouldn't make a difference. In a week's time, yet another Woo-Woo scandal would occur in our family, when Flowery Face, overwhelmed by what she couldn't handle, would kick her own mother down a flight of stairs. On my way out of their foyer, I tried not to look at emaciated Beautiful One, who was still parading around the house.

"Bye, Auntie," I called out, but she did not know it was me and stared disgustedly at a crack in the ceiling.

"Don't talk to me anymore, roof!" she bellowed. "You cannot kill me."

Shuddering, I fled their house, half sprinting, half walking to the SkyTrain station. I could not bear this revelation of sadness and suffocating madness. I would rather confront an axe murderer, because running for my life seemed much simpler than witnessing my poor auntie like this.

Yet the absolute best thing about a Woo-Woo incident that didn't affect the members of your immediate family was that you could exit the dramatic scene and take a break whenever it was most convenient. It was like pressing pause on a deliciously violent movie, and then coming back after you had relieved your bladder and gobbled down a salty snack.

That summer, there were three ongoing cinematic world war experiences.

You might first visit Beautiful One's house, where the structural damage was an irreparable 10 on our Woo-Woo scale, and then stop over at Poh-Poh's house for a solid 7. But with Beautiful One's newfound Woo-Woo, Poh-Poh's viewer ratings had severely declined. By evening, you could finally de-stress by ambling over to my home for a more low-key theatrical production; your continuous Woo-Woo experience might be a 2 or 3. Nowadays, my parents' arguments were only an unsatisfactory magnitude of 1, because my mother was too sad about Beautiful One and the bridge-jumping incident to react anymore.

Who needed the local movie theatre when you had my kind of thrilling relations?

As much as my upbringing was frequently heartbreaking and spastic and extreme, I could say that I had never been bored for one moment. Surely, this was a sign that I'd blossom into something interesting (I did not think of myself as *someone,* an entirely real live person yet). If I was lucky, I'd be much less pedestrian by the time I was in my late twenties. I certainly had enough bizarre anecdotes to last me until I was miserly and thirty-five. Growing up, surely other kids like C.C. had complained about hours spent without internet or decent television, but I got to watch Poh-Poh attack kitchen appliances until she passed out.

Yet it killed me to admit that it was the saddest thing in the whole world seeing my cousin and auntie so completely ruined and unfixable. It was like they had become Poh-Pohs overnight.

CHAPTER 13
THE WOO-WOO'S CHOSEN

Somehow, I had gotten into a school called Columbia University, a higher learning institution in New York City that no one in our family had ever heard of. The *Columbian* University, as my father mispronounced it, had accepted *me* into the master of fine arts non-fiction program, which meant that "anyone, including the bum, can go to higher learning in America!"

For an undergraduate creative writing class, I had clumsily drafted weirdo character profiles on all my relatives, and a few professors thought that I had raw potential. "We can tell that you are a first-time writer," one of them had said, "but you can't fake that voice. Have you thought about graduate school?"

"There are more than a billion book in the library," my father had said when I proudly announced my acceptance, "so how hard can bullshitting story be?"

Since he was only familiar with Canadian Ivy League universities, he did not recognize the Columbian University as a prestigious institution until he checked Wikipedia. "Must be mistake!" he said, looking at me with rodent-like shock. "Maybe you are like Daddy and not so retarded after all!"

Yet he had also sounded so pleased that I was on my way to higher education—his radioactive American dream. Perhaps there was even secret pride too that I had finally done something correct, because an Ivy League school had accepted me.

But New York City fried my brain as soon as I arrived in August. Something happened to my head when I got out of the plane at JFK airport. It was as if the Woo-Woo knew I was here.

Less than fifteen hours later, as I wandered outside my assigned student apartment on 114th Street between Broadway and Amsterdam, I passed out.

Before I did that, I had started to notice that I was falling while standing still. I felt like I was whirling 360 degrees, like I had been skillfully beheaded and my skull was bouncing along the ground. A breezy darkness had eclipsed my vision, and I felt as if my eyeballs had been flipped backwards and I was staring at the unoccupied inkiness of my hard, shameless sockets.

I felt the ground tear open, and I was nose-diving down a feral rabbit hole. I pirouetted backwards, clumsy-toed.

There was a flash of Zeus-like light and soft, shimmery constellations. Then: hammering beat-box music in my bashed-up temples, the lardy scent of fried chicken. I could smell a street fair on 120th and Broadway—what was I even doing in NYC? For a second, I thought that I was having a seizure or a strange hallucination. Although I was not the kind of person who was deeply aware of their feelings, it struck me as odd that I felt absolutely nothing. It had to be a dream, a visceral nightmare, right? Had I taken some designer drug without knowing?

Then a frightening thought struck me—I had gone Woo-Woo and this was a motherfucking delusion. Oh God. I could be lurching down the streets of New York City in a full-blown psychotic state, a grinning, cross-eyed, flesh-chomping zombie.

Was this what had happened to poor Auntie Beautiful One? Did

God suddenly appear in front of her, and had she just been taking basic instructions from Him all along? No wonder she thought she was a modern-day Joan of Arc—the visions were freakish and beautiful and utterly obscene. Had Beautiful One just accepted her Woo-Woo so easily? Did she fight it?

Surely, I thought, this wasn't happening to me when I had been in New York for less than fifteen hours. This had to be severe heatstroke or a formidable case of dehydration. Maybe it was as simple and uncomfortable as a climactic allergy.

But whatever it was, I was bouncing in the blackness, my own unchaperoned madness.

The nice thing about New York City was that if you fainted, no one caused a ruckus. You could somersault into space-age darkness and wake up without an entourage of excited ambulance workers and nosy individuals tugging at your underclothes and asking if you had illegal drugs colonizing your blood.

It was freeing and quite nauseating to go insane, and for a second, I could understand why my relations often did it. But the pain in my head became shooting, and I swear all the parked cars on the street began to levitate. For the first time in my life, I cared whether I lived or expired. I had an alternate path, a potential future in a new country. I was following the trajectory of my immigrant ancestors on my father's side, who had once settled in Manhattan's Chinatown. I had hope for a separate life where no one knew who I was.

Also, I knew that if I didn't care, I'd never find myself again.

I woke up in what I thought was a sweltering deep fryer, but I was lying on the sidewalk. I was freezing even though it was thirty degrees. I stood up and tried to stumble to my three-student shared apartment on West 114th Street. My eyes weren't working, so I couldn't read the signs and I staggered along 112th Street until I asked someone where I was.

The Columbia University Housing Office had mixed up my arrival time by a day, and my room had not yet been prepared. It had been freshly painted, but there was no furniture yet. Groaning, I stumbled to the musty elevator and ended up in the basement storage, where I found an orphaned mattress (duct-taped to keep the yellow stuffing from falling out). Willing myself not to fall over, I dragged the flimsy mattress to my assigned bedroom and kicked it to the corner of my room. As a suburban girl from Canada, I was unaware of bed bugs and how they had plagued the city that year. Then, spinning and feverish, I wrapped myself in a Christmas sweater from my still packed suitcase. I had no blanket or bed sheets, so staggering to right myself, I stole the black-and-white checkered shower curtain from the shared bathroom and used it as a duvet cover.

It was much sweatier under the plastic shower curtain, but somehow, I felt physically safer. Drowning in sweaty fatigue, I fell asleep.

At four a.m., the room came alive and tried to devour me. When I phoned the student health line, the health official suggested that I seek emergency medical attention ASAP. "It could be a stroke," she said cheerfully.

Panicking, I checked into the emergency room at St. Luke's–Roosevelt Hospital, which was conveniently located next door. The nurses jabbed an IV into my arm. The doctors knew I was dehydrated, but they weren't sure of the cause—they had absolutely no idea that I was Woo-Woo and sent me back to the apartment spinning. The doctor assured me that I would be absolutely fine in a few days. The hospital visit would end up totalling $1500. Being from Canada, I was shocked that they had charged me so much for medical care—shouldn't they help a potentially dying person for free?

I missed the first day of orientation and the next.

There was no improvement in my condition; the heavy constellations in my blurred vision lingered. I marvelled at mystical halos that would have been divine miracles if I hadn't been so Woo-Woo.

The next day at Westside Market, where I tried to buy my breakfast, the fantastic sparks of inconceivable colours from the assortment of precooked food made me rotate, and I keeled over in the cheese aisle and squashed the radioactive cheddar. The kindly gouda cooled my muggy brain fever. Like some astounded drunk, I could not right myself for several minutes, tush in the air. Someone called the manager, and I was escorted from the store and told not to come back until I was sober. I was too furious at myself and my condition to be embarrassed.

"You should really consider taking the semester off," the program administrator insisted when I came to see him about my courses. I had only attended a few workshops and lectures but was too dizzy and hallucinatory to commit to the rest.

"I'm absolutely fine," I lied, seeing two shimmering replicas of him: double vision. I didn't know which apparition was real, or if I was even real. His desk was soaring backwards, while I was flying headfirst into it, while he was zooming sideways, and I wondered if we would eventually crash. "It's nothing I can't deal with."

I was terrified that if I admitted that I was sick, I'd have to face the very real possibility that I was having a psychotic break, even if it was a minor one. How did I appear to a complete stranger? Did I speak differently? Did I look like my mother, unhinged and unfocused? These obsessive thoughts made the furniture in the room soar faster.

"Well, please give us a call if you change your mind." (His head was floating like a hot air balloon, up, up, and away!)

"I won't," I managed to stutter, trying to sound gritty and grown-up. *Ignore his flying head, ignore it, ignore it!*

But the breaking point happened on my way out of Dodge Hall, where I bounced forty steps outside the Low Memorial Library and gashed my dummy head. I gave up that moment when my forehead swelled into an arterial-coloured moon. I knew that there was something seriously wrong with me, because when I limped to the student medical building (I sprained my ankle in the fall), the astounding vertigo knocked me into a bush, into a tetragon of flourishing, country-club grass. The student tour guide had said that they had shot the *Spider-Man* movies in this exact spot. Slouching between drooping shrubs to wait out the dizziness, I stared at the reverse blue sky.

Finally, as I cradled my forehead on a prickly mattress of barbed green, I thought that I shouldn't be going Woo-Woo so quickly—that I had at least another twentysomething years. The Woo-Woo had attacked Beautiful One at forty-two, and I thought I was safe at twenty-one. I wanted to scream at the filthy ghosts who had followed me to the East Coast. I had refused to believe in the mystical aspect of our illness, but how could I become so abruptly, coincidentally sick upon arriving?

On my fourth day in New York City I really thought I was having a psychotic break. I saw grinning disembodied faces, whooshing people on flying, mind-bending bicycles, and the excitement of starting my life in New York City spinning wickedly away. Like any effective generational curse, the Woo-Woo gave you an unhealthy amount of hope—and then snatched it all away.

I put off phoning home because I knew my father would be exasperated or furious with me—that was all he knew how to do in times of extreme duress. He still used inappropriate sarcasm as a coping mechanism, humour tainted with serrated annoyance when asked for his assistance. I was beginning to realize that we were so alike that I could instantly predict his behaviour. Bewildered and flustered, my father would tell me to sign up for Retarded Remedial Ivy League Graduate School, i.e., the demands of an MFA program had made me incurably Woo-Woo. And that would be the end of our conversation.

But the fierce, pulsating pain in my head and teeth worsened. It was like battery acid was stewing inside my brain, so I reluctantly pleaded with my mother to "pleasepleasepleasefuckinghelpme." It broke my pride and emotional independence to admit that I needed her assistance—yet I thought that she, being oversensitive to danger, might be more willing to listen to my pleas for help than my father, who would pretend to be My Future and hang up on me.

This would be the turning point of our fraught relationship. When I had to admit that I needed her. As if I were six years old again, living in the food court of the mall, when I desperately needed a mother who could mother me.

I phoned her when I could no longer walk without toppling over, when I could no longer slide out of bed.

"I can't go to New York," my mother said instantly. She was horrified by the idea of air travel. She had not been on a plane since she was eleven and only left the house to go to Costco or the mall. "There are the black and the gay and homeless ghost in New York and I'm very afraid. Your daddy says that I will die if I go to New York City because I will catch all their diseases. And imagine if I saw a black ghost! I won't know what to do!"

"You know, there are black, gay, and homeless ghosts in Vancouver too," I said, pleading with her. "And if you see ghosts, they'll all be transparent anyway. You won't be able to tell what colour they are. Stop being an asshole, okay?"

"No," she repeated, very alarmed, as I expected. "I'm very afraid of the HIV. The ghosts may still be carrying it. You wanted to go to New York, so now you fucking stay there. It sucks to be you!"

Even though my mother was mentally better now—she had not been suicidal or manic for years and had seemed to fully recover from Beautiful One's attempted suicide—she was still highly paranoid about the undead. She had also bonded with my father's Labrador, feeding and walking the animal twice a day, and the routine seemed to soothe her. It seemed as if we had acquired a de facto therapy animal. The dog, she often said, protected her from ghosts.

It had been a long shot, my last resort, to beg my frightened mother to come get me.

Nevertheless, after our conversation, quaking from fear and frustration, I slammed my cellphone into the cakey plastered wall of my bedroom, and the plastic shell shattered.

But she must have heard the humiliating desperation, like liquid laryngitis, in my voice, because she shocked me by flying 4,000 kilometres and showing up at my apartment within seventy-two hours. Her mouth was bleeding and crusty and raw from an intense burn wound. I didn't dare ask her what she had been up to, and she said she had spilled hot tea on herself—nerves from having to travel. She didn't seem to care that she looked scary—a little bit like a horror-movie special effect.

"Hey, retard," she greeted me uneasily when she arrived at the apartment. "Your face is fatter. Are you bingeing on sweets again? I knew you'd have a psychotic breakdown in New York. Didn't I say it? But nothing we can do about it now."

She was nervous, speaking without taking a breath. I said nothing, though I was secretly bothered by her snide remarks. I let her fight her fear through angry chatter.

My mother said that she almost missed her red-eye flight—the security guards thought she had looked extremely suspicious, and she said a female guard had combed through her frizzy hair for buried explosives, "like a monkey!" she exclaimed, scandalized by the airport staff's indecorous behaviour.

Then she proudly handed me a Costco-sized bag of fluorescent jelly beans that Beautiful One had bought for me, as if to celebrate my mental misery. When my mother arrived, I was starving, having eaten nearly nothing in practically three days. My mother said that Beautiful One was still afraid of doctors and dentists and kitchen appliances, but her slurred speech had improved, even while she was insisting that oil of oregano was a major serial killer—the thyme and rosemary in her spice cabinet were in constant danger. Beautiful One seemed to have already forgotten the incident on the stairs with Flowery Face. She had no broken bones from the fall, just a horrific concussion—which my mother said was a major improvement from her previous state of demonic disintegration.

"You fucked up!" she announced, because she could not control herself.

I was only now fully understanding her way of coping was name-calling and unpleasant verbal belligerence. She screamed because she was constantly afraid. I knew that just flying to New York had been incredibly traumatic for her because her eyes were cockroach-sized and twitchy.

"Big time," she added uncertainly, probably scared that there were black/gay/homeless ghosts haunting my apartment. I resisted the urge to teasingly call out to the ghosts, in case she dropped dead from coronary shock, or worse, had a full-blown breakdown, suddenly becoming suicidal, like Auntie Beautiful One on the bridge.

I knew that my mother didn't think that I was lost yet. She wasn't screaming while peeling off twenties and handing me money from our relatives, like we had all done for poor Flowery Face.

My mother did not waste any time, and within half an hour, she had shoved me into a yellow cab, relieved to be taking me home.

"What the fuck?" she repeated all the way to JFK and on our flight to Hongcouver.

Like any proper Chinese mother, she kept smacking my head to see if the ghosts were causing my hallucinatory brain fever. Unfortunately, no ghosts fell out of my inner ear—she expected at least half of one.

"You seriously fucked up, Lindsay," she said, a little more sincerely, while passing me handfuls of gluey jelly beans.

But she did not know why the ghosts were refusing to come out.

"Mind your own business," she barked at the flight attendants, who looked slightly alarmed when they saw her trying to exorcise me, but everyone seemed to understand that my mother meant business.

But I was filled with shitty, disgusted rage—how could I have allowed myself to become so Woo-Woo so quickly? I had always felt that I was in control and resistant to hysteria or psychological malfunction, which seemed to be a precursor for any psychotic breakdown in our family. If this was a sudden test or just fateful DNA, there was nothing I could have done. As usual, the Woo-Woo curse had impeccable timing.

We had not bothered to pack any bags, leaving everything behind in the apartment, and I held out some surreal hope that I'd come back to New York City. That I'd recover and feel refreshed within a week.

But this was not the case, and I felt useless and foolish when I phoned the program administrator and told him that I was going to need that semester break after all. Between my mother's hysterics and the uncertainty of my illness, I couldn't help but believe that I had fallen into madness.

In Hongcouver, with our free health care, there was a twelve-month waiting list to book a decent neurologist and even longer to undergo an MRI. I was relatively young, and I was a graduate student, so I only had to wait four months for a CAT scan. According to my parents, this meant I could skip ahead of dying seniors and homeless drug addicts and the unemployed. The government thought that I still had a starry, infinite future, and I was more valuable than much of the Canadian population. My physician, a family friend, agreed, which led to the Ministry of Health shaving off eight months from my waiting time—just like that.

While I was waiting for my CAT scan appointment, Beautiful One called to check up on her "absolute favourite niece" to see if I could hurry the fuck up and get well so we could go cross-border shopping. Her speech was fast and shrill, but at least she wasn't singsonging anymore.

"Lindsay, none of my kids listen to me," she said in a tangent. "You're the only one who cares."

Unsure how to respond, I stayed quiet, which she took as my unreserved agreement.

I found out later from eavesdropping on my mother's speakerphone calls to one of her sisters that Flowery Face had run away from home. No one had seen my cousin since she had kicked her mother down the stairs a few months ago, and there were rumours among family that she was living in a local mall, where she was "very happy with the pimple because she have lots of fast food and clothing," the auntie solemnly explained to my mother. But my mother wasn't sure if the auntie had mistaken the word "pimple" for "pimp."

In a way, I was jealous that Flowery Face had gotten away, even if she was living in the food court of a mall with a pimp (no one knew for sure). But I couldn't help but wonder if I had been nicer to her, if I had been less honest with her about her mother and our family curse, she would have tried to stay. Was this my punishment for failing her? My own alter ego of Woo-Woo? Was I feeling guilty in some unexpected cousinly way? Her own mother, improving slowly but too mentally unwell to think of her children, had proved to Flowery Face that she could not depend on anyone in our extended family.

Several weeks later, Flowery Face would surprise me with a sickbed visit. My only visitor from outside the Belcarra. She seemed to have recovered from our conversation at her house; her clothes looked expensive, plus she had developed a chain-smoking habit, clutching her Marlboros like crayons. At fourteen, she was living with a new boyfriend, a twenty-one-year-old Vietnamese drug dealer, one of my Poteau neighbours, she said. Flowery Face had found a better life, she explained. And she sincerely hoped that I would fucking recover. I was worried about her but knew that it would do her no good to call the police, in case she decided to never come back. Despite the sadness of her situation, I surmised it could be better than living with a crazy mother. At least someone, albeit unfit, was taking care of my poor cousin.

Frowning, Flowery Face handed me $300, a new digital camera, and a list of essays that she needed to complete to receive her online ninth-grade diploma.

"I'm sorry you're, like, nuts," she said, looking really miserable, "but I really need your help to graduate from English class."

Out of familial obligation and unmitigated shame, I thanked her for the get-well gifts and handwrote all her essays, which was a struggle because of my severe vertigo; she would receive As and one B-minus. Flowery Face talked hysterically non-stop while I scribbled agitatedly, saying that we both could change because she was a new person now, even if she was still furious at our seriously fucked-up family.

This would be the first and final time we would try to talk about anything so honest and optimistic yet sombre. How we both did not fully understand why our families were messed up and aching.

"It's like they don't even try to be happy," she said, her girlish voice breaking.

The Belcarra's yellowing walls suddenly began twisting like wacky funhouse mirrors. I couldn't leave my bed for the deluges of nausea, migraines, and vertigo. Up, down, up again, and sideways, I'd revolve and soar for twenty-four hours, even in my few hours of sleep. Meanwhile, the ceiling would fall and the carpet would automatically push it back up—BOOM! I'd puke twice a day, and in a month, I had lost a good thirty pounds. Becoming Woo-Woo had finally made me slim. I had become one of *them,* now. My pyjamas wore me, and I looked like I was dressed as a ghost for Halloween.

Rather than appease my mother, my weight loss frightened her. She tried again to exorcise me, thumping me in the head like it was amateur boxing night at the Wongs. But no bulky ghosts ever dropped out of my body. I was relieved when she finally gave up.

My father had avoided me by working long hours. Work must have been the only way he could maintain a structured existence—I didn't take it personally; that was how I was raised, how he normally dealt with our chaos. My screaming, however, was what finally summoned him.

"Retarded Lindsay scream like that, just for a little dizzy?" he said, as he ran into my bedroom, sounding scared and simultaneously disgusted. I rolled my eyes as he continued: "Fuck, imagine if she had cancer? She'd wake up the whole block! Thank God Mommy and I are not Woo-Woo like you! Please stop screaming and go back to school!"

"I can't help it," I said, while my mother wailed noisily in the background.

It did absolutely no good to think about what I was missing in frightening and unpredictable New York City, where everyone thought that I had my first psychotic break, including the administration and professors. Instead, I thought of Poh-Poh and how I did not envy her permanent and severe schizophrenia, but at least she did not seem to understand what was going on.

And then I thought about how Beautiful One had despised our family's "psychiatric" care and enjoyed the mental health ward better. At first, I had thought that it was because she wasn't so lonely and unloved at the local psychiatric hospital. But it was much more than that. The doctors and nurses and other patients listened to her and took her pain seriously. Mostly, no one told Auntie to "Shut the fuck up," or if they did, they said it nicely and promised her extra chocolate pudding at dinner. Our family was incredibly fearful of the diseased and dying, and only by being ill could I experience this firsthand. I took my parents' superstitious and impatient reactions, internalizing their reactions as my own inward unhappiness, like septic radioactive shocks to my nervous system. As if I was storing away their collective insensitivity, like fatty tumours, for no purpose or future use. Luckily, I was too nauseated to dwell on their hardness; otherwise, my damaged spirits would have been significantly less optimistic.

That fall, my mother, sobbing and yelling non-stop, began using my bedroom as a personal storage unit—she was a pragmatic lady and didn't think I'd last until Christmas, and I was inclined to agree. My bedroom became a hoarding cell of surplus junk, because we needed more space in the house for all the items she liked to acquire at Costco and Walmart. In her own way, she seemed to be quarantining our family curse, trapping it so that the monsters would not come out—these items were peace offerings for the spiteful ghosts inside me.

But my mother also felt bad for me, so she bought me an expensive new bed, which made the vertigo slightly more cozy and restful.

I had been Chosen by the Woo-Woo, and she was going to do her sacred duty to make sure that I did not end up in the psychiatric ward like her beloved Beautiful One.

But being an invalid truly sickened and shocked me. In those days and months, for the first time in my life, I began to have suicidal thoughts. I considered multiple ways to off myself but was too queasy and dizzy to find the household bleach. Research shows that depressives are less likely to commit suicide than people with manic episodes, like those with bipolar disorder. The depressed simply do not have the energy to die by their own undoing. Also, suicide is no easy feat when your own brain immobilizes you. I thought that if I were to expire in the Belcarra, the family curse meant that I would just become another foul-tempered ghost.

Finally, after the four-month wait, my mother silently drove me downtown for my CAT scan at St. Paul's Hospital. Earlier, the family doctor had casually mentioned that my illness could be caused by a rare brain tumour, which just made me feel numb and more vicious. I bossed my family around for days, shouting orders at them to cut my fingernails and serve me platters of takeout sushi, knowing that I could always blame it on the lump inside me, post-operation.

"You'll be sorry if I have brain cancer," I said to a never-silent-before father as I lounged in bed and he fearfully brought me pillows, obese California rolls, and a taro bubble tea with surplus pearls. I was already destined for Chinese hell, so I felt that I might as well enjoy it. Meanwhile, my mother, wailing, made frequent trips to the mall and the Buddhist temple to divert my ghosts.

At this point, I felt that I had a terminal disease rather than a psychotic break because all my relations seemed giddy and rejuvenated during their episodes. Their Woo-Woo was like going to the spa. I mean, their eyes practically gleamed. Mine had the dull, flat, confused look of frozen fish at the supermarket. Despite the sweet vindication, it was almost a relief, though terrible, if I had a terminal illness, because it meant that my brain was my own and not an extension of my mother's or grandmother's. It would almost be as if I, sickly but victorious, had avoided the illness that broke Beautiful One.

In an underground parking lot downtown, I had to grasp my mother's elbow to toddle down the blurry, undulating streets. A few strangers stared at us with pity. Cringing, I saw myself as they probably did: a crippled girl with gremlin skin who needed her mother to walk a few blocks. Scraggly, demented trees and skewered telephone poles began to soar. They were stalking me to the hospital entrance. Everything was tipsy and chaotic; panicking, I could not tell the blackish sky from the cement ground.

After an arduous few steps, we stopped in an alleyway so I could puke near a Dumpster; the nausea of dangerous, gravity-defying objects was utterly unforgiving. It seemed that nothing in the world could stay where it was supposed to. Commercial trucks floated in the sky like futuristic fantasies, and I could feel myself flying backwards at a billion miles an hour, while the urban landscape whooshed by in the polar opposite direction. Everything was surreal and wrong inside my eyelids. It was almost as if sharp-toothed gravity had gnawed a fabulous black hole around my skull and now the cerebrum was somersaulting about. A constant barrage of acrobatic trees and gymnastic motor vehicles.

"This is what happens when you can't fight your own demons!" my mother admonished, as I wiped vomit off my hair with the tissues that she handed me from her pack-rat purse. I knew that she was trying as hard as she could, but she was too afraid of everything to be a good nurse in a TV medical drama.

Maybe because her rage was as noxious and mean as mine, and her billowing frustration was unbelievable and grating, and because we were much too similar in how we handled disgust and multi-purpose disappointment. But her words detonated some kind of inferno inside me that had been gurgling non-stop.

It really did not help that I had been bedridden for months, and I had not been able to scream at anyone, so I shoved my mother. And of course, being who she was, my mother was up for a quick and dirty fight. It was the first time that I had pushed my mother with so much force. In some ways, assaulting her was like a spurt of demented growth, as it was the only way for her to acknowledge that I was a living person, someone overcome by physical pain and not ghostly possession. My mother looked stunned, and she shoved me back. And this went on, as if we were two seagulls squawking over a rotting french fry, trying our best to resolve years of profound emotional problems.

"You bitch," I screamed, feeling quite wonderful. "I fucking hate you!"

"I'm a bitch? You are the fucking bitch!!" my mother yelled back, louder. "You think I fucking want you for a kid? I didn't get to choose, you know!"

Luckily, there was no one around. We must have looked deranged, but the fight helped me, and I think she must have felt happier too. Attacking each other was so much better than passively suffering, which neither of us had the patience for. Fifteen years of anger had culminated into this one public brawl. I am stunned that we did not just murder each other and leave the bodies in the conveniently close Dumpster. Since the commencement of puberty, I had thought I had put a reasonable amount of effort into not becoming her, but fighting her was like thrashing myself in the face. It made me far too ill to think that I was her daughter, her potential mirror.

"How could you fucking do this to me?" my mother yelled.

That woman was a throaty tornado of horrendous frustration and sadness, and she didn't know it. Yet she had come for me when no one else had, despite her lifelong fear of airplanes and the homeless/black/homosexual ghosts; she had flown to the strange and terrifying realm of New York City to find me and put me in a cab. Despite her irrational fears, she had done her evolutionary job as a mother when I absolutely needed her to be one. She had finally been dependable and competent and helped me. She would never be maternal, not in the kind, conventional sense, but after our clash in the alleyway, she would stubbornly try to earn my forgiveness by becoming my personal chef: frozen dumplings, coronary-sized casseroles—whatever she could buy from Costco and microwave.

"Why did you let yourself get possessed right after Beautiful One?" she carried on. "Why couldn't you wait for next year?"

And then, shockingly, she pleaded with the angry ghost inside me, sounding as heartbreaking and desperate as she ever had, offering herself as the ultimate sacrifice, acting as if she liked me: "New York Ghost, come out now! Ghost from New York, get out of my retarded kid's body! I will let you stay as long as you want in mine!"

After all that fuss, nearly forty-eight hours later, I did not have a brain tumour, not even a lychee-sized wart or ant hole on the cortex. The CAT scan technician claimed that I had "a very unremarkable head." Was my condition semi-psychological or purely psychiatric? No one knew.

The family doctor firmly advised me to take the year off—"You're incredibly young, Lindsay. Graduate school can wait until we know what you have for sure." But his advice rebounded from my mulish ears.

There was no diagnosis for my violent and mysterious illness/

curse, but another month in my storage room facility would have made me more irritable if not crazier. I became certain that similar circumstances and environments had bred people like Ted Bundy and Jack the Ripper. It would be another twelve months of waiting until I could see a neurologist. I did not want to stay in bed for another year.

So without telling anyone, when my episodes of vertigo lessened in speed and frequency, I impulsively booked a plane ticket (with my father's emergency credit card for supernatural disasters) and left Hongcouver in time for the winter semester. *Fuck it!* I lied to the school administrators and claimed that I was cured—there was absolutely no way I was going to lose my place in the current class, or worse, restart the tribulations of graduate school applications and international student visas from the very beginning. What if I applied to the Columbian University again and was rejected? I felt that my original acceptance, black and unholy, had been a miraculous fluke that did not happen very often to people like me. (I did not yet fully trust in my own book-learning abilities, even though I had straight As at UBC.)

But I was still vertiginous and exhausted and hallucinatory most of the time, bone-achingly tired in what seemed like every rheumatic finger to creaky limb, even though the migraines had receded to a ghostly ache. Despite the frequent dizziness and vomiting, I could fumble to class but couldn't function without fourteen to eighteen hours of serious bed rest. I told no one of my illness. Instead, I slowly wrote shitty, irrational essays in bed, tried to read without literally puking (words were capable of rearranging themselves on the page, e.g., *the eth het hte*), and did not leave my apartment except to go to class.

With the ambition of the very young, I had canned soups, beer, and crackers delivered to my doorstep, paid for by the supernatural emergency credit card (my father would analyze the food bill with me each month, lamenting about my spending sixty dollars a week in the Upper West Side on groceries). Like my disappearance to Honolulu, we did not ever speak about my abrupt return to New York City.

Visiting the doctor became a hobby. I saw my general practitioner in the student clinic three times a week, moaning about mysterious fatigue, aches, and fevers, and I was diagnosed with malnutrition. Not once did I mention the vertigo. I was ashamed of my hallucinations. Was I schizophrenic?

Even in my graduate workshops at Dodge Hall, when my brain told me that I was hurling across the long table and my classmates were floating above me like oversized fruit flies in quick, opposing turns, I pretended that I was well.

Don't fuck this up more, I thought. *The professor just told you that your workshop submission needs a quick death.*

At the Columbian University, I became a crippled geriatric spider.

In the smallness of my dirty insectoid soul, I knew that I could not go home, as I could not bear to be with my mother and hear about Auntie Beautiful One's adventures with God and her spice cabinet—she would have said that we were so alike.

CHAPTER 14

THE OTHER MOUNTAIN

The NYPD threatened to break down my door after a roommate/ classmate had a psychotic break at two a.m. and stuck her head inside the oven à la Sylvia Plath to gas us "nasty little people" to death.

In New York, once again, I could not escape the Woo-Woo, but this time it had possessed someone else, someone I wasn't even related to.

Despite my random but chronic episodes of vertigo, I was determined to succeed. Yet I had only been in New York again for two weeks and I already believed that MFAs were the most fickle and melodramatic people on the planet. At the time of the police's arrival, I was knocked out on sleeping pills and possibly carbon monoxide, but another roommate, a quick-thinking mink-wearing law student from Norway, had alerted campus security, who must have phoned the police. It seemed that if I wasn't going to acknowledge the sickness bursting inside my skull, it would manifest physically and find me. For once, I was forced to recognize that I was reacting like my family, denying what was debilitating and right in front of me.

Because of the Columbian University's liking for randomly assigning international students to apartments on West 114th

Street, none of us liked each other very much. I was twenty-one years old, a decade younger than both of my roommates, who found my youth and chronic vertigo somewhat off-putting.

The Mountain, a depressed-looking 300-pound girl from Montreal, had been very meek; she suffered from a twenty-first-century form of kleptomania (stealing food and money and then apologizing via text messages). Every few weeks, she would have an uninspiring workshop critique at our writing school, which meant that she would express her suicidal urges in flamboyant, artistic ways. For instance, she might flop backwards on the kitchen table while you were eating dinner, spreading her legs like a sea monster, splitting them into an enormous rubbery *V*, while bumping over a chipped glass or plate. She did not care that she was seated in a runny casserole dish of wet chicken and gravelly potatoes. Her hair would be in saintly yellow ringlets, garish lipstick blotching her corpse-coloured teeth.

"I'm dying today," she would announce, unafraid. "I'm going to kill myself after workshop. Just you wait."

A few hours before the police arrived, she had begun to scream and cry and accuse the law student and me of breaking into her room and routinely raping her. Her voice had changed, become deeper and more controlled, before she had collapsed into a trembling ball outside my bedroom. I looked at her twitching face, saw the lipstick stains like crusty cranberry sauce, and decided that I did not want to be associated with someone so reminiscent of home. Quickly, I hurtled over her and locked myself inside my room. I was already terrified to acknowledge my own sickness, so how could I confront a stranger's? I craved normalcy and thought I could achieve it by denying my own visual hallucinations. Meanwhile, the law student had gotten hysterical and charged outside to wait at Butler Library across the street.

Angry and shaking, I waited for the Mountain to leave, but she sat outside my door for hours, smoking and screaming sporadically.

"Open the door, Lindsay!" she shrieked. "I just wanna talk!"

I put my headphones on and read a book. I knew the drill: total and absolute inattention would allow me to ignore the wailing outside. The Mountain was blocking my door, but I had my college graduation present: a fantastic plastic chamber pot. My New York grandparents, whom I had only met once before, had mailed this pragmatic and wonderful gift, much more useful than cash. Mah-Mah, my grandmother, had assured me that everyone needed a chamber pot from time to time—this was NYC, and really, how naive was I? I used my pale pink pot while waiting several hours. I had no idea how people in previous centuries managed it—squatting on something so small was incredibly difficult.

It took six police officers to get the Mountain dressed and escort her to the psychiatric ward.

"Bitches!" she screamed at the law student and me. "How dare you tattle on me, you bitches!"

The doctor at the psychiatric ward called shortly afterwards to question me about her symptoms. Hallucinations? Most definitely. Suicidal urges? Yes. Homicidal? God, I hoped not.

I wanted to hang up the phone, because it was like talking about Beautiful One again. I could not handle the fearful reminder. I threw up.

The student dean and I were both in our pyjamas in his office at the Columbian University to discuss the Mountain's assassin-style hit list and the troubling events of the early morning. Without my fourteen hours of requisite sleep the previous night, I was attacked by full-scale vertigo, so I forced myself to believe that I was not plummeting through the air and this interview would be over soon.

The administrator was dressed in his cheerful red flannel because he had picked up the Mountain from the psychiatric ward around four a.m. Not delusional or psychotic enough for the hospital to keep her, my troubled roommate was being lodged in the college's isolated emergency housing quarters. Uncertain and weary, I had thrown a long coat over my pyjamas and yanked a beanie over my unwashed hair as soon as the dean sent his assistant to fetch me at seven. She was accompanied by the college's public safety officers, who threatened to break down the door after I hadn't responded to the dean's emails or multiple voice messages.

"I apologize for how I'm dressed," the dean said when he ushered me into his office. I shrugged, unsure how to respond.

Neither of us had slept after the police incident, and the dean was acting as if someone had just been murdered only a second ago. He was visibly uncomfortable, and so was I. I suppose he was worried about the legal penalties and public relations backlash for the college, but I was not going to sue him; I just wanted to crawl back into bed and forget about the incident ASAP. I wanted to reassure him that there was nothing extraordinary about this early-hours incident, except the Mountain seemed to have multiple personalities, or "many demons," as my mother would have cheerfully said, which made a boring 2 into an exaggerated 4 on the Wong scale. But I had a feeling that this answer would not terminate our meeting, and I did not want to seem insensitive, so I said nothing and stared at the ground. Besides, a fury was burgeoning inside me because I did not want to confront the issue at hand. My Chinese family blatantly ignored our problems, and I had never had to talk about a psychotic episode before. My instinct was to run away and pretend that there was nothing wrong, and this urge made me ashamed.

"Can you please summarize the breakdown you witnessed last night and this morning?" the dean asked, sounding concerned.

"It was like *The Exorcist*," I said, desperate to be back in my apartment. As I blinked, my vision abruptly shifted, and I could feel another sharp spinning. Thankfully, this time it was brief, though unsettling. I inhaled.

"Can you provide more details?"

"Lots of name-calling and profanity. There was a Jerry Springer moment about an alleged rape. Can I go now?"

"Are you taking this seriously, Lindsay?"

"I really don't see how this is my problem," I finally told him, deciding to be direct and honest. But as I leaned forward, the room suddenly flipped upside down, and I had to cling to the desk, desperate to keep from falling off the chair.

Without being nasty or too personal, I could not tell the dean that I had not expected to be housed with someone who might have more than a few people living inside her, someone who was eerily constructed like a messy, genetic Russian nesting doll. And how could he question whether I was serious about the Woo-Woo when I had fought so hard to run away from those who were ferociously afflicted?

I was ill-equipped and not emotionally ready to engage with the subject with any unfeeling distance. I could not separate the Mountain's Woo-Woo from my family's psychotic rages. And being coldly reluctant was my built-in defence system, like an antihistamine against all things to do with severe mental illness. I was too frightened to chatter on about the Woo-Woo, and I didn't know what I was supposed to say to make it go away.

The spinning seemed to be worsening in his cramped office.

Breathe, I thought, my heart exploding. *Breathe!* Every ditzy nerve inside my head was vibrating, like the atmosphere around us had changed magnificently. Like we had taken a sudden trip to the mangy backwaters of deep space. Nauseated and incredibly dizzy, it took every conscientious scrap of willpower not to hurl on the administrator's desk, so I frantically looked around for a garbage can, but he mistook my chilling panic for inattention.

"Lindsay, I need you to listen! Your roommate in the law school is hysterical. She says your other unfortunate roommate told her about a hit list and she's convinced people are going to die. I need to know which students and faculty members are on it. I need to know who she wants to kill in the writing program. We're talking about people's lives here."

I realized that the sensitive topic of a hit list must have occurred in a tense conversation between my two roommates that I hadn't been privy to. Besides, I didn't quite know who *anyone* in the MFA program was. Overwhelmed, I told myself that I couldn't even tell the dean who was worth killing, because I couldn't yet distinguish the seriously talented writers from the mediocre from the most poisonous hacks. Based on those I had briefly met, an exchange of mumbled names and foggy pleasantries, I didn't like half of my peers in the writing school and quite a few of the more disobliging professors, but there was absolutely no reason to have anyone killed, I thought. The Mountain hadn't failed a class yet or, more importantly, her thesis defence. Like my mother, I thought resentfully, my roommate was acting on some contaminated rage, most likely fuelled by her classmates' critiques on her unappreciated writing abilities—which I mentioned.

While the student dean scribbled on his legal pad, I made a mental note that I should never be truthful in a workshop setting in case a classmate had an unusually foul disposition and decided to tuck a semi-automatic in their backpack. And if I had absolutely nothing complimentary to say, if I had run out of lukewarm platitudes to repeat by the second hour, it would be much safer just to be smiley and silent among such damaged and temperamental people.

"Jesus, who knew getting an MFA in America was so ominous?" I tried to joke to calm myself, but the dean gave me a strange look.

Ignoring the Woo-Woo, even in someone outside my family, only made it stronger. I had spent the rest of the day after my meeting with the dean slumbering, so I was well rested and only slightly dizzy when the Mountain came back to pick a fight.

"Let me in!" the Mountain screeched, as she threw her body against the front door, and I, gulping, thought the chain would jerk and shatter. "Let me in! I promise I won't hurt you bitches! I just want to talk!"

Because of some survival trait inherited from my grandparents, who all bragged about surviving the second Japanese invasion of China, I had selected a sharpened knife—a clean utensil that wasn't too hefty to appear unfriendly or intimidating but medium enough to do some damage in case the Woo-Woo was particularly violent. The Mountain still had her keys to the apartment, but I had deadbolted the door after the police incident in the morning—just in case.

"Here, take a knife," I suggested to the law student, who was in the kitchen preparing beefy Norwegian sausages for supper. She was swaddled in an off-white, floor-length mink coat and wore a porcupine-sized fur hat.

Because of the deep anxiety hurtling inside me, I wanted to be prepared. Besides, I thought holding something sharp might make her feel better, if not safer. But she wouldn't take a helpful knife or even a protective metal spoon. I began to gather up all the jagged kitchen implements in a paper shopping bag so we'd have access to a wide arsenal of disposable IKEA weaponry. There was no cellular reception inside our building, so we could not call 9-1-1 unless one of us made it outside. This was assuming either of us would still have our dialling fingers if we managed to escape.

"LET ME IN!" the Mountain was screaming now, as she hurled herself against the door with astounding earth-like willpower. "You stupid little bitches! I am going to fuck you up for telling on me! Come on, just open the door. I just want to talk to you. That's all."

When we did not open the door, she became even more incensed: "YOU STUPID BITCHES! YOU NASTY LITTLE GIRLS! Open up! I said, open up! I live here too, you know."

All our first-floor windows had iron bars on them except for the tiny kitchen, and there was no back exit. Whoever had turned the building into university housing hadn't planned for slighted MFA students. I listened to the planetary thudding—it was as if angsty Jupiter had exploded into grievous Mars. The Mountain crashed against our apartment's entry point, and our train-track hallway shivered from her zealous global quake.

Shit, I thought. *This is a horrible way to die. But at least it's not on the subway.*

From the Belcarra Institute, I had multiple PhDs in intensive horror-movie survival, and I thought I knew what to do. I may have felt completely lost and flailing in my Ivy League graduate studies at the Columbian University, but I thought if I had been the victim of a psychotic murderer, I'd be the very last person alive. If I had faced Jack the Ripper, I felt I would have ended up standing over his gory remains with a fork or butter knife. Anyway, I liked to think that I possessed the killer instinct to outwit any homegrown psychopath, as well as a horde of brain-munching zombies at the end of the world, which was similar to this astonishing start-of-semester incident.

Even if I were stranded on an island after a debilitating plane crash, I told myself, there was no doubt that I'd survive.

Because the difference between me now and only a month ago, I would later recognize, was that I was more aware of what I could be—I was not just some insignificant mosquito or fat louse. I was a grubby human being who didn't deserve to be injured or maimed like a dusty, small-eyed cockroach—and that was why I had run all this time. No one, not even a psycho with a grudge, would get in my way of living what I hoped would be a dull and unexciting life. I realized that I could try to flee from the Woo-Woo, but I could not escape. I might not be able to prevent the Woo-Woo from bursting within my own flailing brain, but I could possibly outwit the lunatic who was trying to bulldoze my front door. Without the Mountain trying to force her way inside, I might never have possessed the bravery to insist on a medical diagnosis for my own internal sickness, for fear it was Poh-Poh's uncontrollable schizophrenia. The shrieking Mountain was a reminder of an alternate future, another self, if I did not figure out a way to fix my hallucinations. If I survived this ordeal, I promised, I would no longer ignore my vertigo.

"What do we do?" the law student shrieked, jolting me back to the crisis at hand. "Lindsay, what do we do?"

I began stripping the gas stove elements of their heavy, blunt coverings (they could easily bash in anyone with an average-sized head) and inventoried all the kill items in the kitchen. I knew from personal experience that the tiny stove lighter could be a powerful tool when wielded like a wild cheerleading baton. I assumed that a fork or spoon could carve up someone's skin like a flabby Christmas turkey, and crushed glass could seriously dismember or kill.

If I shattered the mosquito screen in the kitchen window, if I long-jumped a miraculous three feet to land on the feeble courtyard stairs, I'd only fracture both my ankles and be able to log-roll to safety. Admittedly, this was a terrible escape itinerary, but some of my PhDs in survival had been earned by blatant, improvisatory idiocy.

The law student had worked for the United Nations and was fluent in eight or nine languages yet knew nothing about psychotic breakdowns and was ineffective in a Woo-Woo emergency. So I shoved her in front of me and told her to leap out the window first.

"I'm going to die!" the law student shrieked, but she made no exertion to help herself.

I screamed as sharply as I could, sounding embarrassingly like my father when he wanted to athletically motivate someone: "JESUS FUCKING CHRIST! MOVE!"

In the end, it was the apartment's repairman who saved us; he was fixing some broken tiles in the lobby when he witnessed the Mountain screaming and throwing herself at our door. And I suppose you'd have to be very hard of hearing not to also notice the obscene shrieking from our apartment. He was a robust man carrying a tool box; he shooed the Mountain away.

After the repairman assured us that it was safe, the law student suddenly became unstuck from the window. Hysteria had solidified her muscles.

"You saved my life!" she exclaimed, and then she embraced me, as if we were pals in some campy horror movie.

It was technically the repairman who had saved us, I thought; all I had done was get her wedged into a window frame. But I guessed there was nothing like an attempted assault by a crazed person to make you best friends for life, or until the semester was over.

"Oh, Lindsay," she gushed, "you and I are both proper, well-behaved girls from good families. We don't have outbursts when we are upset! I just don't understand why Columbia would allow in *someone like that*."

I only saw the Mountain once more before she was rumoured to have been sent off to the psych ward for the semester. The dean had allowed her in the building to fetch her mail. I had a public safety restraining order against her, which might explain why she panicked and smashed into a hard-to-miss wall. She smushed her face and hoisted her hands over her head, as if I had pointed a semi-automatic at her back. I felt like I was ordering her bleak execution.

But I could not think of her desperation, while she moaned, "No, no, no, no" in the hallway, as if trying to calm herself. The ground under my feet had begun earthquaking non-stop, so I grabbed onto a staircase railing to stop myself from falling over. *Help,* I thought, frantic, as the walls of Dodge Hall imploded. *The world is collapsing.*

Seven days had passed since the police incident, and I had deleted emails marked with *Highest Priority: Please Respond!* and at least ten or twelve urgent voice messages from the Dean's Office asking to meet. They had also sent maintenance over to change the apartment's locks, but of course it had been much too late. I had thought I had been handed a rare gift with a graduate school acceptance in a faraway place, but the Big Apple was as dangerous as the suburbs of Hongcouver.

Fatigued in the aftermath of the incident, and now suffering from insomnia, my nausea and vertigo returned with unparalleled force. A spooky yellow-orange light permanently coated the edges of my vision like a flashlight, making me feel vicious but faint.

Afraid and ashamed of my weakness, I retreated. I spent a week in my dormitory-style bed, a freshly delivered pizza cradled on my stomach like an open mess of ribboned guts. Even though I was too nauseated to eat, I liked the weight of the cardboard box on me. I was so angry with myself for regressing, but in that moment I was too unsettled to know why. I fiercely debated quitting graduate school and clearing out of the apartment. I had not paid my rent with my father's emergency credit card in more than three months. So I ignored my father's weekly phone call, because he would have said, in another attempt to strengthen my aptitude for suffering, "Oh my God, Lindsay, your future is saying, 'Just suck it up.'"

Swiftly, again, the diagram of my world was churning. This was not fearsome indigestion. My bedroom tilted and warped, and I felt like I was rocking on a wicked ferry. The illicit grease from my pizza had stained the sheets a telltale orange. I wiped my chapped lips on my tumbling sail of bedclothes and belched. I could feel block-like continents suffocating me again, and everything began to float. My bed started to propel forward, as the sadistic hand of the Woo-Woo god picked me up and plunked me backwards. My desk and chair began to crash and slither in every direction. A floor lamp flew at my head like a meteorite. The feral fuzz of my blue floral rug and the adjoining walls began to palpitate, as if they were panicking in a dry, wombatty vibrato.

Help, help, I thought. *I'm flying!*

Bundled in my cheap cotton sheets, I became an airborne corpse. Immobilized, I spun with uncanny velocity—the most severe spinning I'd had in months. There was terror grumbling inside me, and I didn't know what to do about it.

As if to escape the Woo-Woo again, I accepted the law student's invitation to skip a few weeks of classes. We went on vacation—flying to raucous, claustrophobic Miami from La Guardia and then ferrying to the soft, blistering Bahamas.

None of our professors gave a shit about our prolonged absence or missed assignments.

For a while, my vertigo and hallucinations retreated. I returned to the MFA program to finish the semester, believing that I had (barely) outrun the Woo-Woo. Feeling brazen, more socially savvy, I decided to take on a publishing internship, reluctantly declining the law student's offer to spend the four months of summer galloping around her estates in London and Paris before fine-dining through northern Europe.

"Oh, just come with me!" she pleaded, sounding uncomfortably like my former friend C.C. "My family is so grateful that you saved me from that lunatic flatmate. They'll take very good care of you, Lindsay! I keep thinking about how Columbia could let in someone like that. She just *doesn't belong.*"

After her aristocratic invitation, I was filled with gross toadish hope, thrilled that I had somehow fooled her into thinking I was normal and proper and unpsychotic.

For a while, I believed that my bleak and terrifying world could finish earthquaking.

CHAPTER 15
BAD, BAD BRAIN

Fourteen days after my visit to the neurologist in New York, I had no choice but to return to rain-drenched Hongcouver. The specialist had just diagnosed me with the most severe case of migraine-related vestibulopathy that he had ever encountered, and I was bone-shakingly terrified at the prospect of a permanent brain disease. At first, I had been giddy that it wasn't paranoid schizophrenia, but I could not function on my own in New York City. The spinning made me confused, and when I wasn't falling, I was slurring my words as if heavily intoxicated. Without explanation, I quit my summer internship at the midtown publisher and turned down a job offer at a prestigious talent agency.

On the exterior, I looked like a young publishing assistant: uptight, fast-talking, speed-and-Adderall-toting, with a designer purse and matching shoes. When I wasn't in workshop, I made notes about what to say, what to wear, how to appear hard-working and polite. I even had a fake origin story, which I had been prepared to tell in case my boss or co-workers asked (they didn't): only child, parents dead!

Yet inside, I was still fifteen years old—unsure and scared. Afraid that they would discover that I was grossly under-qualified and not smart enough. Being accepted to the Columbian University had taught me that I could fake it well enough to camouflage myself. But now, I was going to quit graduate school and the start of a publishing career.

In Hongcouver, I thought I'd crawl into bed and stay there in perpetuity, feeling like I had failed in NYC, but there was another extravagant dinner party at the oldest auntie's house (attendance was absolutely mandatory), where I saw all the Woo-Woos, and we were paraded in like exotic animals at a zoo. The extended family assumed that I was deeply mentally ill, had, like, one or 200 ghosts inside me, and all my cousins (Flowery Face wasn't there) were afraid to talk to me. This was what it was like to suddenly go Woo-Woo in suburban Hongcouver. To suddenly become something unacknowledged and feared. My cousins avoided eye contact as they swarmed the tables with enough roasted suckling pig, beef, duck, and fish to feed ninety-five people.

"I'm not crazy," I said, but no one was listening, and I repeated myself like Auntie Beautiful One. "I have headaches that make me dizzy. It's the headaches that make me see things that aren't there. It's just a fucking headache that's making me like this."

"Bull-fucking-shit," my mother said, and I sighed, frustrated. I could not convince her otherwise.

"I have a serious brain disease," I explained. "Want me to Google it for you?"

"No such fucking thing as brain disease," she said. "That neurologist is crazy. He doesn't know what the hell he's talking about. He's just giving you bullshit because you paid him. It's the American way. Not like Canada. Besides, white people don't know anything about ghosts. That's why they have so many problems. I am wondering why they don't run out of names for all their different sickness."

My mother had seemingly recovered from her sister's breakdown, despite still being easily panicked. As usual, she kept saying that she was scared for me—I was not safe from the supernatural. What had happened to Beautiful One was now happening to me, she said, handing me a plate of greasy pig ears and chow mein.

I should not have been surprised, but I was suddenly invisible, grouped with the sickly Poh-Poh and starving Beautiful One, who had been sent to sit in a corner of the living room. Muttering to herself, Poh-Poh was heavily medicated on a cocktail of antipsychotics—maybe a new psychiatrist's orders, because she seemed less panicked than usual. Beautiful One was also medicated, and she told anyone who would listen that she had taken up fingerpainting and now thought she was the greatest artist in "the whole wide world." Claiming that she did not need art lessons, Beautiful One proudly presented her impenetrable scrawlings of psychedelic rocks and mutant shrubbery to her family.

"They're ugly," my mother announced, but I thought they weren't too bad. If Beautiful One had heard her sister's insult, she didn't seem to care and smiled, showing all her yellow teeth (she refused to see a dentist, because she feared an ongoing assassination conspiracy from her molars).

"I'm an artist," she said in a terse, horrible monotone. "I'm the best in the world. I could sell these for millions and millions of dollars. I'm Picasso, would you not agree? I'm so good at art that everyone should just pay me all their money. I'm the best artist in the whole world."

Beautiful One had stared at me with her dead eyes, welcoming me into the trio. She grasped my hands and whirled me around, giggling, and asking me to compliment her art for the third or fifth time.

"Very good," I said, and she looked at me, expecting more exorbitant praise, because that was what had defined our relationship. Because I knew what she wanted to hear, I said sadly: "You're incredibly talented, Auntie, the best I've ever seen."

"Duuuuh," she said, and stuck her grey tongue between her teeth.

Wincing, I saw that when you went Woo-Woo, you went directly into the Woo, which was your typical Chinatown aquarium, which had no glassy pebbles carpeting the floor in pearly pink or neon blue. The Woo was undecorated and underfunded. Forget about the little towering castle spires or charming jungle huts in Versailles-inspired gardens. You got a bare holding tank with mildewy green water. An underwater concentration camp that did not discriminate between manic-depressive or paranoid schizophrenic.

In the Woo, all the condemned Woo-Woos hovered on their sides, squeezed on top of each other, yellow eyes bulging, mouths popping to mimic the battered and barely living. That was why my cousin Flowery Face was gone for good; she wanted to find her own secure and hygienic fishbowl in Hongcouver, and I had not seen her since she had visited me at the Belcarra.

Now that I was floating inside our communal Woo, I felt almost bad for batty Beautiful One, who didn't even realize that her daughter was missing, and even sorrier for poor Poh-Poh, who had practically been dumped in its tank as soon as she was born. Going Woo-Woo was just like waiting to be selected by a paying customer so the killing man in the wet and dirty seafood aisle in Chinatown could mercifully end you. Your scales flying everywhere like gleaming fingernail clippings; your noisy thrashing becoming a diluted scream.

The Woo was where I had spent all twenty-two years of my life, and where I might spend the next twenty-two if I didn't get the hell out of there. But it was this instinctive drive, this struggle to run away and to always deny, that had gotten me in trouble in the first place. I wanted to swim around the globe and find my own freshwater space, but it seemed like I was destined to travel in my panicked school of fish.

Throughout my childhood, my mother and I had always just known how to pick the best fish in the Chinatown tanks, the ones that had the most scrap left in them. These were the cold-blooded gladiators, most likely descended from Siamese fighting fish, prepared to thrash to their deaths with ferocious showmanship. These were the most violent survivors. They knew how to give the fish-killing man trouble—they wouldn't let him guillotine their hot, squashy throats. Even if they were too weak to get off the tank's floor, they were the ones who stubbornly flapped their tails back and forth, to prove they were morose and still alive. They were the fools who still thought they could escape, even when the fish-man bashed in their heads and chucked their dismembered faces on the floor of the store, even when their blood pooled on the check-out counter like thick acrylic paint.

In the car once, when I was a little kid, a fish corpse that I had specially chosen for the cleaver jumped and fought me in its clear baggie. I slowly stroked it through the translucent plastic, as if soothing a startled pet. But the zombie fish did not want my sympathy and wrestled me all the way home. And I knew it was total madness: me fighting in the backseat with a decapitated fish, something that didn't even know that it was a goner, that it was in fact missing its head.

"But we killed you!" I had shrieked at the fish that had too much optimism, as I tried to buckle it down with a seat belt.

Anyway, it had tasted delicious and fresh and omnipotent, sprinkled with ginger and garlic and vibrant shallots.

At my aunt's house, I couldn't help but believe in the family curse. The hopelessness in the room felt hot and uncanny, though no one would speak about it openly out of suffocating fear.

I felt that I was the last Woo-Woo in the tank: the very last fish to have my head cleaved off. But I knew I could not be Woo-Woo without a fast, spectacular fight.

"Oooh," Poh-Poh suddenly moaned, and snatched my sleeve with her wrinkled octopus arm. I struggled to get free. "Ooooooooooh, ooooooooooooh."

It sounded like she was moaning "Wooooooo, wooooooo," and I felt as if she was surely condemning me. Was I Woo-Woo like them? Or was my brain afflicted with a rare disease? The neurologist and New York City suddenly seemed unreal.

I shook my head to reassure myself that I was interminably ill, with something thick and rotting in my skull, like a mangy spore or a plucky parasite. *Get out of my fucking head!* I wanted to scream at what I swore was an extraterrestrial worm drilling a home inside my brain—a burgeoning migraine. I was relieved when the room rotated upside down, as if to confirm the neurologist's diagnosis.

"But I'm pretty," Beautiful One suddenly whispered at me, flicking her slovenly, sea-addled hair. "Don't they see that I'm not old? I'm only sixteen. Why can't they see that I'm very beautiful?"

"Fucked in the head, all of them," my mother muttered, gesturing at us with maddening distrust, and this made me laugh a little at her continued defiance.

"Hey," she barked at one of my many, almost identical little cousins, who were scuttling around the house like nervous ants with plates full of food, "do you want end up like them? Come here, brat. I want to show you what the fucking crazy looks like so you don't end up over here. If you are weak and think too much, you'll end up like Grandma over here! Or your retarded cousin, Lindsay!"

Reeling from dizziness and disbelief, I couldn't be around the inhabitants of the Woo anymore, so I stumbled down the stairs and locked myself in the basement bathroom, where my mother had hidden when Beautiful One had tried to slit her wrists almost two years ago. For the rest of the dinner party, I refused to come out; I flopped on the floor and prayed that my amphibian claustrophobia would stop.

The midtown neurologist had prescribed me beta blockers and anti-anxiety and epilepsy medications, which were real proof that I wasn't crazy, that I had done a stint out in the oceanic world, I told myself, shuddering.

It didn't occur to me until much later that the strangeness I was feeling was a newfound empathy for everyone I knew who was trapped in the Woo. Like one of those bratty, insensitive heroines who doesn't quite understand the wretched plights of others until some significant monetary loss befalls her, I could actually *feel something* now.

It would take me a long time to relinquish all my numbing fury, but in the bathroom, I could feel something dark and isolated. I could feel the pebbly hopelessness of the dinner party upstairs, the obsession to finish our barbecued pig and beef and salty fish so we could stare at our possessed patients. And there was always that fishy warning, a low and steady hum, trying to circulate in our Woo-Woo filtration systems in all our seemingly perfect McMansions. But our aquatic system was certainly broken, because everyone eventually became poisoned and sick.

Our family was determined to hold on to our supernatural beliefs; it was far easier to blame ghosts for our hurt than believe there were genetic miseries making us lash out at one another.

It was suddenly like the insides of my stomach had spilled out. Every spineless, godawful emotion was pouring out. And it was so sad and frustrating and decidedly overwhelming. I did not understand what each sentiment meant. But I thought that it was wonderful that I could finally experience something.

For two months of summer, I was forced to stay in bed until the migraines and dizziness began to lessen. The world would occasionally tilt and whirl, but the wicked episodes of instability became less frequent. From the crippling nausea, I lost another fifteen pounds and my skin faded to a ghostly brown-green. I was as skinny as a ten-year-old girl. My mother began to talk about us checking into a nursing home together, maybe in ten years, when she was in her sixties and sufficiently old; the dawdling environment might do my "fucked-up head good," she concluded, nodding to herself. I shuddered and imagined us as roommates in a cozy retirement palace. And I realized that my mother did not expect me to recover. At that time, I also did not think that I'd ever be able to leave my bed that was becoming a crypt.

When I could walk again without falling, and became tired of watching thick raindrops sizzle against my window on the Poteau, I ambled around the Belcarra, sneezing and suffocating because I had developed a serious allergy to the Labrador. The family doctor spoke to my father, saying it was "Lindsay or the dog: one of them has to immediately go."

"Oh, not even a choice," my father joked and, because he said he loved the dog the most, bought me a one-way ticket to New York.

"But I can't finish my program," I said, mimicking my father's derisive tone. I was terrified to return for the upcoming fall semester, but I also knew I desperately needed to finish what I had started to prove to myself that I was capable of success. Without my awful allergy to the dog, I'd have never gone back to graduate school.

"It's too hard," I said, hating to declare defeat. I felt that I couldn't cope with my long-term disease alone. "I'm too stupid for school. I have to quit. Besides, I'm sick."

"We all know how much you like to suck," he snapped, not even noticing that I was imitating him. And he made my choice for me. "But Retarded Lindsay has to go, too bad. Daddy doesn't want to see you anymore. Seriously, Daddy is very sick of you because you cry and moan all day. You fail piano, and now you fail the Columbian University. You think you can't function even if you are Woo? Fake it until you make it. How come Beautiful One so Woo-Woo she can still be business owner, huh? Why people trust her is a big mystery to me."

I had no choice. The vertigo now came on mostly at night, and I could stumble around for up to six or eight hours without fainting. According to my father, that was good enough to finish a master's degree. "It's not like you do PhD," he said, rolling his eyes.

But during my last-minute red-eye flight from Hongcouver to JFK, the engine caught fire twice, and there were two emergency landings. I could not have made up this anecdotal horror production if I tried. At the risk of sounding neurotic and narcissistic (not to mention spastic and delusional), it was almost as if the universe was plotting against me, and I couldn't leave Hongcouver.

When the plane smacked back down in Hongcouver for the second time that night, all the passengers were given a crusty egg sandwich for our flammable troubles. The tiny palm-sized sandwich was supposed to keep us preoccupied as we evacuated the aircraft. But I finished my sandwich long before the fire trucks arrived. From the very back and centre of the plane, I could not see anything but

assumed the fire was dire from the grimacing of the flight crew. I
was most definitely not going to expire on an empty stomach.

I had been quite pleased that the plane's door did not drop
off while we were pinned to the reticent purple sky. The aircraft
could not fly more than a few hours outside of Hongcouver, as if
the ghosts haunting my mother's family were hauling it down with
their undetectable gravity. Their aerial bodies were weighing on the
wings—the spirited friction causing the mid-air blaze.

During both takeoffs, the air smelled a lot like barbecuing plastic
and shoe polish with the brassy undertone of overcooked leather. I
was surprised that my fellow seatmates couldn't smell our impending
mid-air plummet. It was the seedy plastic of the airplane seats tinged
with fire and the unmistakable smell of the Woo-Woo, which lingered
longer than the smelliest junkyard perfume.

When we landed for the second time, I was thrilled that the
plane did not implode, and then I was worried when I had to spend
the night in room 666 at the Sheraton near the Vancouver airport.

"Room 666 is in a separate tower. It's not in this building," the
front desk manager had muttered, handing me a mystical plastic key
to an isolated dimension.

It was four a.m., and my mother called to see if I had landed in
New York yet.

"You're in room 666?!" she interrogated me, not really interested
that my flight had caught fire. "It means the ghosts are angry at you!
This is what happens when you try to leave Vancouver!"

An hour later, to add to the surreal horror and implausibility
of the night, there was a clipped and very Chinese pounding
on my hotel room door, as my parents had arrived to de-possess
me. Being obsessive ghost hunters, my mother and father were

always equipped for supernatural emergencies. No other parents, except in a made-for-TV Lifetime movie, would have driven to the airport to de-possess their eldest child.

I was sure my mother had scurried to the pickup truck as soon as she finished our phone call. My parents had no difficulty finding room 666 in its special, private hell-tower, and I knew that this was all part of our family's perverse curse—Chinese and Western superstition always got scrambled together. The number 666 was a Western, religious superstition, but it sounded dangerous enough—they had watched enough mainstream horror movies to believe in fiendish numerology.

I was clearly being punished for leaving, and I thought my mother had come to gloat. But they probably thought they were being "Best Mom and Dad in World" by rescuing me from supernatural disaster. In their obsessive way, I realize now that this was how they showed affection. Despite screaming profanities at everyone and each other, my parents, teeming with frustration, still only sought to protect their offspring from dead people.

"Surprise!" my father said, handing me an emergency pack of rations (a bucket of leftover KFC from last night's dinner). "Your mommy insist we get rid of the demon for you! She make me drive here to help you. Here we are! Lindsay's special helpers!"

"WHERE IS THE GHOST?" my mother demanded, peeking into the bathtub. "ARE THEY HIDING FROM ME?" She frantically checked under the bed, and then scourged the room's closets and drawers, expecting shifty apparitions of dead people to jump out and murder her. She screamed: "You can't leave! We leave you alone and you made the plane catch fire! It's all your fault! ALL OF IT! The ghosts are giving us a warning!"

I could tell that she was terrified, even more upset that I was responsible for making a plane combust, not once but twice.

"You can't go to New York," she kept repeating, but her warnings were no longer crazy and nihilistic, just cheerless, broken, and a little pathetic. I felt bad for her, so I said nothing and allowed her to vent, which seemed to make her feel better. "You need me to fight off the fucking ghosts for you, Lindsay," she pleaded. I knew she thought that I needed her, but what she needed was a licensed psychiatrist and a husband who didn't spend his spare time collecting dog fur.

"You're too fucking retarded to function on your own," she said, peering under a sterile dresser. My father moved the hulking decoration from the wall so she could conduct a more thorough psychic investigation. For nearly thirty minutes, we flipped over queen-sized mattresses and gently combed between the bleached sheets—as if checking for bed bugs, but we were looking for deceased people playing hide-and-seek in room 666.

Eventually, my mother relaxed a bit, and she gulped down her sleeping pills and conked out on one of the pillowy beds—the room was ghost-free and safe. We were obviously insane, but we were meticulous in our methodology.

Exhausted, I fell asleep eating my bucket of fried chicken on the other bed.

Almost three hours later, my father insisted that I "go now." He shook me awake and fetched my luggage and carry-on for me.

"What the fuck are you doing?" I asked him, dazed. Fried chicken grease was on my pillowcase and a drumstick was tucked beside me, a reminder that I was still a gruesome mess. "I haven't eaten breakfast yet, and you don't know if the airline cancelled the flight," I said, stalling.

"Use your head, retard!" he announced in an irritated whisper.

"Get up now! Time to go! Your stupid mommy sleeping. So Daddy is helping Retarded Lindsay to make sure she don't blow up plane with her fucked-up thinking. Also, I really want to make airline pay Daddy back fourteen dollar for parking in stupid hotel."

"I don't think I should be flying so soon," I said nervously, wondering if my next flight would enthusiastically explode as soon as we smashed through an inconsequential cumulous cloud. "My plane just caught fire, twice, you know."

"You let little thing like plane burning bother you?" my father said, looking disappointed. "Geez, I thought you tougher than that. Are you loser or a winning Wong? You still have two arm, two leg, and two eye, nothing wrong. Even dead people in body bag fly, so why can't you?"

His prime parenting plan had always been to harden me, and in the hotel his expression seemed to say that he took my reluctance as another of his personal failings. Yet this time, his decade-long strategy for teaching me to endure mass misfortune worked. For I had no argument for him about dead bodies flying, so instead, I looked at my mother snoring on the bordering bed. She was still wearing her puffy winter jacket and looked like the Abominable Snowman. Especially in her sleep, she looked small and scared. I shuddered. For I knew we were somewhat alike, but I was more like my father—derisive, frequently insensitive, but un–Woo-Woo.

Yet leaving my mother in the hotel room felt like I was abandoning some grizzled fraction of myself that was not good or evil, lazy or nice. Like I was amputating an arthritic finger that I could not use, but it had been an intrinsic part of me for so long. Goddammit, I wanted to be somebody different from my mother, or at least, grow up to be someone with a job. I collected my plastic bags drooping with fobby MSG snacks that she had packed, as I still could not refuse free food.

"I'm not a loser," I said, and my father looked relieved.

My father, not one to waste time, drove us to the airport terminal in less than a minute. He shocked me by submitting to the airline's demand and buying me a stand-by replacement ticket to New York, which would be refunded later. And then, blaming the airline for his expenses, he pocketed a twenty from the poor airline clerk, who was probably too afraid to argue with my cheap father. Never bothering with social niceties, my father had waved his hotel receipt like a fluttering paper weapon and demanded, "Parking refurbish NOW."

"Why the fuck you just standing there for?" he asked me, impatient. "You have ticket."

For a panicked moment, I wondered if he had glimpsed my mother's Woo-Woo decaying in my brain and veins and was going to order me to leave it behind with him, like a diseased piece of poultry that was not allowed past US agricultural customs.

"You want hug or something?" he barked at me instead. "Last night, I watch FBI show on TV and people in airport always want hug. Don't tell me you want one too?"

"No," I said, still shocked that my father was being so goddamn *nice*. My father had never been actively helpful before, and I was absolutely terrified. "I don't want a fucking hug."

"Okay, good," he announced, reassured and more convinced that I was "normal," like him. "If you want one, then you ask stranger next to you."

In his outlandish way, I believe that my father wanted to send me away from my mother and her relations—perhaps he was trying to protect her from witnessing me leave; perhaps he also knew that I would languish in bed, citing vertigo and permanent immobility, if he did not force me to finish graduate school in a strange country. He needed to believe that I could be different from my relations in Hongcouver, that I was more like him than Poh-Poh and my mother.

And I was. By flying for a third time in less than twelve hours, I proved that I was not afraid of the supernatural. Like him, I could pretend to be obnoxiously fearless.

Before I went through airport security, my father handed me my carry-on, and I imagined him driving home to the rank aquarium of the Woo, tempted to leave my mother behind at the hotel. If she woke up alone in room 666, she'd start screaming and sobbing about her malevolent ghosts. She'd probably require a tranquilizer, and the hotel concierge might even have to call 9-1-1. But I knew that my father would dutifully wake her, and they'd go to their favourite mall or parking lot to run a blockbuster marathon to lose the demons, and then they'd make their lonely trek up Pot Mountain without me. And then, because he probably loved her, they'd share a frothy beer or five together before bed.

To leave the Woo, I had cheated, lied as often as I could, and stubbornly bashed and smashed my way through every bizarre and totally unbelievable situation. And now, I was being handed a free pass—by my father. No one would ever believe me if I told them about all the wondrous and terrible and fantastical things that had happened to me. I would be an idiot if I didn't snatch this opportunity and tornado brazenly through airport security before something else caught fire.

I knew I needed to go back to New York to avoid the family curse and my premature future as a young, mummified corpse in a government-run nursing home. With my genetically resilient, zombie-evolved spores, I convinced myself that I did not need to worry. I decided that I was going to be the last creature left on both sides of the wobbly continent, even if unlucky Manhattan decided to capsize when I got there.

In forty-eight hours, I was also supposed to meet C.C., who had forgiven my nastiness in Europe, for a jaunt around New York. She was on vacation from Oxford and had already scheduled a list of notable restaurants, cafés, and bakeries that we would visit. I was excited to eat.

"Use your fucking head and everything will be okay!" my father shouted, as if to reassure himself as much as me.

I wish I could have told myself that I was going to be more than a little okay. That I could finally stop inflicting misery on others. That I could feel cactus-like crumbs of kindness and any wide-ranging species of emotions, like any malleable human being. I was no longer a thing or object, to be formed by irrational beliefs.

But I was also too scared to think about a possibly bleak future. Because the truth might have been that I was just another giddy scuba diver fleeing the stagnant aquarium of Hongcouver. This new Lindsay had a *third* chance to discover a normal, un-marine life outside the Woo, and she was going to jostle and push her way to the front of the lineup at airport security.

I turned around to see my father. He still looked miserable and moustached like Hitler, but under the twinkling airport lights, in his agitated pacing, he began to resemble an idea of a human being, a half-formed question mark of someone who might be capable of cantankerous emotional reasoning.

"Good riddance to your bad, bad brain," he called. "Don't fucking suck too much in the Bad Apple, okay?"

"Fuck you," I said sadly, knowing that he was doing his best to be constructive and helpful, but I couldn't help feeling resentful of him at the same time. "Worry about your own brain."

I felt that I had not been entirely Chosen by the Woo-Woo, and I was somewhat safe for now. So I slipped off my shoes, removed my jacket and belt, and watched them float, as if by sheer miraculous gravitation, past me on the conveyor belt.

EPILOGUE

From 2008 to 2010, Beautiful One continued plotting her suicide on every national holiday, but thankfully, did not carry through. She is eighty-five percent recovered from her bridge-jumping attempt. The family pretends that Canada Day 2008 never happened. Flowery Face graduated from high school and has a job in finance. She and her mother have forgiven each other.

My mother is attempting to make amends with her children. She is still deathly afraid of ghosts. In 2012, my father was diagnosed with colon cancer; he is in remission, and everyone in the family agrees that the experience made him a more compassionate person.

Gung-Gung (my grandfather) died in 2006 from bronchial pneumonia, nearly two years after the family took sanctuary at Walmart. Poh-Poh (my grandmother) is still alive. She still does not know that her husband is dead (no one has told her yet).

Eventually, with the steadfast support of friends, professors, my mother, and my father, I graduated from Columbia University with an MFA in non-fiction. Even though there are days when writing, reading, and fundamental tasks are difficult, I am learning to live with migraine-associated vertigo. I work part time as a freelance editor and college admissions consultant.

Deep Thinker is a recently certified veterinarian in Australia. We are estranged.

Make Lots of Money is a graduate student in Hongcouver.

We didn't speak for many years, until he needed assistance with a portfolio for admission into a prestigious writing program. But, God help him, he's a writer too.

ACKNOWLEDGMENTS

Writing makes me want to gouge out my eyeballs.

This is why I have to thank and salute the following people for their incredible belief in my work: the indefatigable Carly Watters and the team at P.S. Literary; the wonderful Brian Lam, editor extraordinaire Shirarose Wilensky, the talented Oliver McPartlin, word-savvy Doretta Lau, Robert Ballantyne, and Cynara Geissler at Arsenal Pulp Press.

Immense gratitude to the irreplaceable and exceptional Marni Berger, Rowan Hisayo Buchanan, and Marie-Hélène Westgate; thanks also to Jill Rothenberg, Gina Leola Woolsey, and everyone else who read discordant fragments of the manuscript. Alexis Marie, for your rare, unshakeable friendship; Teri Cho and A.H. Reaume for your support. My family for teaching me not to accept failure but to seize the microscopic improbabilities of the universe.

To my brilliant Columbia professors for patiently showing this bumbling rookie how to write: Richard Locke, Sonya Chung, Cris Beam, Patricia O'Toole, Lis Harris, Leslie Sharpe, Rebecca Curtis; all my talented classmates, especially Shira Schindel and Jennifer Ohrstrom. My generous mentors at UBC: Linda Svendsen, Mary Schlendlinger, Alison Acheson, and Andreas Schroeder.

I'm also incredibly grateful to the Canada Council for the Arts, the Kimmel Harding Nelson Center in Nebraska City, Joy Kogawa House, Studios of Key West, Caldera Arts in Oregon, and of course, the Bank of Mom and Dad, Inc. Thank you for your patronage.

Photo by Shimon

LINDSAY WONG holds a BFA in creative writing from the University of British Columbia and an MFA in literary non-fiction from Columbia University. Her fiction and non-fiction have appeared in *No Tokens, The Fiddlehead, Ricepaper,* and *Apogee Journal.* She is the recipient of many awards and fellowships, including from The Studios of Key West, Caldera Arts, and Historic Joy Kogawa House. She lives in Vancouver.

lindsaymwong.wordpress.com